Praise for *The Bogle Effect*

"We are on the threshold of a new era, one in which the power of large numbers beats expertise. Where network effects and mass distribution overwhelm traditional structures of authority. To fully understand it, one must go back to Jack Bogle's revolution, the effects of which are only now beginning to be felt everywhere. Let Eric Balchunas be your guide as we leave behind the old world and go charging into the new one."
—Downtown Josh Brown, CEO of Ritholtz Wealth Management, star of CNBC's *The Halftime Report*

"Eric Balchunas has not only written the definitive professional biography of John Bogle, but he has done so with a penetrating honesty and narrative grace rare in the genre. Read, enjoy, and, most important, absorb the wisdom of the most important investor ever to have lived."
—William J. Bernstein, author of *The Four Pillars of Investing* and *A Splendid Exchange*

"Balchunas has written a rare beast: a delightful read that humanizes one of the icons of finance, while at the same time providing a meaty argument for how our modern financial world has been shaped by the genius, goodness, luck, and perhaps arrogance of one man."
—Dave Nadig, Director of Research and CIO, ETF Trends and ETF Database

"A riveting story of a once in a lifetime, transformational figure for the fund industry. A candid look at the birth of passive investing and its subsequent revolution."
—Aye Soe, Head of Product, S&P Dow Jones Indices

"Eric Balchunas's *The Bogle Effect* is a powerful and captivating exploration of how John Bogle and Vanguard revolutionized the entire financial industry. A must-read for Wall Street beginners and veterans alike."
—Arthur Levitt, Former Chairman, the Securities and Exchange Commission

"Thanks to Jack Bogle, there's no longer any dumb money in the stock market. Also thanks to Jack Bogle, the smart money has to work that much harder to prove they're worth the fees they charge to beat the market. In *The Bogle Effect*, Eric Balchunas expertly shows how Jack Bogle built Vanguard into the Amazon of the asset management industry: a disruptive, disintermediary and deflationary force that's left its competitors scrambling. This is a must-read for anyone wondering how buy and hold became a winning strategy."
—Scarlet Fu, Quicktake Anchor, Bloomberg, and senior markets editor, Bloomberg Television

"Balchunas provides one of the first ever exhaustive looks behind the veil of the high fee asset management business and the dramatic impact that John Bogle played (and still plays) in saving the retail investor billions of dollars. This is a must read for anyone who wants to understand the past, present, and future of the asset management world and portfolio management."

—Cullen Roche, Founder, Discipline Funds

"The Bogle Effect will change the way you look at the financial industry forever. Balchunas's insights give readers a fresh and unique look at how Bogle and The Vanguard Group revolutionized both portfolios and Wall Street. A must-read for all."

—Mary Schapiro, Vice Chair for Global Public Policy, Bloomberg, and Former Chair, US Securities and Exchange Commission

"Jack Bogle did more for investors than anyone else, ever. He was brave enough to wave a pirate flag, take on Wall Street, and change the world. And no one will help you appreciate Bogle's radical simplicity quite like Eric Balchunas."

—Joel Weber, Editor, *Bloomberg Businessweek*

"Jack Bogle is famous and revered—but not nearly as famous and revered as he should be. Eric Balchunas's new book should help on both counts. Read it and learn. Read it and be amazed what one determined man did for the average investor."

—Alan Blinder, the Gordon S. Rentschler Memorial Professor of Economics and Public Affairs at Princeton University and Former Vice Chair of the Federal Reserve

THE
BOGLE
EFFECT

Also by Eric Balchunas

The Institutional ETF Toolbox (2016)

THE
BOGLE
EFFECT

How John Bogle and Vanguard Turned Wall Street Inside Out and Saved Investors Trillions

ERIC BALCHUNAS

Matt Holt Books
An Imprint of BenBella Books, Inc.
Dallas, TX

BenBella Books, Inc.
10440 N. Central Expressway
Suite 800
Dallas, TX 75231
www.benbellabooks.com
Send feedback to feedback@benbellabooks.com.

BenBella and *Matt Holt* are federally registered trademarks.

Printed in the United States of America.
10 9 8 7 6 5 4 3 2 1

Library of Congress Cataloging-in-Publication Data: 2021049927
ISBN 9781637740712 (cloth)
ISBN 9781637740729 (ebook)

Copyediting by Nancy Ellen Shore
Proofreading by Michael Fedison and Lisa Story
Indexing by WordCo
Text design and composition by PerfecType, Nashville, TN
Cover design by Brigid Pearson
Cover image © Shutterstock / HolyCrazyLady (texture) and Alexander Kalina (origami)
Printed by Lake Book Manufacturing

To my grandparents, Joe, Aldona, Dan, and Pat
(and the rest of the World War II generation)

CONTENTS

FOREWORD

I didn't expect to learn much from this book.

That's the honest truth.

Having spent twelve years in the ETF industry, I knew the story of John "Jack" Bogle well: his early days at Wellington, his split to form Vanguard, the subsequent growth. As CEO of ETF.com, I had the pleasure of interviewing Bogle multiple times; I even edited a number of articles he wrote for *The Journal of Indexes*, arguing with him over word choice.

Jack is also a personal hero of mine. I've read his books, studied his speeches, and use him as a north star when making decisions. What more could I learn about a man I consider one of the greatest Americans?

But Eric is a good friend and a great writer, so when he asked me to read his book, I obliged.

I was blown away.

The thing that separates good biographies from great biographies is simple. Good biographies tell us what happened—the upbringing, early career, and formative moments in the lives of our leaders. This book does that well, bringing stories to life that even I didn't know.

But great biographies gaze forward, weaving threads from a person's life and accomplishments to craft a tapestry of what lies ahead.

And here, in Eric's hands, Bogle's story is transformed.

At a time when America's relationship with the financial system is fraught—when the common narrative is that Wall Street takes more than it gives—this book is a reminder that it can go the other way.

As Eric shows, the scale of Bogle's impact to date is staggering. The creation of Vanguard and Bogle's relentless focus on costs have taken $1 trillion out of the claws of Wall Street and stuffed it into the pockets of everyday Americans.

That figure is likely to triple in the next ten years: The equivalent of 95 million years of college tuition, 36 million down payments on the average American home, or 27 million years of private nursing home care, all saved by the simple idea—that fund companies should pass along economies of scale rather than arrogating the proceeds for themselves.

Eric uses clever techniques to bring Bogle's story into the present. He sprinkles in dozens of interviews with some of the biggest names in finance—from iShares founder Lee Kranefuss to Berkshire Hathaway's Warren Buffett to Morningstar's Christine Benz—showcasing Bogle's profound influence on the industry's pioneers.

He also wades directly into the toughest challenges the industry faces today, from concerns that indexing has gotten too big to discussions on ESG, thematic investing, and meme stocks. Driven by Eric's framing, we can meet these challenges from Bogle's perspective and see a clear path forward.

Eric is also unafraid to weave his own views into the mix, tackling issues like the common arguments made against ETFs. Though he wouldn't admit it, Eric is a big part of the modern Bogleian movement—using words, research, and insights to push the investing industry toward a better future.

Importantly, being Eric, he does it with wit and style. Who else could write: "*[B]laming the stock market bubble on index funds or ETFs is like blaming MP3s for the rise of Nickelback*"?

Readers may wonder how I came to write the foreword for a book about Jack Bogle. After all, I left the ETF industry in 2018 to become the chief investment officer for one of the world's largest crypto asset managers. We run crypto index funds, but still: Jack would have raged against my current career. He didn't like investments without cash flows, and he spat fury at anything that smelled of speculation. Bitcoin would have driven him nuts.

But the principles he championed are a daily inspiration to me. Seek efficiency, but always with the goal of improving lives. Open new doors. Don't fear the raised eyebrow. And always remember you serve your investors, not the other way around.

That's the really extraordinary thing about Jack Bogle: You could disagree with him over an asset class or a word choice, but at the end of the day you couldn't help but be drawn to his wisdom and his character.

—Matt Hougan, Chief Investment Officer at Bitwise Asset Management

INTRODUCTION

"If a statue is ever erected to honor the person who has done the most for American investors, the hands-down choice should be Jack Bogle."
—WARREN BUFFETT

realized about five years ago how relatively unknown and under-appreciated John Clifton "Jack" Bogle was after I had written an article for *Bloomberg Opinion* deconstructing how much money Vanguard had saved investors. Soon after, *The Billfold*, a millennial-focused personal finance site, published a follow-up piece using the BuzzFeed-esque headline "Some Guy You've Never Heard of Has Saved Us All Billions of Dollars."

That headline was spot-on and spoke to the need for a book. Because when all is said and done, Jack Bogle will likely end up having had a bigger impact on both investors and the global financial industry than any other human being. Through Vanguard, he is already responsible for funneling more than a trillion dollars from Wall Street to Main Street, enriching the lives of about fifty million people, and installing a fiduciary mindset in a financial industry that was losing its way. Yet many outside—and inside—the financial bubble don't really know who he is beyond the "father of the index fund" label. There's a lot more to his story and impact than that. When you really sit back, think about it, and trace it out, his story and legacy are truly mind-blowing. I tried to capture all of it in this book.

The Last Company

During the past decade, there has been nothing short of a total sea change in investing as the amount of assets in index funds and exchange-traded funds (ETFs) has exploded to $11 trillion in the United States and $15 trillion globally. By the time you read this, it will probably be much more. Each year, about a third of all the net new cash invested by Americans goes to Vanguard. And most of the rest goes to Vanguard-esque low-cost index products from one of its competitors. And this isn't fickle money chasing the latest shiny object or star manager—it is migrating to a permanent home.

I often call Vanguard investors' last fund company. If they invest with Vanguard, they probably would not have a motivation to move their money elsewhere.

—Christine Benz

By setting up Vanguard in such a way that the fund investors are also the owners of the company—a decision motivated by a desperate attempt to save his job as much as, or more than, altruism—Bogle changed everything. For him, it was a chance to keep his career going as well as to start the financial world over again by creating a company that aligned its incentives with those of its investors. Profits would not be spent on making everyone at the company rich but rather on lowering the fees in the funds.

The bigger Vanguard grew, the lower its fees got. And the lower its fees got, the more cash came in and Vanguard grew even bigger, which resulted in still lower fees. Rinse and repeat for forty-five years, and you reach the point at which investors today can now get a fully diversified portfolio for basically no cost.

This book aims to show that without Bogle and Vanguard's "mutual" structure, the boom in passive funds wouldn't have been a boom at all but rather a tiny fraction of itself. It took the unique structure of Vanguard, combined with the unique makeup of Bogle himself—a force of nature with vision, patience, and unrelenting evangelism about the importance of costs— to win the hearts and minds, as well as the assets, of American investors.

Google Is Wrong

And while some would say that Bogle's impact is fairly well-known, I would argue that it is wildly underrated—and even misunderstood. For example, when you google *Jack Bogle,* the search engine brings up an image of him with the label "American Investor," but that's really incorrect. That is a more fitting description of Warren Buffett, Peter Lynch, or Cathie Wood. Those are the kind of investors people are used to seeing books written about. But Bogle was something entirely different. He was more like a combination of Steve Jobs and Martin Luther.

Jack Bogle was on a different trip. And I think folks who had the unbelievable honor and privilege of spending any time with him—or his team, because he assembled some amazing people around himself over his career—all would report what I would report: he was not playing the same game we were playing. And more importantly, he wasn't playing it for the same reasons. He was not a charlatan. He was a true believer, and I think he felt he had a moral obligation to do what he was doing. Never once in countless meetings with him and speeches that I saw did I ever get the sense that he was anything but 100 percent convinced that he was doing the right thing for the American people, for the world. And I think sometimes that rubbed some people the wrong way. But I also think it was true.

—Dave Nadig

I challenge you to give me someone who is more of a revolutionary in investment than Jack Bogle. You just can't.

—Jim Wiandt

Addition by Subtraction

Bogle definitely had attributes of a revolutionary, a preacher, and even a punk rocker. He was known to be abrasive and was more comfortable swimming upstream than down. He loved sticking it to the "establishment" and calling out gimmickry, excess, and corruption. And his overall investment philosophy, spearheaded by the index fund, was all about *addition by subtraction*—a hallmark of punk songs and the title I almost gave to this book. Just as the punk genre was built by removing all the stuff its pioneers didn't like from rock music at the time, Bogle built an entire genre of investing by eliminating all the stuff he didn't like that just gets in the way of investors' fair share of returns—management fees, brokers, trading costs, attempts at market timing, or even human bias and emotion. A cheap index fund is basically investing distilled to its purest form. There's no fat or indulgence. This is why it will likely never go out of style.

Bogle was highly creative and passionate, but he could also be egotistical, unbending, and difficult to work with. After all, he essentially got booted against his will from *both* of the companies that he ran and loved so much. He remained feisty and fired up right until the end, too (which I'm convinced is the secret to longevity). In fact, one of the last things Bogle ever wrote—on the final pages of his last book, *Stay the Course: The Story of Vanguard and the Index Revolution*—was this quote from the poet Dylan Thomas: "Do not go gentle into the good night. Rage, rage against the dying of the light."

For many, even those of us inside the industry, it was easy to miss the punk-rockery of Bogle, because although his words and ideas were explosive, he looked and sounded so grandfatherly and folksy. Not to mention, we're talking about mutual funds—a subject most find as interesting as watching C-SPAN. But this industry's relevance can't be overstated as it sits between the value created by our nation's businesses and the trillions in investment savings of everyday Americans. It's an easy place to get greedy and extract unwarranted value. In retrospect, this was actually the perfect industry for a guy like Bogle. You'll see why in the upcoming chapters.

Why Did He Do It?

One of the questions I've always had and made sure to explore in this book is: Why has no one in all these years copied Vanguard's mutual ownership structure? Clearly, Vanguard's had such amazing success with it, you'd think some would follow suit. But they haven't. No one has followed. The perhaps obvious answer is that there's no economic incentive for an aspiring asset manager to turn over ownership of their company to the investors of the fund. And generally, people who go to Wall Street want to make a ton of money. OK, fine. So then why did Bogle do it?

This question sent me on an even deeper journey and sparked an entire chapter in this book that wasn't even in my original outline. How could it not? Here's a guy who created the biggest fund company the world has ever seen, and yet he himself wouldn't even rank in the top one thousand richest people in finance. It defies logic and all the laws of Wall Street physics.

The thing that makes Bogle different is that he literally chose not to make any money from his innovation. It was the most powerful innovation in finance in, like, fifty years. He could have been a billionaire, and he deliberately chose not to do that.

—Jared Dillian

He did very well for himself, but he also did much better for other people. This is a great lesson. It shows that the financial industry doesn't have to be predatory. This industry tends to attract people for all the wrong reasons. But you can be in finance and not be the Wolf of Wall Street. There's another path. And you can do a lot of good. He showed that.

—Anthony Isola

Although this book is largely very favorable toward Bogle, I try to give the full picture, which means showing his less attractive traits, as well as the huge part circumstance played in his career. That said, here, "net positive" is the accurate framing. One fact that confirmed this is the people closest to him seemed to respect and admire him the most. You sometimes read about a historical figure—a world leader or entertainer, for example—who was beloved by millions but neglected their own family or treated the staff like garbage. That was not the case here, as Bogle's family and former assistants are among his biggest fans.

Even his competitors seemed to really respect him. I tried in vain to find someone who went toe-to-toe with Vanguard and would talk about how big a pain in the rear Bogle was. I thought I had found that person in Lee Kranefuss, who ran BlackRock's iShares ETFs at the same time that Vanguard launched its ETFs, which you'd think would be *really* annoying given the company's reputation for causing fee compression wherever it went. But Kranefuss was happy Vanguard came into the market. He ended up becoming friends with Bogle. They became email buddies.

I hope he gets the credit he deserves. It's huge. I used to say to Jack sometimes that those of us that came after you in the ETF and index world are standing on your giant shoulders here. Because Jack introduced what can be a very esoteric concept, in terms of the effective proof and theory, to individual investors. From there forward, it has been the amplification of that idea. He broke the ice. Everyone associates Jack Bogle with indexing, and I hope they continue to. He was really a pioneer, and he was the first one who cut the trail through the jungle. His impact has been huge.

—Lee Kranefuss

Pushing the Industry

This was a pattern I would see again and again in all the folks I spoke with. Even when I brought up one of Bogle's savage comments about their area of the financial ecosystem, they'd sort of smile and laugh, like, "That's just Jack being Jack, and I love him anyway." I think the reason is twofold: he was just such a colorful character in an old-school way, and deep down his competitors actually liked being pushed to align more with the investor.

People want to feel good about what they do every day. Bogle almost single-handedly increased the amount of "I'm doing good for my clients" sentiment in the financial industry. He made finance people—and the industry as a whole—better.

Another reason it was hard to find Bogle haters is that he was very good about separating someone's job from the human being that they were. Even if he bashed someone's investment strategy, their company, or their whole industry, he didn't use that to judge them as a person. "You can have different ideas with people," Bogle told me. "What are ideas? Ideas are a dime a dozen, and friends are much more important."

Even active managers tended to be friends with him or draw inspiration from him.

I can't think of another figure, current or historical, who has championed an initially less-loved cause, persevered, and thereby benefited more everyday investors than Jack. In fact, it's not close. I can't think of a number two on the list that isn't a ridiculous comparison with the Great Man. Despite the fact that no human is perfect (disagreeing with me being the definition of imperfect!), he truly earned the sobriquet Saint Jack. And, on a personal note, he was a kind, witty man and great company. I will always really miss him.

—Cliff Asness

And yet, Bogle could be pretty savage when it came to almost every area of the financial industry. And a lot of that savagery is in this book. Let me say right now, if you currently work in the financial services industry, there will likely be times while reading this book that you feel a little judged and maybe even attacked. You aren't alone though; Bogle was an equal opportunity offender on that front. As an ETF analyst, the host of an ETF podcast, and the author of a book on ETFs, Bogle was just as brutal toward my world and livelihood. Moreover, some of his more pointed criticisms were aimed at Vanguard itself, which we will look at in the book. No one was spared. He even trashed himself on occasion.

Abnormal Guy

I was fortunate enough to be able to interview Bogle in his office on three separate occasions for more than an hour each time in the five years before he passed away. When I was first looking to speak with him, in early 2015, I reached out to my colleague Michael Regan of Bloomberg News, who had just written a profile of Bogle for the *Bloomberg Markets* magazine. He gave me Bogle's email and said he would probably reply. He was right. Bogle replied within a few hours and we set up the meeting.

When I first arrived at Bogle's office, I told him how abnormal it was for someone of his stature to be so easy to get a hold of. He replied, "Well, I am abnormal in more ways than that, my friend." And that is how our relationship began. During the next five years, we would do in-person interviews as well as exchange regular emails. He was also a recurring guest on a TV show I cohosted for Bloomberg Television, *ETF IQ*, as well as one of the key speakers at the first ETF event at Bloomberg, which I organized. Michael Bloomberg had introduced him as "one of the deans of our industry," and Bogle responded by encouraging Mike to run for president. It was a cool moment.

My first interview with Bogle was for my book on ETFs. The second one was for a book I never ended up writing, about passive portfolio management, although some of that interview is in this book. The third one was for a Bloomberg ETF podcast that I cohost, *Trillions*. All told, I have about four hours' worth of his views on just about everything, and I knew if I just let those interviews sit there, trapped in my Dictaphone, I'd probably come to regret it.

While his eighty-year-old body was clearly weakening and his lifestyle was that of a senior citizen, his mind was still sharp, evidenced by his feistiness as well as his quick wit and self-deprecation. For example, when testing audio before our podcast interview at his office, our technician asked him to say what he had for breakfast. Bogle replied, "I had raisin bran, a banana, a large glass of orange juice, and twenty-three pills."

When asked what he did last weekend, he replied: "I have a family, and my daughter came over for dinner Friday night. Can't remember what we did Saturday night, and my daughter and her husband came over Sunday night. And then, as I am shameless about saying, I need a nap every day. The only thing that interferes with my nap is the *New York Times* crossword puzzle on Sunday."

In addition to my own interviews with Bogle, I used his own writing as a foundation for this book. Bogle was a gifted and prolific writer, penning twelve books, most of which I've read both before and during this project. He wrote all but one of those books after he stepped down as Vanguard CEO, in 1996. Personally, I probably would have moved to the beach to focus on fishing and tennis, but Bogle is not normal, so he continued working out of a small office on the Vanguard campus, where he wrote like crazy for more than twenty years. The guy was seriously inspired—on a mission, as you will learn throughout the book.

Things to Know Before Reading

You will see me use the terms *passive, index funds,* and *ETFs* almost interchangeably to denote funds that track indexes and have set rules versus, say, a fund that is run at the discretion of a human portfolio manager who has ultimate control over what goes in and out of it ("active"). When I say *passive,* I am referring to the fund, not the investor. If I am talking about an ETF that happens to be actively managed, I will state that clearly; otherwise, just assume *passive* means a rules-based index fund or ETF.

I will also use *basis points* or *bps* on occasion—especially when describing fees. It just means a hundredth of a percentage. For example, 0.20 percent would be twenty basis points. You will also see *NAV* (net asset value), which is simply the fair value of a fund based on the value of its holdings divided by its shares outstanding. In short, the fair price for the fund based on what it holds.

More Than a Biography

While you will get to know the man and what made him tick and learn the story of Vanguard's inception in this book, it is not meant to be a biography, a textbook, or a how-to guide to investing. There are elements of all those things, but swimming in just one lane is not my style. What Bogle did is in itself multidimensional, so I wanted the book to reflect that.

I also wanted the book to feel like a semi-documentary. And so I went and interviewed about fifty people whose commentary helps give color to the topics and stories. Many of them worked with or knew Bogle personally, while some only saw him from a distance. I spoke to some people who disagreed with him or offered criticism. After all, Bogle was human, and he and Vanguard aren't beyond reproach. Here is a list of all the people (in alphabetical order) that I interviewed exclusively for this book. Thank you.

Theodore "Ted" Aronson: founder and managing principal of Philadelphia-based AJO

Erin Arvedlund: columnist for the *Philadelphia Inquirer*

Cliff Asness: founder, managing principal, and chief investment officer of AQR Capital Management

Victoria Bailey: Bogle scholar and financial advisor

Christine Benz: director of personal finance and retirement planning at Morningstar

David Blitzer: former managing director and chairman of the Index Committee, S&P Dow Jones Indices

John C. Bogle Jr.: founder of Bogle Investment Management

Nicole Boyson: professor of finance, D'Amore-McKim School of Business, Northeastern University

Warren Buffett: chairman and CEO of Berkshire Hathaway

Ben Carlson: director of institutional asset management at Ritholtz Wealth Management

Jamie Catherwood: client portfolio associate at O'Shaughnessy Asset Management

Anthony D'Amato: Bogle scholar and singer-songwriter

Jared Dillian: editor and publisher of *The Daily Dirtnap* and columnist for *Bloomberg Opinion*

Rob Du Boff: ESG research analyst, Global Equity, Bloomberg Intelligence

Dan Egan: vice president of behavioral finance and investing at Betterment

Donnie Ethier: senior director, Wealth Management for Cerulli Associates

Rick Ferri: founder of Ferri Investment Solutions and president of the John C. Bogle Center for Financial Literacy

Deborah Fuhr: managing partner, founder, owner of ETFGI

Sheryl Garrett: founder of Garrett Planning Network

Nate Geraci: chairman and president of the ETF Store and host of the *ETF Prime* podcast

Wesley Gray: founder and CEO of Alpha Architect and former captain in the United States Marine Corps

Victor Haghani: founder of Elm Partners

Amy Hollands: director of development at LEAP Innovations

Anthony Isola: investment advisor at Ritholtz Wealth Management

Elisabeth Kashner: VP, director of global fund analytics at FactSet

Brad Katsuyama: cofounder and CEO of IEX Group

Michael Kitces: head of planning strategy for Buckingham Wealth Partners

Lee Kranefuss: founding member at The Kranefuss Group LLC

Taylor Larimore: author of *The Bogleheads' Guide to the Three-Fund Portfolio*

Michael Lewis: author

Burton Malkiel: professor emeritus of economics at Princeton University

John Mulvey: professor of operations research and financial engineering at Princeton University

Dave Nadig: chief investment officer and director of research of ETF Trends and ETF Database

Jim Norris: former managing director of Vanguard International and one-time assistant to John Bogle

Ken Nuttall: chief investment officer of BlackDiamond Wealth Management

Eric Posner: law professor at the University of Chicago Law School

Robin Powell: editor of *The Evidence-Based Investor*

Athanasios Psarofagis: ETF analyst at Bloomberg Intelligence

Salim Ramji: senior managing director and global head of iShares and index investments at BlackRock

James Riepe: retired vice chairman and former senior advisor at T. Rowe Price and previous Vanguard executive vice president and assistant to John Bogle

Barry Ritholtz: chairman and chief investment officer of Ritholtz Wealth Management

Todd Rosenbluth: senior director of ETF and mutual fund research at CFRA

Tyrone V. Ross Jr: CEO/cofounder of Onramp Invest

Gus Sauter: former chief investment officer of Vanguard

Jerry Schlichter: founder and managing partner of Schlichter Bogard & Denton

Jan Twardowski: former president of Frank Russell and former senior vice president of Vanguard

Nerina Visser: independent ETF strategist and advisor

Jim Wiandt: founder and CEO of Spark Network and IndexUniverse (now ETF.com) and the *Journal of Indexes*

Dan Wiener: coeditor of *The Independent Advisor for Vanguard Investors*

Catherine Wood: founder, CEO, CIO of ARK Investment Management

Jason Zweig: investing columnist for the *Wall Street Journal*

Yes, Warren Buffett is on this list. The fact that he even replied to my inquiry to offer some thoughts on Bogle is telling. He is famously tough to reach, so I figured my long-shot request would go unfulfilled. But Buffett replied, within a few hours to boot, with, "I'm swamped with requests, but I'll try to help on a couple of items about Jack."

And he wasn't alone. Almost everyone I reached out to got right back to me. There was genuine love and respect there, not for me or just to be quoted in a book, but for Bogle. People miss him. They still think about him. And they had plenty to say, as you'll see.

1

The Vanguard Colossus

"I was never in this business to build a colossus. But I was too stupid to realize if we gave investors the best deal they would ever get, I'd be building a colossus. So here we are."

Many people are well aware that Vanguard is a big asset manager. But there's so much more to it that isn't all that well-known because Vanguard isn't a publicly traded company like BlackRock or Goldman Sachs, so it largely lives off the radar. It physically exists off the radar, too, headquartered in Malvern, Pennsylvania, which is one hundred miles from New York City but might as well be five light-years away.

Even folks inside the industry probably do not realize the extent of Vanguard's growth rate, reach, and impact. The firm has gotten so big that Bogle—a true wordsmith, as you will learn throughout this book—called it a colossus. And its impact is only just beginning.

As I write this sentence, Vanguard manages $8.3 trillion for upwards of thirty million investors—and likely more by the time you read this. Those assets are in funds in a variety of asset classes as the firm spearheaded equity index funds and bond index funds, as well as money market funds and a variety of other financial products that we will explore.

Vanguard is currently the second-biggest asset manager by total assets but the biggest in US fund assets. Only BlackRock, which manages a lot of institutional money, is bigger overall, but barely and likely not for long, given that Vanguard regularly attracts more new cash every year. Vanguard has taken in an average of $1 billion every day for the last ten years. For most asset managers or advisors, $500 million in new money would be a good year. Vanguard sees that much come in by lunchtime.

Add up all those days, and you have a sum total of about $2.3 trillion in flows for Vanguard since 2010. In second place is BlackRock, with about half that, and then you need binoculars to see third place. Moreover, many asset managers have seen *outflows*.

Vanguard Annual U.S. Flows ($B)

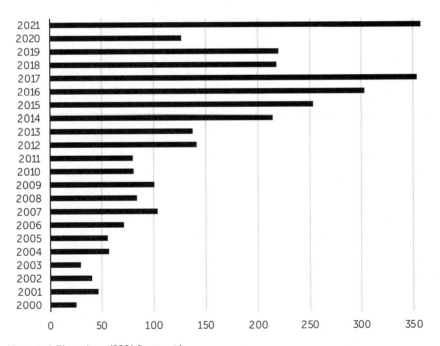

Vanguard, Bloomberg (2021 flows est.)

These numbers are even more astonishing considering every dime came from investors seeking out Vanguard as opposed to the company paying an intermediary, which it has always refused to do even though that is how much of the industry operates and was built.

Vanguard was not paying to be on brokerage platforms. It was doing limited, if any, advertising. Its products don't have cute tickers. They just are what they are, which is well diversified and cheap. And the firm is very diligent about what products they roll out to the marketplace, which is why people keep coming back to them time and again—because they know what they are getting.

—Todd Rosenbluth

One important factor to remember is that this isn't Vanguard's money but rather the money of thirty million–plus investors who were fed up with overpaying for underperformance and sought out the low-fee pastures of Vanguard. And this populist investor revolt has now reached fever pitch. If you were to rank the top ten biggest funds in the world, you'd find that Vanguard has *six* of them, including the *top three*. And this is in a fund industry that has about 750 companies with about 30,000 competing funds.

The biggest of them all, the Vanguard Total Stock Market Index Fund, is also the first and only fund to ever eclipse $1 trillion in assets. The fund serves up 99 percent of the entire US stock market for almost no cost. It's pure, uncut exposure to the whole enchilada. This fund is Bogle's *Mona Lisa*.

It is also notable that three of the remaining four funds in the top ten—the SPDR S&P 500 ETF Trust (SPY), the iShares Core S&P 500 ETF (IVV), and the Fidelity® 500 Index Fund (FXAIX)—are also dirt-cheap index funds offered by Vanguard's competitors, who essentially launched them after they saw all the success Vanguard was having (a development I refer to as the Vanguard Effect or the Bogle Effect throughout the book). And then there is the Growth Fund of America, the sole high-cost active mutual fund hanging on for dear life to a top-ten spot—a far cry from only twenty years ago, when active funds made up the majority of this list.

Top 10 Biggest Funds in the US

Name	Ticker	Active or Passive	Fund Asset Class Focus	Total Assets $B
Vanguard Total Stock Market Index Fund	VTSMX	Passive	Equity	1304.95
Vanguard 500 Index Fund	VFINX	Passive	Equity	796.24
Vanguard Total International Stock Index Fund	VGTSX	Passive	Equity	417.70
SPDR S&P 500 ETF Trust	SPY	Passive	Equity	384.85
Fidelity 500 Index Fund	FXAIX	Passive	Equity	350.33
Vanguard Total Bond Market Index Fund	VBTIX	Passive	Fixed Income	318.13
Vanguard Institutional Index Fund	VINIX	Passive	Equity	298.03
iShares Core S&P 500 ETF	IVV	Passive	Equity	286.71
Growth Fund of America	AGTHX	Active	Equity	278.81
Vanguard Total Bond Market II Index Fund	VTBIX	Passive	Fixed Income	254.31

Bloomberg

Add it all up, and Vanguard has a 29 percent market share of US fund assets. In the one hundred years that the fund industry has existed, no asset manager has ever come close to this level of dominance. The previous two leaders and their high-water marks were Investors Diversified Services (IDS) with 16 percent in 1964 and Fidelity with 14 percent in 1999. Anyone over the age of forty can attest to how invincible Fidelity seemed back in the day.

Fidelity was so big. It was just unfathomable that we would ever be bigger than Fidelity. It was so much bigger at the time.

—Jim Norris

Vanguard has about *double* Fidelity's assets today. In fact, Vanguard has blown both of those leaders' records away, and its market share is likely to go even higher given how dominant and consistent it is when it comes to inflows.

Staying Power

Unlike those other former top dogs, though, Vanguard's asset growth is not based on beating the market or having a star manager as much as it is on simply owning the market. Moreover, what makes Vanguard different is that despite having a 29 percent market share in assets, it only accounts for 5 percent of the industry's total revenue thanks to its superlow fees. That gap is why it is so popular with investors, and it may be the most telling stat in the whole book as it foreshadows the huge changes (shrinkage) coming to the financial industry.

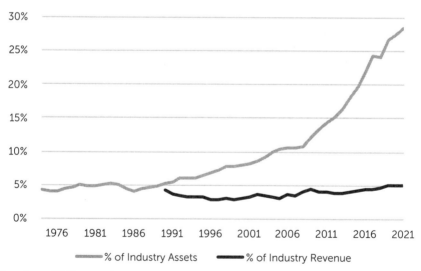

Vanguard's Market Share of US Fund Assets

Bloomberg, ICI, Vanguard

With no chance of underperforming the market (because the funds largely track the market) Vanguard's reign at the top is much more likely to last than its predecessors. Bogle purposely set it up this way. He had seen how fickle flows could be in his early years in the industry. He called it "the curse of the mutual fund industry" in a 1994 speech to the crew (his term for Vanguard's employees and staff):

> *We have tried to avoid, with some degree of success, the curse of the mutual fund industry: huge cash flows from investors after spectacular perfor-mance gains have been achieved and huge outflows after commensurate losses have occurred . . . This has always been a cyclical, market-sensitive business; it remains so today. But sooner or later, the investment pendu-lum, having swung to the speculative extreme, swings back to the defen-sive extreme, finally coming to repose in the conservative center, before repeating the cycle again.*

Bogle knew the history of the fund business better than anyone, and in *Stay the Course* he meditated on what it would take to ensure that Vanguard, with its edge of having a highly trusted name and low fees, would be able to stay on top:

> *By 2004, Vanguard had become the fourth firm to hold the crown of lead-ership in the mutual fund industry since its inception in 1924. At some point in their lives, our predecessors were all powerful firms, but some-where along the way, they lost their bearings and proved unable to deal with the changes in the investment environment, investor preferences, and the industry's distribution systems. Vanguard is different. We began following our guiding star of "shareholders first" 30 years before our rise to prominence in 2004, and we have continued to follow that star. Staying the course with our mutual structure and our index strategy should assure Vanguard's leadership for decades to come.*

Good Money vs. Bad Money

Another reason for Vanguard's staying power is its strong core of long-term-minded investors that was partially a result of it filtering out the "wrong" clients at the beginning. Bogle didn't want "hot" money that was going to use the fund short term and potentially incur costs for the long-term investors.

The first week I was at Vanguard was maybe the best lesson I ever learned. I'm there running the index fund, and I remember we had somebody who wanted to put a fair amount of money in. If it came in at more than $100k, I had to approve it, and this was more than that. It was significant enough that I talked to Jack about it.

I remember him saying, "Do we really want that money? There's a difference between good money and bad money."

It was a great lesson. Bad money comes in and stays for six months. You incur transaction costs coming in and transaction costs getting it out, and it does nothing but hurt the existing long-term investors. And that was what we were all about. [Rejecting that money] was absolutely the right thing to do, which is what drove Vanguard—being sure we were doing the right thing for our existing investors.

—Gus Sauter

The idea of turning down investors isn't unusual if you are some kind of private equity fund or small cap fund that can only take in a certain amount due to the limited liquidity of the market you are investing in. But it is highly unusual—borderline unprecedented—if you are a mainstream mutual fund company investing in big liquid markets, especially one that is young, small, and looking to grow. Stories like these help add a level of consistency to Bogle that is rare to find. He walked the walk even when it was inconvenient and would delay the company's success.

While Bogle relished the early years when he had to claw and scratch for the flows—"Honestly, I love the years of struggle," he said; "the years of momentum do very little for me"—he was nevertheless surprised at how *long* Vanguard struggled, given how good a deal it offered investors. "I'm disappointed by how long it took. Forty years is a long time."

Once the company took root, however, and the world came around, Vanguard's asset ascent was stunningly parabolic as evidenced by the fact that $7.3 trillion (88 percent) of Vanguard's $8.3 trillion in assets came after the firm's thirtieth birthday, in 2004. It is a textbook example of the Ernest Hemingway "gradually, then suddenly" line. The pace and level of Vanguard's ascent blew Bogle away—and perhaps even alarmed him a little. Here's what he told attendees at a Grant's Conference at the Plaza Hotel in 2017:

Indexing is growing at an astonishing rate and, for someone who never intended to build a colossus, a kind of frightening rate. When we passed the $4 trillion mark in assets at Vanguard, I recalled a speech I gave to our crew—I used to do it quite frequently—called "Which Axiom?" I gave it when Vanguard's assets crossed $8 billion. I used to give the speech every billion in the old days, and now we're taking in a billion a day. Go figure.

Vanguard's Total Assets

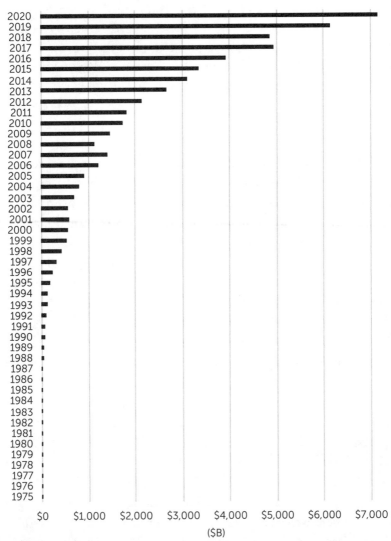

($B)

Vanguard, Bloomberg

The compounding effect that Vanguard experienced would become a fitting parallel to the compounding effect of the buy-and-hold, low-cost index investing that Bogle preached relentlessly for about fifty years.

In short: hang in there and don't do anything stupid because *it will start to add up.*

A Trillion Dollars in Savings

Speaking of adding up, the amount of money that Vanguard's rise has saved investors is pretty astonishing, and it's one of the reasons I was drawn to this topic. The sum of the savings is currently more than $1 trillion and growing exponentially. This is money that would have otherwise belonged to the financial industry—and why I sometimes say Vanguard's gain is Wall Street's pain. I'll walk you through how I came up with those numbers.

Average Active Fund Fee vs. Average Vanguard Fee

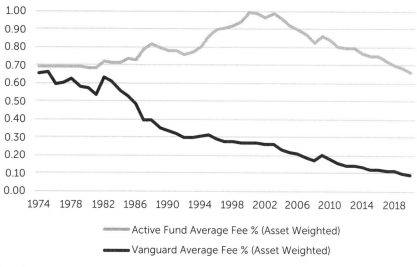

Active Fund Average Fee % (Asset Weighted)

Vanguard Average Fee % (Asset Weighted)

Bloomberg

First, investors have saved about $300 billion since Vanguard launched its first fund in 1976 via lower expense ratios, which is the term for the percentage of the assets in the fund that the fund company takes each year. This is calculated by assuming what those assets would currently be charged if Vanguard didn't exist. That spread has varied over the years, but generally it is about 0.60 percent more. That may seem small, but when it's multiplied by the trillions in Vanguard funds, it suddenly becomes big.

This number doesn't even include sales loads, which are onetime distribution fees (usually around 5 percent) that an investor pays to a broker. While Vanguard funds do not have loads, I didn't include them in this calculation because that is part of the shift in how advisors get paid—which we will look at shortly. But those savings could arguably be added to the total as well.

Investors save another $250 billion in the form of lower trading costs by having very minimal portfolio turnover. Every time a mutual fund manager makes a trade, it costs a tiny amount. Generally speaking, every additional 1 percent in turnover comes with 0.01 percent in extra costs. Active mutual funds have an average turnover that is approximately 50 percentage points higher than that of a Vanguard fund. Again, we multiply that difference by Vanguard's assets each year.

The turnover loss is why assets going to Vanguard stings both asset managers and Wall Street banks. Market makers and Wall Street banks facilitate much of the trading that happens each day. Using casino-speak, they are like the house and they get a tiny cut of each trade. When money moves to Vanguard, it basically leaves the casino entirely and lessens the amount that active managers—some of the casino's most prized customers—have available to trade. This is why you could make the case that the ethos behind Vanguard is similar to that of "DeFi," or decentralized finance.

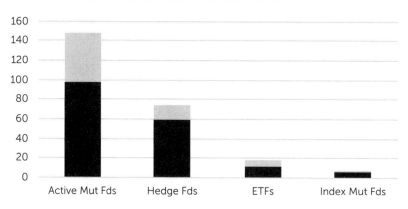

Estimated Annual Fee and Trading Revenue Generated in 2020

- Est Annual Trading Revenue Generated ($B)
- Est Annual Fee Revenue Generated ($B)

Bloomberg

Last, but certainly not least, there is the Vanguard Effect, or the company's influence on other financial firms to lower their fees in order to better compete. As Bogle put it in a 1989 speech to the crew, "Vanguard's very existence has established price competition—long overdue—in this industry, and if our competitors are dragged kicking and screaming into giving their customers a fair shake, well, that is not without redeeming social value, even if it slows our growth."

The Vanguard Effect has largely come at the expense of Vanguard's own assets since that is money that probably would have gone to the company but is now going to its competitors' low-cost funds instead. Yet the idea of others copying Vanguard's low-cost formula wasn't a problem for Bogle—in fact, it was the *perfect situation*. In *Character Counts: The Creation and Building of the Vanguard Group*, he recalls a 1991 speech to the crew:

And if our competitors will finally compete on lower price and higher value, rather than on higher spending on dubious marketing, they will make the mutual fund world even more competitive. Indeed, as I told the Harvard Business School class, the first sign that Vanguard's mission has created a better world for the investor will be when our market share begins to erode.

I'm not sure anyone else in the history of business—let alone the history of asset management—has ever wished for their market share to erode. It's somehow anticapitalist yet supercapitalist at the same time. It really speaks to the different trip Bogle was on. *Mission* really is the perfect word for it.

It's almost as if he is selfless as to how his goal gets accomplished. The thing about him was I always wanted to be more cynical about him than the material would permit. Whenever I tried to take it to the next level and [call him out], I'd sort of hit the wall and be like, no, he's not really motivated the same way everybody else is.

—Jason Zweig

That was absolutely [Vanguard's] mission, to basically do good for all investors. Heck, there are investors in Australia that don't realize the benefit they get because of what Vanguard did in the US. And the rest of the world have lowered fees because of Vanguard, and investors who have never heard of Vanguard are benefiting from it. It's the title of your book, The Bogle Effect.

—Gus Sauter

And while there was definitely some "kicking and screaming" among Vanguard's peers, many have also embraced the idea of offering low-cost index funds and ETFs because they know how beneficial it is to the client. They like being in tune with the end investor, and they deserve their due.

Bogle had incredible clarity of vision and was a huge advocate for individual investors, particularly in the United States. He was a pioneer. We spend a lot of time making investing more accessible and affordable, and I think if Bogle were alive, he would approve.

—Salim Ramji

Let's try to calculate the savings from the Vanguard Effect starting with active funds, which have seen fees drop from 0.99 percent in 2000 (when Vanguard and indexing started to get popular) to 0.66 percent today. Again, that seemingly small decline adds up because it is multiplied by trillions each year. That's about $200 billion in total savings from Vanguard's influence on active mutual funds to lower their fees as well as on investors to choose cheaper funds.

On the passive side of the equation, the Vanguard Effect is even greater. Think about it: every single issuer that launches a cheap index mutual fund or ETF (such as Fidelity, BlackRock, or State Street) is largely doing it because they need to better compete with Vanguard or serve a client that was influenced by Bogle's low-cost preaching. For example, the very first ETF launched in 1993, the SPDR S&P 500 ETF Trust (SPY), was inspired by and priced to match the fee of the Vanguard 500 Index Fund, which was 0.20 percent.

Today Vanguard has about 50 percent market share of the $11 trillion in total passive fund assets, but it influenced almost all the rest. And those non-Vanguard cheap passive funds have an asset weighted average fee of about 0.18 percent. If there were no Vanguard, this money would also likely be paying the active mutual fund rate. Thus, investors get another $250 billion in savings via the Vanguard Effect.

Interestingly, almost everyone I spoke with brought up the point that Vanguard offered low-cost index funds because it *wanted* to while others did it because they *had* to, and that difference mattered to them.

[Bogle] forced the hand of so many different places who have had to cut costs, kicking and screaming. Vanguard made them do this. It's not like they wanted to do this on their own.

—Ben Carlson

The only reason many of these other asset managers are offering and marketing low-cost index funds is because they have to. They don't have any other choice. If Vanguard was not in existence, trust me, Fidelity would not have zero-fee index funds.

—Anthony Isola

To sum up the savings:

Expense ratio: $300 billion
Turnover: $250 billion
Vanguard Effect (active): $200 billion
Vanguard Effect (passive): $250 billion
TOTAL: $1 trillion

But There's More

That's how I get to $1 trillion. But the real number is arguably even bigger than that. What I just walked you through was an updated version of my original math when I sketched this out in an article for *Bloomberg Opinion* in 2016. About ten days after the piece came out, my colleague Matt Miller asked Bogle what he thought about my article during a Bloomberg Television interview, and here's what he said:

> *Actually, it may even be understated. [Eric] doesn't take the savings each year and earn a return on the accumulated savings. If you put some kind of a return on the money we save investors each year and look at it over twenty years or so, you'll find a huge and staggering number. It's big. It's very big. And it's good for the investor. That's the important thing.*

OK, so let's add in the money that was likely made by reinvesting the savings people got each year and letting that compound. That results in *another* $400 billion. We could also throw in the international markets, which have about $3 trillion and counting in low-cost passive fund assets.

Either way, this puts the total savings at well over $1 trillion. And by the time you read this, the number will be higher than that since the amount saved is not static—rather, it grows by about $100 billion a year. And as assets grow, that $100 billion annual number will also grow. We could realistically reach $3 trillion or $4 trillion in savings in the next ten years, especially if the investor obsession with low fees persists—and I can almost guarantee that it will. Remember, this isn't total assets (that's going to be in the tens of trillions)—this is just the fee revenue that would have gone into the financial industry instead of investors' pockets.

Further, everything I've covered so far is just funds. Vanguard is now expanding into other areas as well. For example, the firm has launched an advisory business that charges a fraction of the industry average, which we will cover in a later chapter. It's also helped bring down the cost of trading after it announced commission-free ETF trading on its platform before other big discount brokerages did. It won't end there. Vanguard is making a push into Europe and Asia. It just made a first step into private equity. There's talk of launching a custody business. It could even get into crypto at some point. Anywhere it applies its unique structure and mission it is likely to disrupt the status quo and wreak havoc on any firm that has been overcharging and underdelivering.

The Faces Behind the Flows

Who exactly are these thirty million people (more if you add investors in competitors' index funds) that have "found" Vanguard and are enjoying that $1 trillion in savings? We in the media tend to focus too heavily on the supply side of the business. But it is important to understand and dig into the demand side, too. Without investors, there is no Vanguard and there is no $11 trillion in passive fund assets. Bogle made sure to keep the focus on the people behind the numbers. In *Character Counts*, he referred to them as "souls, all of whom with their own hopes and fears, their own financial objectives, and their own trust in us. And we have never let them down."

These investors, or souls, take many forms but can largely be broken down into four categories: The first is self-directed retail investors who found Vanguard directly. Then there are retail investors that have come through defined contribution (DC) plans such as a 401(k). The second group—and one of the fastest growing—is advisors, who are ultimately putting their clients into Vanguard because they consider themselves fiduciaries and feel it is the best move. Third is institutions, though most tend to do their own investing or favor alternative strategies like hedge funds and private equity. That said, Vanguard has a fair share of small- and midsize institutions that outsource their investment plans to it. We will look more at them later in the book. The final category is international investors, which is one of the newer but fast-growing areas for the firm.

Vanguard Assets by Investor Type

% of Vanguard AUM

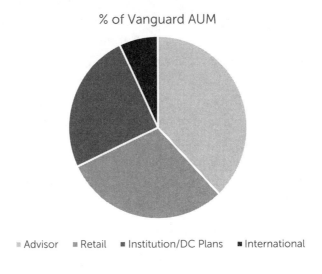

■ Advisor   ■ Retail   ■ Institution/DC Plans   ■ International

Vanguard

DIY Retail

Do-it-yourself retail investors make up about 30 percent of Vanguard's total assets but account for 90 percent of the firm's DNA. These are the original core assets, the ones Bogle obsessed over protecting in the early years. These are the doctors, dentists, schoolteachers, accountants, software developers, electricians, graphic artists, office clerks and managers, entertainers, athletes, PR people, plumbers, and financial industry professionals. These people were not looking to invest for fun or excitement but rather to achieve real goals, like sending their kids to college, buying a second home, and enjoying a comfortable retirement. Bogle lived for these investors.

He saved every single letter he ever received from an investor, and he showed me copies of them. He would talk about having to write back to some of them. That practically brought me to tears because who does that? Nobody. One letter he showed me was from a doorman who wrote him to say thank you because he was able to save for his kids' education and his retirement and he couldn't have done it without [Bogle]. He derived a lot of personal satisfaction from those

*[letters], especially as the passive investment movement got so big.
I think it was the only way he felt he could have a personal effect.*
—Erin Arvedlund

In a way, you could say that Bogle *had* to correspond with these investors because they were the owners of his company. They were, in effect, his boss. In fact, one of the earliest Vanguard investors would end up becoming something of a compass for the company to use in making decisions.

---

*We had this mythical character named Toby Choate. From the day
I got there, everybody kept talking about Toby Choate. Everything
was subject to the Toby Choate test. The legend went that Toby
Choate would ask, "Why do I want you to spend money on—" whatever
it might be, advertising or a holiday party or whatever. So we
always had that test: Would Toby Choate be OK with us spending
this money? If we couldn't justify spending Toby Choate's money,
because ultimately it was the investors' money, then we didn't do it.
And it wasn't until about ten years ago that I found out Toby Choate
was a real person. Back in the early eighties, he was challenging
Jack, "Do I want you to spend this money?" So I think Jack really felt
a fiduciary responsibility for the investors' money and are we getting
any sort of return for these people if we go out and spend a big wad
on marketing?*
—Gus Sauter

Not spending on advertising is right in line with Bogle's *Field of Dreams–*esque "Build it and they will come" approach. As he told the crew in a 1980 speech: "We are beholden to no army of outside sales staff. Rather, we depend on the investor to come directly to us." And they did. By waiting for people to come to it, Vanguard ended up attracting the best kind of "sticky" investors. In *Character Counts*, Bogle comments:

We have always known that our typical Vanguard client is better educated and wealthier than the typical fund investor. We know that, in addition, he or she is more ready, willing, and able to move his or her assets among our funds. In short, our prototypical client is a financially astute investor who knows what he or she wants, when he or she wants it and how to get it.

Celebrity Indexers

To Bogle's point, some of Vanguard's retail investors include some pretty prominent, high-profile people who use index funds when it comes to their personal money. One example is Salomon Brothers bond trader–turned-writer Michael Lewis, who has taken deep dives into many of the corners of Wall Street in his best-selling books, including *The Big Short* and *Flash Boys*. Here's what he told MarketWatch in an interview:

I've always been a boring and conservative investor. I own index funds, and I don't time the market . . . I put it away and I don't look at it very much . . . I think the best way is a low-cost index fund. I do not think people really should be making individual stock picks with their savings. I think that's generally been demonstrated to be not such a good idea. If you want to do it as entertainment like gambling—like you bet on football games—fine, but I think you're better off in a low-cost index fund, like a Vanguard index fund.

Another high-profile retail investor—if you could call him that—is Warren Buffett, who in a 2013 letter said he planned to put the vast majority of his wealth in an index fund:

My money, I should add, is where my mouth is: What I advise here is essentially identical to certain instructions I've laid out in my will. One bequest provides that cash will be delivered to a trustee for my wife's benefit. (I have to use cash for individual bequests, because all of my Berkshire shares will be fully distributed to certain philanthropic organizations over the ten years following the closing of my estate.) My advice to the trustee could not be more simple: Put 10 percent of the cash in short-term government bonds and 90 percent in a very low-cost S&P 500 index fund. (I suggest Vanguard's.) I believe the trust's long-term results from this policy will be superior to those attained by most investors—whether pension funds, institutions or individuals—who employ high-fee managers.

I asked him about this and he confirmed that it was still the plan.

Buffett's 90/10 portfolio is very similar to what former secretary of state Hillary Clinton's portfolio—as well as former president Barack Obama's—looks like, at least according to their financial disclosures. Both are strikingly simple but potent relative to many of their political peers, whose portfolios typically involve multiple funds from multiple fund families with a lot of overlap. Clinton reported to have about $5 million in the Vanguard 500 Fund. She also had around $75,000 in short-term treasuries.

Like Clinton, Obama has in the neighborhood of $600,000 in Vanguard index funds as well as some Treasury bills and notes, according to his 2016 financial disclosure. Vanguard is the only fund company listed in his disclosures. Like many, he has simplified his investments and kept them low-cost.

Academics

One of Vanguard's first-ever investors included renowned academic Paul Samuelson. An MIT professor for his entire career, he was the first economist in America to win the Nobel Prize in Economics. He was also an advisor to former presidents John F. Kennedy and Lyndon B. Johnson and wrote one of the textbooks Bogle used during college. He became friendly with Bogle and ended up writing the foreword to Bogle's first book: "I have no association with The Vanguard Group of funds other than as a charter member investor, along with numerous children and innumerable grandchildren."

Samuelson was the first of what would be a long line of academics who not only endorsed Vanguard and low-cost indexing and worked it into the curriculum but also became friends with Bogle. Here's Bogle talking about it on the *Bogleheads* podcast:

Another great source of our strength is academia. Few business school courses in investment do not take the index as book—the Bogle message. It's an academic community. So it's not just the man or woman on the street, worthy of help and worthy of honor, but it's the man off the street, too, in the ivory tower of education and sophisticated concepts that has also been a great asset.

The Ultimate Compliment

Some of these astute index investors include Vanguard's own competitors.

People used to say stuff about Bogle like, he's so sanctimonious, he's such a hypocrite. But on the other hand, they all owned Vanguard funds. To me, that was the funniest thing of all. What I learned from putting alcohol into these fund industry CEOs and talking to them—in five minutes they'd be like, "Yeah, most of my money is in Vanguard funds." So they hated him but they were customers at the same time.

—Jason Zweig

You would be amazed at how many analysts on Wall Street I used to manage money for that are index fund investors. A lot of Wall Street has their money and their family's money in index funds.

—Rick Ferri

"Look at all the directors of our mutual fund competitors," Bogle said on this topic during one of our interviews. "You know what they own when they buy their kids' college plans? They're going to Vanguard. Look at a securities salesman at Merrill Lynch when his uncle comes in and doesn't know what to do. He says, 'Buy Vanguard,' because it keeps him from looking like an idiot."

The Bogleheads

Some of the investors that found Vanguard have turned into something akin to missionaries in an effort to advance Bogle's cause and enlighten other investors. Dubbed the Bogleheads, the group started small and informally but has blossomed into a mini-institution with some *serious* reach. The roots of the annual conferences were formed by Mel Lindauer and Taylor Larimore, a World War II veteran who fought in the Battle of the Bulge and whom Bogle once dubbed "King of the Bogleheads," as a way to discuss, debate, and spread Bogle's message and philosophy of low-cost investing. The Bogleheads' conferences, individual chapters, and online forum have been very effective in spreading the "gospel," and Bogle appreciated it and was always available to the group. Here he is on the *Bogleheads on Investing Podcast*:

> *The Bogleheads have been a staggeringly large asset to Vanguard . . . The Bogleheads have not only helped one another but they are also independent and have nothing to do with us. They have nothing to sell but good grace and good advice. So the Bogleheads stand alone in being a huge asset to Vanguard and a huge asset to indexing.*

The Bogleheads are quick to say they are not a Vanguard fan club; they're more about Bogle-osophy. As such, the Bogleheads' forums often highlight the value-add of non-Vanguard funds, such as those from Charles Schwab or BlackRock. The forums are divided into personal investments, investing theory, and news and personal finance. A quick scan of topics shows people discussing nonqualified savings investments, ideas for diversification, protecting against inflation, dividends, and whether a 401(k) is worth it.

The Bogleheads forum is now the largest noncommercial financial forum in the world. When I wrote my last book (The Bogleheads' Guide to the Three-Fund Portfolio), the Bogleheads forum was receiving over 4.5 million hits per day with more than 70,000 registered members. Mel Lindauer and I held the first Bogleheads Conference in my living room in Miami in 2001. Everyone on the forum was invited. Mr. Bogle and twenty-one Bogleheads attended. We have held annual Bogleheads Conferences ever since. They are extremely successful and sell out within a few days.

—Taylor Larimore

The group's no-frills, ad-free, 1998-looking website is very Bogle. The site has no bells and whistles to divert from the content—which is the message boards and the discussions about all things investing. The Bogleheads run a tight ship, which means not allowing any solicitations at all, which I found out firsthand when I tried to solicit a few people to interview for this book and was immediately banned. To be fair, I did violate one of their rules, and they did write an email explaining that and gave me a second chance. I actually respect their dedication to the purity of the forum.

It really is a cohesive group with a cohesive view. And what's interesting about the group is, now that Bogle is gone, the hagiography can move to the back burner. They don't have to be dedicated to talking constantly about how great he was. They seem to be transitioning to advocating for his core ideas: buy and hold a diversified portfolio of low-cost index funds, don't trade, and be tax smart when you do. And that's kind of it. It's very simple. It's very clean. It's very sensible. And it has a lot of appeal for people. I think it probably is sustainable.
—Jason Zweig

The Bogleheads could be a force to come for generations. These hard-core groups tend to not last long in the investing world because they are typically built around an active manager. When the performance stops or falters or the manager retires or dies, the cult aspect goes away. But with Bogleheads, it is likely to grow as time goes on, because it isn't rooted in Bogle as a cult figure—although there is a little of that—as much as it is in the evergreen ideas he put forth and the focus on low-cost, prudent investing.

Reformed Brokers

Another big chunk of Vanguard's investor base—and the fastest growing—is advisors, who collectively manage a whopping $25.7 trillion in assets according to Cerulli Associates. They put together people's portfolios and in many cases also give them financial advice or do full financial planning. This group is currently undergoing a monumental sea change that has been one of the biggest (if not the biggest) catalysts for flows into Vanguard, index funds, and ETFs.

Back in the eighties and nineties, they were typically called brokers and they got paid via a commission, which was essentially a kickback from the mutual fund (although the money didn't come from the mutual fund company, it came from the end investor). That meant retail investors were paying a lot to the broker only to be put into high-cost, fee-laden, underperforming funds simply because the broker got commissions, even if the brokers knew deep down the fund was bad and they would never invest in it themselves.

This may seem like a horrible way to structure incentives because it is. Many of these brokers knew it, and it weighed on the conscience of some. They could see that this was not doing good for their clients and ran counter to their role as a fiduciary to just put clients into whatever fund paid them or their firm told them to push. But they didn't have much choice—or knowledge—in the pre-internet era.

The only thing you learned [back then] is what you learn at conferences or what your firm teaches you. And if you worked for a broker dealer, the only thing the firm taught you is what the firm sells. Once you become aware that there is something on the other side of the mountain, some people start becoming curious and trek across the mountain to see if the grass is greener on the other side. And it turns out, for a lot of advisors the grass is greener, and so you see a twenty-year flow from the broker world into the RIA world.
—Michael Kitces

Many of them became RIAs (registered investment advisors that commit to a fiduciary duty to their clients) and either fully or partially switched to a fee-based or asset-based model, in which they get paid not by commissions from the mutual fund but rather as a percentage of the client's assets—typically around 1 percent. Instead of working for and being a distribution agent for the mutual fund companies, they were now working for their clients. This incentivized them to pick funds that were both good for the client and cost as little as possible.

All this has helped create the torrent of flows we now see into passive funds. I spoke with many advisors who talked about having had an aha moment, or epiphany, and some have credited Bogle. After all, he had been out there pounding the table about this approach for two decades by then.

Rick Ferri was a broker at Smith Barney, where they put clients into active mutual funds that paid the brokerage firm. He was listening to Bogle talk at the CFA Institute annual meeting in Atlanta in the early nineties when he recognized that Bogle was saying the exact same thing he'd experienced independently.

"I realized that, wow, this indexing concept is something I need to look into more," says Ferri. "So I picked up a copy of [*Bogle on Mutual Funds: New Perspectives for the Intelligent Investor*]. I could not believe what he was writing in this book. It was exactly what I was seeing firsthand. I had this overwhelming realization—an epiphany—that, my gosh, there are people out there just like me. And you know what? We're right. This guy is right. Then I just consumed the rest of that book. And I decided this is what I have to do, because I was all about the client rather than making money for the firm."

Inspired by his epiphany, Ferri first proposed using Vanguard funds to his boss at the brokerage but got immediately shot down because Vanguard wouldn't pay the company to be on its platform. So he left and became an independent RIA. "I wanted to do what Bogle was saying," says Ferri, "but I couldn't do it where I was."

Ferri and others couldn't do it because Vanguard did not pay for distribution—which is one of the main reasons it took Vanguard so long to grow big despite having such a strong value proposition. It was like making a great movie but none of the theaters or TV channels would show it. How do you get people to come to you? You have to inspire them to leave the other system, which is not easy.

But this is what Bogle's message did. Once it really hit someone, it usually changed their life. They couldn't go back to seeing things the same way again. It was powerful.

Once you go indexing and you really understand why you are doing it, and you had the aha moment, the epiphany, you don't go back [to active]. It's like changing religions. Now all you do is get closer to the altar and eventually you join the choir.

—Rick Ferri

It was interesting how it felt like a religious conversion that the people who had previously been wildly enthusiastic about their own financial advice and their own financial acumen had come to conclude that actually they didn't have any. And they were then proselytizers for that idea that nobody knew anything, which is kind of the basis of it all.

—Michael Lewis

Once advisors stopped getting kickbacks from mutual fund companies and started getting paid as a percent of the clients' assets, it put all funds on a level playing field. And when index funds and Vanguard are on a level playing field, they almost always win that fight—and usually very easily. Thus, the shift to this new model for advisors is a huge, underrated factor behind the current rise of Vanguard, index funds, and ETFs.

Underlying the move to the fee-based model is a fiduciary obligation to do what is in the best interest of clients, and at the end of the day, if you look at the data that is out there, focusing on minimizing fund fees and taking an index-based approach over the long term tends to result in better investor outcomes . . . Bottom line is, if you are a fiduciary advisor, and you aren't paying attention to the data on cost and underperformance of active management, then I think you'll have a hard time justifying your role as a fiduciary.

—Nate Geraci

Many of the larger advisor networks have also followed suit. About 70 percent of the industry's revenue is now derived from asset-based fees as of 2020 and is estimated to hit 74 percent in 2022, according to Donnie Ethier, senior director of Wealth Management at Cerulli Associates, who conducts advisor surveys. That is up from about 51 percent ten years ago in a similar survey conducted by Cerulli.

"Whether you look at the fee-based trend by head count or assets," said Ethier, "the growth has been explosive over the last twenty years. And I think passive funds are a big, big reason. Almost every trend points back to that."

Institutional Investors

Institutional investors are another—albeit smaller—part of Vanguard's asset base. While some have moved toward Vanguard and passive, they have not done so with the same intensity as retail investors or advisors. It isn't in the nature of many institutions—especially the big ones such as pensions, endowments, family offices, and insurance companies—to go full Vanguard. They are basically married to alternative investments such as hedge funds, private equity, and real assets such as real estate (aka the Yale Model). While they have different needs and goals than smaller investors, there are unnatural conflicts of interest in that world that keep them from moving the funds into a low-cost, simple portfolio.

Having been in that [institutional world], it's just so much more intellectually stimulating in talking to all these venture capitalists, private equity people, and money managers and having this stable of managers to talk to. It gives them something to talk about and something to brag about to their committees or alumni. A lot of it is the signaling behind it. Where I used to be, we had fifty or sixty managers—it made no sense at all. That's why I wanted to get out. Talking about the index fund to your board is just not going to fly, especially when these places are so worried about quarterly performance, what's happening, and who on our list of managers we should take off.
—Ben Carlson

That said, some of these institutions are increasingly under pressure from stakeholders to stop using high-cost alternatives. For example, a few years back, eleven members of the Harvard Class of 1969 wrote a letter to Harvard's president lobbying to move half of its $40 billion endowment into low-cost index funds:

> *If half the endowment . . . had been in the S&P 500 index, where it would have cost literally nothing to manage, then Harvard would have saved half the payments to Harvard Management, amounting to $68.8 million—enough to pay a $43 million tax bill with a good deal more to spare.*

In all likelihood, we will see many of the mid- to small-size institutions that can't possibly get access to the top hedge funds—or don't need the intellectual stimulation—continue to shift to the Vanguard model. It just makes sense. Meanwhile, most of the bigger institutions will likely stick with the Yale Model.

International Investors

While the Bogle Effect and overall move to indexing is in full bloom in the US, it is really only just beginning in other parts of the world. The hang-up is that most of the rest of the world still has a system of brokers that get paid by the funds in the form of commissions. That stacks the deck against Vanguard and passive. That, along with the fragmentation of so many different countries, as well as a lack of defined contribution plans, makes the international market a much tougher nut to crack than the US one.

Especially in Europe, there is so much mediation that happens in the banks. The DIY investor, who is Vanguard's bread and butter, is operating in a different environment there. I do think the influence is growing and there is room for growth, but market structure and incentives can be an obstacle.

—Elisabeth Kashner

Another thing Europe doesn't have is a force of nature like Bogle, who is able to break through the clutter and really stir things up.

No one has taken on the messianic role in Europe, which should be even more sympathetic to the "you're getting screwed by Wall Street" story. I mean, they are getting more screwed there than in the US. It's ridiculous.

—Jim Wiandt

[Bogle] is much less known here in Europe than in the US. It wasn't until the last few years of his life that he entered the consciousness here. We are very much behind the US in terms of the public's awareness of how hard it is to beat the stock market. We've kept the illusion going a bit longer than you have. Thankfully, things have now started to change.

—Robin Powell

Vanguard is having as much success as any new entrant can have. They are growing their market share and they didn't buy their way in. They didn't do acquisition. They are steadily getting the Vanguard message out. And breaking into Europe is not that easy. Hard market to do it in. It's just a different animal.

—Athanasios Psarofagis

Outside of Australia, Asia is arguably even worse than Europe when it comes to the embedded commission-based system and intermediaries. Regardless, for many issuers, Asia is well worth the effort given the sheer number of people. Asia has six times the number of people as Europe and nine times the number as North America. That's a lot of retail investors who have yet to discover how much they can save by going from 2 percent to 0.20 percent in fees. This is why the Bogle Effect is only in the third inning.

The advisor is still paid to sell product everywhere in Asia except in Australia. So they are being paid to sell structured products and mutual funds, not ETFs. The other big challenge is that [Asia is] unlike Europe, which benefits from the EU UCITS regime (regulatory framework that allows for the sale of funds across Europe). You can create a fund under UCITS, and you can sell it in many places, including Asia. When you create a fund in Hong Kong, you can't go sell it in Singapore. You can't go sell it in Taiwan. You can't sell it in Japan or Malaysia. Asia today is very much a country-by-country silo, so there's no economies of scale.

—Deborah Fuhr

Vanguard's Non-US Fund Assets

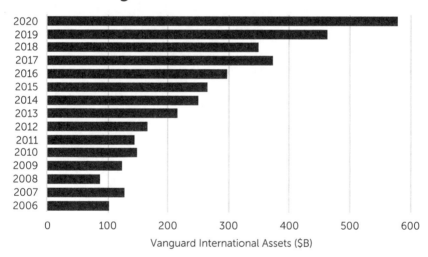

Vanguard International Assets ($B)

Vanguard

All told, about 7 percent of Vanguard investors are international, which adds up to a very healthy $578 billion. And passive overall is about $2 trillion. There's no doubt it will grow, however, for the same reasons it did in the US. It starts with the early adopters and then spreads to everyone else.

There are some people everywhere who understand [the risks of] investing in active funds that charge high fees but can't consistently deliver that alpha or are unlikely to. But there's a "do what your parents did [mentality]," and so you buy active funds. So it is slow to take off.

—Deborah Fuhr

Every country we'd go to, we'd hear, "It's different here." Really? Let's find out. We know it's not different. It can't be different. The math is always the same. So we have had to make the case for indexing in Canada, the case for indexing in the UK, the case for indexing in Australia. We have to go country by country and do the case for indexing just to prove the math is the math. The challenge, though, is the advisors and how they are paid.

—Jim Norris

The Retail Host Organism

Winning the hearts, minds, and assets of retail investors—and the advisors that serve them—across the globe is a major disruptive force inside the financial industry because retail investors tend to generate the highest fees for asset managers (institutional investors already get everything for near-free costs because they have so much money to pony up). Many asset managers live off them, which is why I call them "the retail host organism."

Once people get used to paying five to ten basis points for their entire portfolio, there's no chance they will ever go back to paying 1 to 2 percent. This is a *major* shift.

While most inside the industry are well aware of the revolutionary bomb that Bogle dropped on them—as they could feel it—few outside the bubble have really grasped the populist revolt Bogle was leading. One person who did was Hamilton Nolan, who in 2016 wrote this about Bogle in an article in Deadspin, which was a reaction to the Bloomberg Opinion piece I had written about the cost savings:

Che Guevara looks good in a beret, and Eldridge Cleaver had his moments, but today let us all take a moment to honor Real Motherfucking Hero of the People: John motherfucking Bogle . . . who has done more than any crusading socialist (in America) to take money out of the pockets of Wall Street . . . and keep money in the pockets of regular people. John Bogle founded a multi-trillion-dollar investment firm and did not use it to make himself into a multibillionaire but instead used it to produce a good product at a fair price that saves money for everyone who uses it . . . Wall Street hates this guy but I love him and so should you. It's good to Occupy Wall Street and it's good to regulate Wall Street and it's good to put the fear of populist insurrection into the heart of Wall Street every once in a while . . . Not all revolutionaries carry machine guns. Some carry knowledge of compound interest, which is just as cool.

New Fiduciary Society

Bogle relished the idea of leading a revolution. He built his whole life around it. Most of his books are largely rallying cries for a better business and investment world. He would have been perfectly cast had he been around in 1770s Philadelphia. In his book *The Clash of the Cultures: Investment vs. Speculation*, he says, "What we must do is build a new fiduciary society," and he lays out an investing bill of rights that includes eliminating conflict of interest, making the client king, and disclosing dollar fees along with fee rates, as well as providing good stewardship when it comes to voting shares.

This populist uprising is why Vanguard's massive size should be viewed very differently than, say, a gigantic tech company that has too much pricing power or can inhibit freedoms. This is what current Vanguard CEO Mortimer "Tim" Buckley thinks as well. Here's what he told ETF.com in a 2018 interview: "I might argue we aren't big enough. Five trillion is a big number, but that's our clients' money, not ours. Our revenue is $5 billion. We're hardly Amazon."

Nonetheless, Vanguard's size has become an increasing topic of concern—even for Bogle before his death. But for now, let's just leave this chapter alone as a testament to an idea whose time has come—and then some.

His impact is so underrated. He is one of the biggest philanthropists in the world if you think about all the money he has saved the average person. That money is now going into more productive things instead of these high-cost funds inflating the already inflated salaries of people who shouldn't be getting that much. His biggest legacy is the trillions of dollars he saved people. I don't think people really understand it in that way. It's extraordinary.

—Anthony Isola

And none of it would have happened if it weren't for a massive bear market and Bogle getting fired from his own company.

2
Declaration of Independence

"My goal was to create an enterprise that was only of the shareholder, by the shareholder, and for the shareholder."

f you trace the path of Vanguard's tremendous success—the rise of passive, ETFs, and a whole host of trends that dominate the investing landscape today—you will ultimately end up in the early seventies inside young Jack Bogle's brain and his decision to set up a new kind of fund company using a *mutual ownership* structure. That wonky-sounding—even boring—term is utterly powerful in practice and made the formation of Vanguard something akin to a declaration of independence, not just for Bogle at the time but also for investors.

The reason the mutual ownership structure is so powerful is simple—the company is owned by the funds and the investors own the funds. Thus, the investors own the company. The shareholders and the investors are no longer two different groups of people but one and the same. When there are extra revenues from assets increasing, the shareholders—who are the investors— tend to opt to lower fees (or reinvest in the company) via an elected board representing them.

The ownership structure is 100 percent the reason for Vanguard's success. A lot of people think Vanguard is a nonprofit or a not-for-profit corporation. Vanguard is a Subchapter C Corporation, just like all other corporations with every intention of making money. It's just a question of who you are making the money for. In all cases, you are making it for the owners of the firm, and the owners of the firm happen to be the investors in our funds.

—Gus Sauter

If you polled Vanguard investors, I would bet 75 percent of them have no idea that the mutual ownership structure is the nucleus and source of it all. They think it is something else. They don't really know. They don't think about it. But it was the breakthrough.

—Ted Aronson

Bogle totally agreed with this assessment as well. I asked Bogle point-blank in one of our interviews about which was more important—the mutual structure or the index fund?

"Well, in my mind, there's no question that the mutual structure is the founding block," he replied. "The basic block. Because you have a mutual structure, your whole idea is to see how cost can be kept down and to capitalize on low cost."

All one has to do is look at the expense ratio of the Vanguard 500 Fund over the years to see this structure in action. The fee has dropped from 0.43 percent in 1976 to 0.03 percent in 2021. What's notable about that decline is that most of the cuts happened when people really didn't care that much about fees as they do today. Investors weren't really demanding this. But that's just how the structure rolls. The more assets that come in, the lower the fees get.

Vanguard Fund Fees

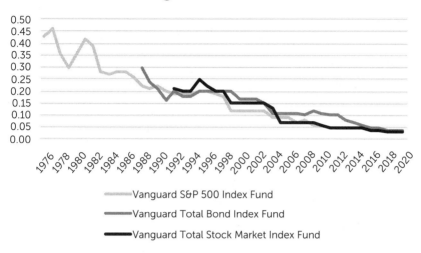

Vanguard S&P 500 Index Fund
Vanguard Total Bond Index Fund
Vanguard Total Stock Market Index Fund

Vanguard

The fact that Vanguard's shareholders are its mutual fund owners makes it very clear who everyone is answerable to, and so it short-cuts the principal agent problem. I think what both the mutual ownership structure and indexing have in common is the theme of efficiency.

—Elisabeth Kashner

The mutual ownership structure permeates the incentives. You might worry about a for-profit company doing sketchy things. You have to keep your eyes on them, at least in terms of incentives. But Vanguard has a different set of incentives. You own the fund. You are an owner of the company. So you are not just buying into the fund but into the fundamental structure. And if [you] commit to this fund, it is probably just going to get better over time.

—Dan Egan

One Master

Despite the obvious benefits of aligning the incentives of the fund company and its investors, to this day Vanguard is still basically the only fund company structured this way. So how are the rest structured? Well, about half of fund companies, such as industry giants Fidelity or Capital Group, are private, so the partners own the company. And the other half, such as Black-Rock or State Street, are publicly owned, so outside equity shareholders own the company. Both of these situations have the potential for conflict since the owners want profits and the investors want better returns and lower fees. Bogle talked about this discrepancy to anyone who would listen. Here he is in *Don't Count on It! Reflections on Investment Illusions, Capitalism, "Mutual" Funds, Indexing, Entrepreneurship, Idealism, and Heroes*:

> *Public ownership is anathema to any kind of fiduciary duty. You have two gods . . . Most mistakes and major faults of the financial era that has drawn to a close will be ascribed to the failure to observe the fiduciary duty, the precept as old as holy writ, that "a man cannot serve two masters" . . . It was high time that any conflicts between the profession of investing and the business of investing be reconciled in favor of the client.*

Now, to be fair, this doesn't mean people who work at publicly traded or privately owned asset management firms are bad people looking to exploit their investors. But they do have to deal with the inherent tension caused by two opposing forces. What's good for the shareholders may not always be good for the investors.

The author and Princeton professor emeritus Burton Malkiel spent twenty-eight years on the board of Vanguard and got an up-close view of the structure in action. "What always impressed me about Vanguard," Malkiel says, "is it not only talked the talk but walked the walk. It really did that. There was never any argument [over whether to lower fees with new profits]. That is the DNA of the company, and I think it's one of the few in the world that is truly mutual."

Given how crucial and rare this structure is, I think it is worth going through the story of how it happened. I honestly didn't realize just how wild, volatile, and serendipitous it all was until I researched it for this book.

But I suppose that is what it would take to form a company with a structure that there is no economic incentive to create.

Selling Doughnuts

The year is 1965. Lyndon Johnson is president and the Beatles had just released *Rubber Soul* while *The Sound of Music* was the number one movie. Meanwhile, a thirtysomething Jack Bogle was quickly climbing the ranks at the Philadelphia-based Wellington Management, one of the biggest asset managers of the day, which had hired him right out of college. Wellington managed one of the most popular, albeit conservative, active funds of that era. This fund was holding a prudent balance of stocks and bonds, and in the first half of the go-go sixties decade it was up a mere 5 percent, versus 87 percent for the S&P 500 Index. Meanwhile, many active managers who invested in some of the more high-flying growth stocks were returning much more than the market.

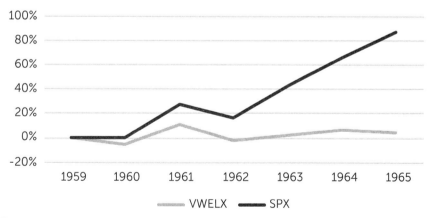

Wellington Fund vs. S&P 500 in the Early 1960s

Bloomberg

As you can imagine, investors were pouring money into the high-flying equity funds while ignoring the conservative Wellington Fund, which saw its share of cash flow fall from 40 percent to 1 percent. Wellington's founder,

Walter Morgan, turned over the reins to Bogle, his heir apparent, and asked him to "do whatever it takes to solve our problems."

Bogle was immediately faced with what most would consider a tough dilemma. Do you stick to your prudent roots and wait for the market euphoria to end, or do you try to adapt to the supposed new-normal era and join the party? For Bogle, it was a no-brainer. As he wrote in *Stay the Course*:

> *Perhaps overly confident, I thought the solution was obvious. Imagine you run a bagel shop and your customers are deserting you in droves, buying doughnuts from the shop across the street. To survive—or so I reasoned—you must start selling doughnuts yourself.*

His idea was to partner with a firm that was strong in equities and could modernize Wellington and give it some edge. Bogle initially asked American Funds (aka Capital Group), which said no. He then went to Franklin Custodian Funds (known as Franklin Templeton today), as well as a few other firms, and all of them politely declined. Eventually, he found a group of equity managers in Boston named Thorndike, Doran, Paine & Lewis, Inc., who ran a popular growth fund called the Ivest Fund. Bogle saw this as his best opportunity, although it was not his first choice. But he had to act because of the bagels and doughnuts situation. He gave the group 40 percent of Wellington's shares, which was effective voting control, as well as some board seats, in exchange for its talent and the Ivest Fund.

The Good Times

The partnership was an instant success. Growth stocks like Xerox, Polaroid, IBM, and Avon surged to the point where their price-to-earnings ratios were in the neighborhood of fifty, way above the long-term average of fifteen for the S&P 500. The funds were doing really well at first. They made the cover of *Institutional Investor* in 1968.

Here's an excerpt from that article:

The four from Boston had built a tidy investment counseling business bearing their names—Thorndike, Doran, Paine & Lewis, Inc.—and they had also built a reputation managing the Ivest Fund. Putting together Wellington's vast assets, elegant reputation, and marketing ability and the Ivest group's research and investment management talents and the winning reputation of its fund seemed like an extremely felicitous combination . . . The payoff came quickly. After a sales decline for Wellington Management from $168 million in 1965 to $151 million in 1966, the curve swung sharply up again in fiscal 1967, reaching to $180 million.

Bogle felt justified. His idea worked. The flows had reversed. But then things slowly got hairy. According to Bogle, his new partners "couldn't wait to get their hands on" the conservative Wellington Fund, which they ultimately altered to include more equities. The fund's manager during this period was Walter Cabot, who articulated why he changed the fund's strategy in 1967 during a nice run in the stock market:

Times change. We decided we too should change to bring the portfolio more into line with modern concepts and opportunities. We have chosen "dynamic conservatism" as our philosophy, with emphasis on companies that demonstrate the ability to meet, shape, and profit from change.

The Party's Over

The fund became much riskier than its original incarnation. And I'll bet you can guess what happened next. The raging bull market had decided to turn into a nasty bear market at the end of 1972, which would see the S&P 500 Index fall 37 percent during the next two years. The party was over.

1973 and '74 were the equivalent of 2008 plus March 2020. Everybody was walking around like freakin' zombies.

—Ted Aronson

Wellington Fund vs. S&P 500 During 1973 and 1974

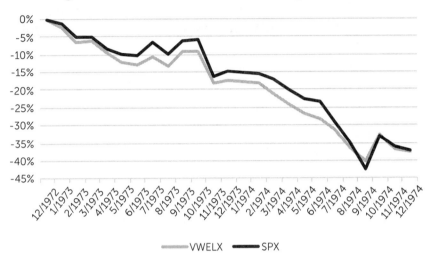

VWELX ■■■ SPX

Bloomberg

The Ivest Fund lost much more, about 65 percent, as the high-flying growth stock holdings took the brunt of the selling. It had lived by the sword and was now dying by the sword. Even worse, though—and ultimately heartbreaking for Bogle—was that the Wellington Fund went down the same amount as the stock market. In fact, in the first eighteen months of the bear market, the Wellington Fund did no better than the S&P 500 Index, dropping some 38 percent. That was a far cry from its relatively sturdy performance during the Wall Street Crash of 1929, in which it was buffered from the steep downside of the crash, declining only 3 percent in October 1929 versus 20 percent for the S&P 500.

This time, though, the "balanced" fund did not provide any balance. There was no buffer. It betrayed its objective and reputation. Had it stuck to its original objective—holding more bonds—it would have gone down much less than it did.

The regretful feeling must have been intense—especially because Bogle predicted this would happen, as evidenced by a memo he sent in March of 1972, mere months before disaster hit, warning Cabot and company to revert Wellington back to its original conservative focus from the equity fund it had turned into. He wrote:

Wellington has become a different fund than it was in the past . . . Yet the one characteristic that Wellington Fund has consistently offered to its shareholders has been relatively good downside protection (the result of its balanced asset allocation between bonds and equities). I conclude that our failure to show reasonable stability in the next market decline—and there will be one—would be "the last straw."

Cabot responded without addressing many of Bogle's points except to say the fund "has good downside protection" and that he thought they should not return it to its original form. When the bear market iceberg hit, it sunk Wellington. And then things turned really ugly internally.

The Bifurcation Period

The firm was losing assets. Wellington's stock price was on a decline that would see it fall from fifty to five dollars in a little more than five years. Bogle and his new colleagues disagreed entirely on how to move forward. They basically hated one another. Something had to give.

Bogle's tech-whiz assistant, Jan Twardowski, watched the whole thing play out. "They [TDP&L] were the hot guys," he says. "Bogle felt under pressure because he was running a stodgy old firm. He tried to buy them but ended up merging with them. Then their performance tanked. Of course it did. The go-go years ended. His timing was awful. But they had voting trust and they got control. And so they were going to throw him out . . . He was going to get fired. There were enormous personality clashes."

Despite Bogle having courted them and despite their horrible returns in the market decline, Thorndike, Doran, Paine & Lewis banded together, fired Bogle, and named one of their own, Robert Doran, as the new CEO. Bogle claims he was a scapegoat, although he was reportedly no picnic to deal with either during this period, according to people close to the situation. But it didn't matter. His colleagues had the voting control, and he was out.

Bogle was utterly savage about it years later in a 2016 interview with *Bloomberg Markets*:

The first five years you would have described Bogle as a genius. And at the end of the first ten years, roughly, you would have said: the worst merger in history, including AOL and Time Warner. It all fell apart. Their management skills were zero. They ruined the fund they started, Ivest. They started two more and ruined both. And they ruined Wellington Fund. The company started to shrink radically, and they who had done the damage decided to fire me.

However, while the Thorndike crew had voting control of the Wellington Management Company, Bogle was still chairman of the eleven funds for which Wellington served as advisor. This is a wonky detail but absolutely key as mutual funds are like shell companies or general contractors, and they get to choose the investment manager, administrator, distributor, and so on. In short, they controlled the contracts.

They (Thorndike and Doran) fired him. Well, they asked him to resign. But he wouldn't do that, so they fired him. But they made a very serious mistake, because they were not mutual fund people. They didn't recognize that the mutual fund boards had enormous power because they controlled the management contract. The fund boards had more Philadelphia directors that knew Jack well than Boston directors. So after deliberation they said, "You guys made a terrible mistake, and we are going to work through this, and you are going to continue to have Jack as president of the fund during this period, and you are going to pay him." That began what Jack and I used to call the bifurcation period.

—Jim Riepe

Even though Bogle was chairman of the board of the funds, he couldn't act unilaterally. He would need to get the board members' buy-in. There were nine people on the board, six of whom were "Philadelphia people" appointed by Bogle's mentor, Walter Morgan—who generally liked Bogle and wanted to keep him—while three were Thorndike appointees, who likely weren't Bogle's biggest fans.

At this point, Bogle could have just called it quits. If it were me, I probably would have taken a few months off to lick my wounds, hang out with my family, and then go find a new job rather than stay in such a toxic atmosphere—but that's just not Bogle's nature. Plus this was all very personal for him, given that Morgan had left Wellington in his care.

He decided to dig in, fight, and exploit this oversight that the Thorndike crew had made in not realizing that Bogle was still chairman and president of the funds themselves and there was nothing they could do about it. This kind of civil war (aka the bifurcation period) between mutual funds and their independent advisor was unheard of, as the boards of the funds and the advisor have large overlap. But an unheard-of situation is exactly what it would take to create a largely unheard-of structure for the asset management business.

We Need a Solution

In early 1974, the board of the funds—looking for a way to resolve the chaotic situation—requested that Bogle present some options for them to consider.

While the board was arguably tilted spiritually in Bogle's favor, it was also taking its independent role seriously, and it told him the vote had to be unanimous to proceed—meaning the three Thorndike appointees had to agree, too. This forced Bogle to get creative. How could he keep his job while breaking free from the hotshots who had just booted him from his own company—*and* do it in a way that would satisfy the board?

In Bogle's book *Stay the Course*, he says he relished this challenge, so he and his assistant Jan Twardowski—in what sounded like a scene from the movie *Jerry Maguire*—ended up cramming to write a 250-page study to be presented to the board, titled "The Future Structure of the Wellington Group of Companies."

He had me issuing all kinds of different reports, suggestions, analysis, and stuff. And then he came up with this big thing, which I produced all the numbers for and wrote the technical stuff. He wrote the business stuff. There were several iterations.

—Jan Twardowski

They presented seven options to the board, four of which the board decided to focus on:

1. Status Quo: A continuation of all existing relationships.
2. Internal Administration: Administer the eleven funds by themselves and use Wellington Management as investment advisor and distributor.
3. Internal Administration and Distribution: Bring everything in-house but still use Wellington Management as the investment advisor.
4. Mutualization: The Wellington mutual funds would acquire Wellington Management.

For Bogle, mutualization would be a way for the funds to acquire the management company and basically "unscramble the egg" of the failed merger. He thought this was a way for the eleven funds (of which he was chairman) to gain independence from Wellington Management Company (the company he was just fired from)—and more importantly to save his job. In Bogle's mind, the eleven funds were like the thirteen colonies, and Wellington Management Company was King George III.

Of course, this mutual structure wasn't invented by Bogle. It had been around for centuries and was common in the insurance industry (which is how Bogle knew about it). That said, this structure was and is highly rare in the asset management business due to the lack of economic incentives. No one wants to turn over all the potential power and money like that. On the flip side, companies structured as mutuals tend to last for long periods of time because the incentive system is aligned with the clients.

A Compromise Is Reached

Ultimately the board decided on the least disruptive choice, which was option two—bring the administration of the funds in-house. It would create a new company that would be owned by the funds themselves. Its purpose would be to provide administration for the eleven Wellington funds, and Bogle would be CEO. Meanwhile, Wellington Management Company would continue as investment advisor and distributor for the funds, which is what it liked doing anyway.

Jack and I recommended several options to the fund directors and we knew some of them were a bridge too far, such as "turn the whole business over to us." What they settled on was "you guys can set up your own administration so we are not dependent on the manager for overseeing our funds." We are going to take over finance, accounting, shareholder services, and communications—and Jack would stay as chairman of the funds.

—James Riepe

[Jack] was able to convince them that he was going to start a new type of organization and he was not going to get into [the] investment management business and compete with them: "I'm going to do the ugly part of your biz that you don't like anyway. The distribution and back-office stuff. You guys want to focus on investing." So he convinced the Wellington board that it was good for them. And he was able to sell it to them because it was novel that he wasn't just going to generate a tremendous amount of profit to put into his pocket but he was really going to benefit the investors in their funds.

—Gus Sauter

While this arrangement wasn't Bogle's desired scenario by any stretch, as he wanted the funds to acquire Wellington Management Company outright, it allowed him to keep his job and gave him enough rope to work with. He was able to take twenty-eight people with him, which included his trusted assistants James Riepe and Jan Twardowski. He decided to name this new back-office company *Vanguard,* after a British navy ship commandeered by Vice-Admiral Horatio Nelson that helped to beat the French and kill Napoleon's dreams of world domination. Bogle loved the symbolism.

It Oughta Be True

And that's how the almighty Vanguard and its mutual structure was born. While saving his job and living to fight another day were his main objectives, Bogle said much later on that he had been bothered for years by Wellington trying to "serve two masters" by being a publicly traded mutual fund company. So he'd had this grand altruistic vision all along. Others who witnessed the situation say it was more circumstance than vision. But as one of his former assistants told me, "When it comes to Jack, if isn't true, it oughta be."

Was he a saint? No. Did he have a once-in-a-century idea? Yes. Did he like to rewrite history and say he was a great guy all along? Definitely.
—Erin Arvedlund

One of my pet theories about Jack is that he cast himself as the outsider, like Shane riding in on the horse. But he was the ultimate insider. What happened is he got thrown out from the inner circle. Running Wellington Management in the late sixties is hardly an outsider job. It's sort of like being secretary of state or Speaker of the House. He was not only an insider but he was also in the innermost circle. Then he got thrown out. And what did he do? He made a virtue out of necessity.
—Jason Zweig

Zweig also pointed to a speech that Bogle gave in the early seventies at the Investment Company Institute [ICI] general membership meeting while he was still running Wellington, which the company called "The Future of Mutual Funds," in which he essentially defends active mutual funds from some articles critical of their performance. He basically says active mutual funds are doing a good job and that the S&P 500 isn't a fair benchmark (wait, what?). He even defended distribution fees and industry compensation. Reading the speech was a very weird experience, because while it is written in Bogle's signature fiery voice, it is largely making the *opposite* case that you'd expect from him. Here are a few lines:

> *With respect to performance, I do not see how the mutual fund industry's long-term record of performance could be very much better . . . it is, on an absolute basis, excellent and on a relative basis, superior to even the toughest market index . . . The negative comments are based principally on a comparison of the S&P 500 Index with the Lipper Average of 530 mutual funds . . . it really is comparing apples and oranges.*

This speech—as well as the fact that he was happy running Wellington (he wrote, "I assumed that I would be at Wellington forever" in *Stay the Course*) until disaster struck—gives credence to the "virtue out of necessity" argument and counterbalances the hagiography tendencies in writing about Bogle.

Young but Experienced

While Bogle's motive may not have been as saintly as he liked to present it, no one disagrees that once Vanguard happened, he was all in and a total warrior for the cause. Plus, Bogle was also in the sweet spot of having a lot of time on his side. He was in his early forties, armed with some hard-won life lessons about market cycles and self-betrayal. That experience would fuel the discipline it took to not take the "market cycle" bait again—no matter how many years have to pass in which everyone wants doughnuts and you are selling nutritious bagels, which is what has happened about half a dozen times since.

The story of how getting fired turned into the best thing for someone is not uncommon. It isn't dissimilar to Steve Jobs, who was ousted from Apple, or Michael Bloomberg, the founder of Bloomberg L.P. who was sent from the glamorous equity trading desk to the IT department and ultimately fired from Salomon Brothers after the company was sold.

There's definitely something about getting rejected that can end up being a blessing in disguise—like fate's way of nudging you toward something greater or the place you really belong. If it happens to the right person, it can change the world. As the great Bob Marley put it, "When one door is closed, don't you know, another is open."

Had Jack Bogle not been fired, I don't think there would have been a Vanguard. On the other hand, once it happened, Jack was absolutely, positively all in.

—Jim Norris

Born in Strife

Despite the colossus that Vanguard would ultimately become, there was no initial excitement or press about the company's birth or its unique structure. It was no overnight success. In fact, it was just the opposite. Officially formed in 1974, Vanguard spent its first decade in relative oblivion and then its next decade in slightly less oblivion. It took the company about twenty-five years to get to a 10 percent market share of fund assets. Luckily for Bogle—at forty-five-years young—he had the time.

People don't focus as much on the entrepreneur aspect of him. He was so young when he did this, and a lot of the ideas he had were groundbreaking. It's almost lost a little bit because it's now so taken as a given.

—Ben Carlson

But initially Vanguard just seemed like a small back-office company administering eleven funds, which is what it was. Further, those eleven funds were in the middle of what would end up being *eighty straight months* of outflows. An unimaginable streak considering the inflow-machine Vanguard is today.

Vanguard has had one negative month of cash flow in the last fifteen years, and he had eighty months in a row of negative cash flow. You can imagine a CEO after year one, year two, year three, year four, year five, year six thinking, Maybe this was a bad idea. *Particularly someone as competitive as Jack.*

—Jim Norris

Vanguard's Net Flows from 1974 to 1980

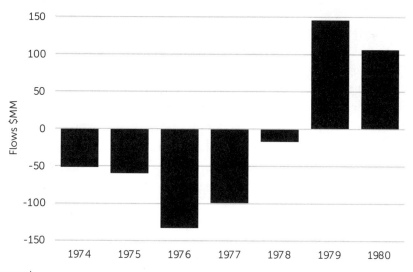

Vanguard

This is why Bogle liked to quote *Miss Saigon* when describing Vanguard's inception as being "conceived in hell, and born in strife." But while Bogle knew his timing was not opportune, he says he was never discouraged. He knew he had something unique—separate from Wellington the company and his former partners—that he could build on and experiment with.

> There was Wellington management and then there's this other thing. That separation allowed him to be in his own petri dish. And it created an explosion.
>
> **—Ted Aronson**

> I think it was essential that Vanguard didn't have profits as a motivator, as that allowed Bogle to be a lot more experimental than it otherwise would be.
>
> **—Christine Benz**

"You Will Destroy This Industry"

While the media didn't really notice the potential of Vanguard, the company definitely caught the attention of its competitors—after all, Bogle was a well-known figure inside the industry. In July 1974, within a few months of the board's approval of the new subsidiary—Bogle hadn't even chosen the name Vanguard yet—Bogle met Jonathan Lovelace, the head of American Funds (Capital Group) in an airport. In *Stay the Course*, Bogle recalls what Lovelace told him: "If you create a mutual structure, you will destroy this industry."

Note that Lovelace's comment came two years before Vanguard launched its first index fund. This was *solely regarding the structure.* He knew that it probably didn't even matter what kind of funds were offered; it would ultimately feed on itself by lowering costs, which would attract assets, which would allow it to lower costs more. This would then force everyone else to follow suit, à la when a Walmart opens in a town. And he was spot on. That's *exactly* what happened.

Ironically, Lovelace was the first person that Bogle reached out to when he was seeking an equity partner in the mid-sixties. Given their good relationship at the time, if they had become partners, it is very likely that there would not have been a falling-out and thus no bifurcation period, which was necessary for the formation of Vanguard. The idea of that alternate reality led me to imagine some other what-ifs: What if one of the more conservative asset managers Bogle first approached, such as Franklin, had said yes? What if the bear market in the seventies hadn't been as bad? Would Bogle have remained the happy CEO of an actively managed mutual fund company?

We'll never know. I lean toward yes, Bogle would have stayed a happy CEO running an active mutual fund company. Perhaps he would have applied some investor-focused initiatives, but it is hard to imagine anything like a Vanguard happening had fate not intervened. It took a freak situation to provide the motive to create a freakishly rare structure.

Proof positive of this is the fact that despite Vanguard's tremendous success, it has yet to truly be copied by anyone in the *fifty years* since the company was formed—which always fascinated me and is one of the reasons I wanted to write this book. I asked most people I interviewed why they thought this was and most gave roughly the same answer:

Nobody's ever going to do it because people don't commit financial suicide willingly. Why would I forgo hundreds of millions of dollars in net worth and millions of dollars in annual comp to drive a Volvo like Jack did?

—Jason Zweig

The only way an existing fund business could mutualize is to give up all its revenue or have the mutual funds buy it out. So the economics just didn't work for existing fund managers, and if you wanted to start a mutualized fund company, who is going to give you the capital to do it?

—James Riepe

It's anticapitalist. That's the fundamental reason. In a normal economy, pools of capital seek ways to grow, so they build businesses that have high margins that can be exploited, so their $100 million becomes $200 million. The Vanguard model is not that. And that is why it is difficult for someone to step in and replace it.

—Dave Nadig

I asked Bogle this question as well. His response: "The simple but somewhat bragging answer is: all the damn money goes to the investors."

No *Forbes* Lists

Setting up the company as a mutual meant Bogle would have to forgo any potentially massive amount of upside and personal enrichment. That said, he was already fairly wealthy at the time of his ejection from Wellington. And he was paid a handsome salary during his years at Vanguard, ending up with a net worth of $80 million—a large sum to most people, although far below that of his peers.

For example, Bogle's net worth is 225 times less than that of Fidelity Investments' CEO Abigail Johnson, whose net worth is an estimated $26 *billion*, according to *Forbes*, and it is twenty times less than that of the retired bond manager and Pacific Investment Management Co. (PIMCO) cofounder William Gross, who has a net worth of $1.5 billion and once got an annual bonus of $290 million (which sparked an investor lawsuit). In short, he never made any of the *Forbes* richest lists.

It's incredible that he only ended up with $80 million. I thought you were going to say $2 billion, and even then I would have thought, "Wow, he really left a lot on the table." He commandeered trillions of dollars, and he only made a few million himself. In the history of Wall Street, the ratio of money touched to money taken was never so high.

—Michael Lewis

He lost billions of dollars in opportunity profits when he didn't set it up as a Fidelity-like operation. I asked him about that, and he would say, "Well, I have enough money," so I thought that was pretty admirable.

—John Mulvey

Bogle was well aware of this point. He said at times it made him jealous not to be on the lists, but overall he wore it like a badge of honor, even weaponizing it. As he wrote in his book *Enough: True Measures of Money, Business, and Life*:

> *I have never played in that billon-dollar-plus major league, nor for that matter, even in its hundred-million-dollar-plus league. Why not? Simply because as the founder of Vanguard, I created a firm in which the lion's share of the rewards would be bestowed on the shareholders of the truly mutual mutual funds that compose the Vanguard Group . . . So I'm something of a financial failure compared to my peers in this business. But I'm doing just fine, thank you. I was born and raised to save rather than spend.*

Now it's easy to shame all these billionaires as greedy when you aren't one. But the thing is, 99.9 percent of us don't have a choice in the matter. We don't have the vision, dedication, work ethic, and luck all coming together like that. But Bogle did—he had the choice to go the megarich route. And moreover, he had just started a family with six kids. There was plenty of incentive to look for something with much more upside potential. So why didn't Bogle?

Enough

He had enough. He didn't need to be the primary shareholder in a $7 trillion company to have enough. He had enough at a much lower bar, and at the point that you had enough, why bother doing more? He created a structure in which you have enough. That's actually part of Bogle's legacy writ large—he was the guy who talked about having enough and what it meant to have enough. But the truest manifestation of that is he built the company that way, and it mattered.

—Michael Kitces

Enough, one of Bogle's books, is about how much better the corporate and investing worlds would be if leaders learned to be happy with enough instead of always wanting more. The book opens with this story, which may as well be Bogle's thesis statement for life:

At a party given by a billionaire on Shelter Island, Kurt Vonnegut informs his pal Joseph Heller that their host, a hedge fund manager, had made more money in a single day than Heller had earned from his wildly popular novel Catch-22 *over its whole history. Heller responds, "Yes, but I have something he will never have . . . enough."*

His notion of "enough" was in his soul. He was like a Puritan or a Calvinist. He liked money and he got some good money, but enough was enough. If there hadn't been the "enough" part of Bogle's personality, it wouldn't have happened. It's the money for most people. We active managers salivate over it. We get excited.

—Ted Aronson

I think that is something people should think about, the quality of life, not just how big your boat is. Several decades ago I was working with an investor down in Palm Beach, and he had a 120-foot boat, and we'd go there for lunch, and he was so jealous of the person who had a 180-foot boat next to him.

—John Mulvey

I remember hearing stories about Bogle's thriftiness—that he never flew first class—and to be honest, I was a little skeptical. But most people I interviewed said these stories were largely true.

I once asked his secretary if it was true that Jack flew in coach. She assured me that he flew coach class whenever he could. I have seen him take home the uneaten part of his sandwich at a Bogleheads convention.

—Taylor Larimore

Bogle shared this frugal style with Warren Buffett, who is famous for living in the same house in Omaha that he bought in 1958, eating at McDonald's, and drinking Cherry Coke. It is perhaps one of the ultimate ironies that the richest and most successful active manager of all time and the "father of the index fund" were cut from the same cloth and mutual admirers.

Jack told me that when he had met Warren Buffett, he was in an airport and he saw Buffett waiting for an airplane and noticed that Buffett had on a ruffled suit, and he went over and introduced himself, and he thought, "This is my kind of guy."

—Burt Malkiel

The funny thing about my dad is that by the standards of just about any industry he was very successful in his career and made a good amount of money, but he was never really motivated by the money. He didn't spend money—ever. He wore old, beat-up clothing. He wore the khaki pants that he must have had for forty years, and they looked terrible, but he didn't care. That's just the way he was.

—John C. Bogle Jr.

Now, of course, what Bogle didn't get in megawealth he did make up for in appreciation from Vanguard investors—which is ironically something he could never get "enough" of (I will explore this in chapter four). According to people close to him, that was much more a motivator than money.

3
Average Is the New Great

"Our stock-in-trade is to guarantee you your fair share of the stock market returns. That's good today and that's good tomorrow. It's good in rising markets and it's not good in declining markets."

While Vanguard's mutual structure—and having Bogle as its leader—would have helped the company find success even if it only offered actively managed funds, the index fund was really the ultimate vehicle. As Bogle explains in *The Little Book of Common Sense Investing: The Only Way to Guarantee Your Fair Share of Stock Market Returns*:

Simple arithmetic suggests, and history confirms, that the winning strategy for investing in stocks is to own all of the nation's publicly held businesses at a very low cost. By doing so you are guaranteed to capture the return that these businesses generate in the form of dividends and earnings growth. The best way to implement this strategy is simple: Buy a fund that holds this all-market portfolio, and hold it forever. Such a fund is called an index fund . . . Index funds make up for their lack of short-term excitement by their truly exciting long-term productivity. Thanks

to the growth, productivity, resourcefulness, and innovation of our cor-
porations, capitalism creates wealth, a positive sum game for its owners.

There have been thousands of books written about investing, but these 120 words are arguably all you really need to know.

Not only did the index fund fit hand in glove with Vanguard's mutual structure, it was an idea whose time had come. The concept of indexing as an investment strategy had been kicking around in the academic and institutional worlds for a couple of years but had yet to see anyone champion it for the masses. Investors and advisors alike were becoming exhausted by the time-consuming and largely futile process of trying to pick active managers amid boom-and-bust cycles.

While the logic of an index fund as an investment may seem obvious today, it was not so back in the day and perhaps still isn't to some. An index fund can be counterintuitive to anyone living in a capitalist society. Investing in all the companies in the market and weighting them by their size— which requires almost no thought at all—seems like a very average and dull way to invest. As one of Vanguard's competitors once put it, "Who wants to be operated on by an average surgeon or be advised by an average lawyer?"

The concept of indexing is really counterintuitive, and it's just not something that gets people's blood racing. Investors primarily care about two things: making as much money as possible and losing as little money as possible. And indexing doesn't sound like a way to do either. It's also stupefyingly boring. There's nothing to say. There's nothing to do.

—Jason Zweig

It's boring as shit. But good investing should be boring.

—Barry Ritholtz

It really is very boring—from the way the index is designed to the patience needed to do it well. You basically just take a section of the market and buy the stocks in proportion to how big they are as measured by market capitalization. While there are some other criteria that can differ between indexes, for the most part, index funds are McDonald's simple. Just look at the top holdings of the Vanguard 500 Index Fund:

Top 12 Holdings of the Vanguard 500 Index Fund

Security	Ticker	% Weighting
Apple Inc	AAPL US	6.22
Microsoft Corp	MSFT US	5.94
Amazon.com Inc	AMZN US	3.89
Alphabet Inc Class A	GOOGL US	2.27
Alphabet Inc Class C	GOOG US	2.16
Meta Platforms Inc Class A	MVRS US	2.37
Tesla Inc	TSLA US	1.48
Berkshire Hathaway Inc CLASS B	BRK/B US	1.41
NVIDIA Corp	NVDA US	1.46
JPMorgan Chase & Co	JPM US	1.26
Johnson & Johnson	JNJ US	1.19
Visa Inc Class A	V US	1.01

Bloomberg

While these are all great companies to own, the way they are assembled can come off as overly generic. This is one of the reasons the concept took so long to take off. American consumers naturally want the best. They like competition and winners. It's in our DNA. Active investing simply fits our culture much better. But, over time—and largely due to Bogle's dogged persistence and evangelism—people have realized that investing in an index fund is, in fact, winning.

To put it in baseball terms, investing in an index fund is like guaranteeing yourself a double or a triple. You do give up the glorious, dopamine-rush home run, but you get an extra base hit, and you also ensure that you don't strike out, which is a trade-off most are willing to make when it comes to their retirement savings.

The case for indexing shines when you look at how, during a ten-year period, about 80 percent of active mutual-fund managers—outside of a few niche categories—lag their benchmarks, according to the S&P Indices Versus Active (SPIVA) Scorecard. Thus, by buying an index fund, you are basically guaranteeing yourself a fund that lands in the top 20 percent of all funds on a performance basis. Further, the active funds that managed to win in the past decade are almost guaranteed to lose in the next. SPIVA also does a persistence scorecard that shows that only a small fraction of the benchmark-beating funds can repeat the feat. The numbers get worse for active the longer the time frame, too. Thus, you could argue that index-fund investing is, in fact, hitting a home run, if you can hang in there long enough.

Bogle was brilliant to position index funds this way. If you go by the numbers, they *are* star managers. Here's Bogle on this in *The Clash of the Cultures*:

> *Thinking of this extraordinary performance, I once had a dream that when I started the [Vanguard 500] fund, I decided not to disclose that it was an index fund. I told investors that I would be the portfolio manager. In the dream, I was named the most successful equity-fund manager of the past quarter century.*

I spent a lot of time over the years learning about behavioral finance, so I was always a little skeptical of Bogle's vision that people would just settle for average. And, of course, part of his brilliance was that's not how he framed it. That's how his enemies framed it. He was sharp enough to realize that you could never get anyone to buy index funds if you told them it was a way to be average.

—Jason Zweig

One of the most effective ways that Bogle framed it was by putting the returns into dollars-and-cents charts that people can relate to. He loved to use the "Growth of $10,000" chart to drive home this point—in which $10,000 grows to $294,600 in fifty years assuming a 7 percent annual return but only $114,700 if 2 percent a year in costs are applied. Basically the investor only gets about 40 percent of the market return over those fifty years despite putting up 100 percent of the capital. The now-famous chart, which Bogle used in *The Little Book of Common Sense Investing*, is so powerful because it translates those seemingly innocent fee-percentage differences into dollars and cents.

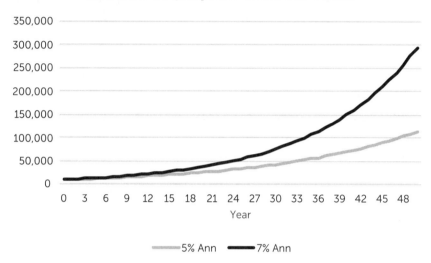

Growth of $10,000 Over 50 Years

5% Ann 7% Ann

Bloomberg

Bogle made the dollar terms case to me in one of our interviews as easily as if he were breathing air. This was probably the millionth time he had said something like this:

> *The stock market gives us 7 percent a year. All the investors in a stock fund get that same 7 percent, and there's no way around that because we are all in a little circle limited to the return generated by a corporation. A dollar will grow to thirty dollars in fifty years. And those active stock funds will get seven dollars but spend two dollars on turnover, expense ratio, and sales loads and give their investors five dollars. If you get five percent for fifty years, your dollar grows to ten dollars. When you retire, do you want ten dollars or do you want thirty dollars?*

He constantly framed index funds in mathematical terms to reinforce that the problem is the costs, not the brains or skill of the active managers. The challenge is that only a minority of them can "win" after costs are deducted. "By and large, these managers are smart, well-educated, experienced, knowledgeable, and honest," he wrote in *The Little Book of Common Sense Investing*. "But they are competing with one another. When one buys a stock, another sells it. There is no net gain to fund shareholders as a group." Bogle frequently used the imagery of a circle of people trading with one another, which is effective because it helps provide a visual for the market. They are all betting against one another as if at a figurative poker table. For me to win, you have to lose.

Jack knew what we clearly know today. He just knew intuitively back then the whole math problem of active management. And we'd get into this whole philosophical debate, and he'd say there's nothing philosophical about this debate at all. It's just mathematics.

—Jim Norris

He'd weaponize the math even further by throwing in the odds of outperforming persistently. Here he is in *Enough*:

> *Don't forget that your incredible success in consistently making each move at the right time in the market is my pathetic failure in making each move at the wrong time . . . And if the odds of making the decision are, because of costs, even less than 50–50, the odds of making two right decisions are even less than one in four. And the odds of making, say, a dozen correct timing decisions—hardly excessive for a strategy based on market timing—seem doomed to failure. Over, say, 20 years, betting at those odds would give you just one chance out of 4,096 to win.*

And, ironically, as many investors have heeded this message and gone into index funds, which is like leaving the casino altogether, it's arguably even *harder* to win because those left are highly trained professionals with tons of computer power betting against one another.

> *Think about Peter Lynch and John Neff back in the seventies. Taking nothing away from their skills, they were competing with amateurs. We know it is a zero-sum game. So when the other side of their trades were mom-and-pop retail investors trading stocks, having no idea what they were doing, the professionals were feasting on them. And you can see that as the US market got more and more professionalized, it got harder. There's no dumb money in the market anymore. There's no alpha to be had.*
> **—Jim Norris**

This has been a tough pill to swallow for active managers. There are so many people out there who have dedicated their lives to trying to figure out and beat the market. And why not? It's fun. It's like one big, highly stimulating brainteaser. In fact, one of the reasons why I got into this industry is that I liked how covering the markets sent my mind into all these various places. There's something that feels right about trying to figure out how everything works and is interrelated, along with identifying new trends and what will happen next in the markets. And yet, in what is perhaps cruel irony, it is arguably better to know almost nothing—if the goal is to build wealth.

The Hedgehog

Beyond the math, Bogle loved to use parables to make his case for index funds as well. For example, he would tell the story of *The Hedgehog and the Fox*, an Isaiah Berlin essay. The gist of the tale is that the fox knows many things and is a very smart and cunning creature devising ever more complex strategies to deliver a sneak attack on the hedgehog, a small creature with a cone-shaped head and short legs and porcupine-like quills. Each time the fox thinks he has outwitted the hedgehog, it simply rolls into a ball of spikes and the fox must retreat.

Not exactly a riveting tale, but the moral of the story is that the fox knows many things and is clever but the hedgehog knows one great thing. That one great thing for Bogle was buying and holding an index fund. You really don't need to know anything else. He saw Vanguard investors as hedgehogs in a world full of foxes.

The story also shines a light on the deeper point of investing. What are we really trying to do here? What is the goal? For the vast majority, the whole point is to earn money on your investment and get a decent return above inflation so you can pay for the big things in life like raising kids, buying a house, and enjoying a comfortable retirement.

And why is investing in stocks a good way to do this? Well, because every day, hundreds of millions of people wake up, go to work, and produce goods and services at companies. Ultimately, by being an owner in those companies, you'll get paid for their efforts via dividends and earnings growth. It's like riding capitalism's coattails.

And to be fair to active funds, index funds are also in many ways riding active's coattails. Index funds track and weight stocks based on market cap, and that is set by active players trading all day. If active managers do research on a company, like it, and buy it, the company will have a bigger market cap and thus get a bigger weighting in index funds.

If you think about what active investors are doing, they are making sure securities are correctly priced. They are buying the cheap ones and selling the rich ones, and they are pushing prices toward fair value. Basically, index funds are free-riding off the efforts of active investors. The index fund assumes everything is correctly priced and invests in everything indiscriminately, but it relies on the work of active investors to do that.

—Jared Dillian

Where Stock Market Returns Come From

Another creative way that Bogle was able to make the case for indexing was by focusing on the two sources of investment returns: dividends and earnings growth. Those two things are what you should realistically hope for and expect as a stock investor. That is the internal rate of return (IRR), or the intrinsic value of stocks. Bogle argued if you can just be happy with this value, you will win. The key is to ignore the third source: speculative return.

Speculative return is dictated by supply and demand of all the trading in the market, along with investor psychology. This source is unpredictable, tends to result in bubbles, and can make people lose their minds with euphoria or fear. But it is a smoke screen and only temporary. In the end, prices and valuations tend to revert to the mean and you see investment returns.

As such, the investment return of stocks has been highly consistent each decade going back to the 1900s, returning between 8 percent and 13 percent annually, with only one negative decade: the 1930s, following the Great Depression. But when you add in speculative return, the total returns are all over the place. Some decades are up big, some are down, and some are flat. It turns a calm walk in the park into a roller-coaster ride. But as Bogle put it, "In the long run, reality rules." As he wrote in the *Little Book of Common Sense Investing*:

> *I believe that the US economy will continue to grow over the long-term and that the intrinsic value of the stock market will reflect that growth. Why? Because that intrinsic value is created by dividend yields and earnings growth, which historically have had a high correlation of about 0.96 with our nation's economic growth as measured by GDP. Of course, there will be times when stock market prices rise above (or fall below) that intrinsic value. But in the long run, prices have always, finally, converged on intrinsic value. I believe (with Warren Buffett) that's just the way things are, totally rational.*

Not a Fan of Commodities

The lack of intrinsic value—dividends and earnings growth created by the work and innovation output every day by the American workforce—was the main reason Bogle (and Buffett as well) was not a fan of commodities (such as gold, silver, oil, or crypto, for that matter).

"Commodities are a real loser's game," he told me. "In the long run they have no internal rate of return. You buy a commodity—gold is a good example—you are betting you can sell it to somebody for more than you paid for it. I don't have an intelligent comment for that. It's absolute rank speculation. Investing in stocks has an element of speculation. But with stocks, it is about what corporations produce. The returns don't come from the stock market, the returns come from the corporation. The stock market is just a derivative to allow investors to invest in corporations. And there's no underlying thing like that in commodities."

For Bogle, to maximize your fair share of this fruitful internal rate of return of businesses, you just need two things: low costs and patience. Low cost is crucial because it gets all the middlemen and frictions out of the way that tend to confiscate some of those returns. Again, it's addition by subtraction.

Bogle argued that a low-cost index fund is a practical tool in which to get those investment returns as well as minimize taxes. Not only was the tool available but you don't need to know much about anything finance related. You could spend your time and brainpower on other things.

I always thought the index fund had this other knock-on effect in the value it had for people's lives because they could just stop thinking about this stuff. That's what it has done for me. Instead of checking my portfolio five times a day and thinking about what I should do, I don't think about it at all. And it's enabled me to be a much better writer because I'm not worrying about that. And that's a big unmeasured benefit to what he did.

—Michael Lewis

Bogle removed the need to have to try to pick the good manager. You can now pick the average of all managers but without their costs. This frees up your attention and time to focus on other things. You can now start to think about higher-value things instead, like tax planning, your goals, a financial plan. So he took out something that was a time-and-attention suck from what wealth management used to be.

—Dan Egan

The Origins of Indexing

Just as Steve Jobs didn't invent computers, neither did Bogle invent the concept of indexing. It was first formed in the academic and institutional worlds. There was growing evidence in the sixties that active managers may not be that good and that just holding a diversified basket of all the stocks on the exchange could be a better way. There were even some attempts at actual index funds that predate Vanguard. In 1971, Batterymarch Financial Management had pitched the idea of an index fund, but it didn't go anywhere. In 1975, American Express also filed for an S&P 500 index fund to be made available to institutional clients but withdrew the filing a year later. Most notably, in the early seventies, John "Mac" McQuown had worked with many now–Nobel laureates at Wells Fargo to develop a short-lived equal-weighted index fund for a pension client.

"Everyone talks about that damn Wells Fargo fund," said Bogle in one of our interviews. "Even our legal department says they were the first index fund. First off, they weren't a fund; they never had a registration statement. It's not weighted by market cap. It's a nightmare. It was a total failure. We are the first index mutual fund."

McQuown, who would ultimately become friends with Bogle, would have liked to launch retail index funds but was prohibited by the Glass-Steagall Act, which forbade commercial banks from offering mutual funds to the public. Unable to move forward where he was—but wanting to see the idea become reality—he freely shared his research with Bogle. This cleared the way for Vanguard to become the only game in town for a long time and for Bogle to become the face of the index fund.

There were these theories coming out of MIT, Chicago, and all these other places, and that was great, but you needed Vanguard to actually get those terrific theories to have an impact. It all funneled through Vanguard. It needed Bogle.

—Victor Haghani

It wasn't like Bogle invented the idea of indexing or had the first fund. He simply brought it to the masses.

—Dan Wiener

"Bolt of Lightning"

The story of how Vanguard launched the first index mutual fund is yet another twist of fate, once again born as much out of necessity and convenience as it was out of some grand vision or altruism. According to Bogle, the idea of an index fund had first crossed his mind in 1951 when he wrote in his thesis at Princeton that "[active] mutual funds can make no claim of superiority over the market averages." But there wasn't much he could do about it, given that the concept of indexing hadn't been invented yet—plus he was in college and had no money or business experience.

What Bogle did have going for him was a habit of regularly reading trade publications, journals, and business magazines—a trait that would pay dividends regularly. And as luck would have it, one month after he started Vanguard, in October 1974, the inaugural issue of the *Journal of Portfolio Management* was published. It included an article by the famed economist Paul Samuelson that laid out the case for why active managers cannot "deliver the goods" and are weighed down by "deadweight transaction costs" and that someone should launch an index fund to show it.

Here's the paragraph in that article that would change the course of investment history:

> *At the least, some large foundation should set up an in-house portfolio that tracks the S&P 500 Index—if only for the purpose of setting up a naive model against which their in-house gunslingers can measure their prowess.*

This caused the neurons to start firing in Bogle's brain, as is evident in this excerpt from *Stay the Course*:

> *Dr. Samuelson's challenge struck me like a bolt of lightning, igniting my conviction that upstart Vanguard had a remarkable, even unique opportunity to operate a passively managed, low-cost index fund and have the*

market to ourselves for at least a few years . . . What an amazing—and happy—coincidence that I read that profound article only moments after founding the new firm! The timing couldn't have been more perfect.

Selling It to the Board

After deciding to take up Samuelson's challenge, Bogle made a pitch to Vanguard's board that it should launch an index fund. He came with numbers, showing the board members that the annual returns for each equity mutual fund from 1945 to 1975 were 9.7 percent versus 11.3 percent for the S&P 500 Index. Thus, indexing had a 1.6 percent annual advantage, which was not coincidentally about the same as the average cost (expense ratio plus turnover) of an active fund.

It was simple math. Bogle readily admitted that he was basically ignorant of complex algorithms and applied statistics such as those that were being developed at the time at the University of Chicago. The college produced many future stars with PhDs who would become successful in their own right, namely in quantitative investing—the idea of relying on computers, mathematical models, rules, and lots of historical data to do active management. Bogle did not have any advanced degrees, in contrast to many of his peers in the industry or many of the assistants that he hired.

I was his techie guy. I was doing all the analysis, all the numbers. This was pre-PC days. This was close to abacus. There were only mainframes. You had to share it. It was called time-sharing. You would issue instructions and get results back. That's how all data analysis, performance analysis, and creating tables were done. When he asked me about the indexing idea, I didn't know if the databases existed. It seems simple now, but I didn't know if I could get at the data. So it took a few days to figure it out.

—Jan Twardowski

Some of Vanguard's board members were a bit skeptical and thought this could be a violation of Vanguard's limited mandate, which prevented it from doing investment management or marketing. Bogle argued that the index wouldn't be managed and would need no investment advisor. Here is Bogle describing it in *Enough*:

> *The fact that investment management was outside of Vanguard's mandate led me within months to develop a great idea I had toyed with for years . . . The argument that we were not overstepping our narrow initial mandate just squeaked past approval by the board of directors. The trick of the index fund, I contended, is it didn't need to be managed.*

"Believe it or not, they bought it," Bogle said years later, in a 2016 interview with *Bloomberg Markets*. "I think they figured, 'This won't amount to much, let's throw a little candy to Bogle.' Plus, I had the intellectual backing of Paul Samuelson."

We were only allowed to exist as an administrative function. We were not allowed to run money in any form or anything related to it. But the index funds were Jack's way of backing into it. That's why they wouldn't call me a portfolio manager. I was a "portfolio administrator," which I kind of resented, but it was politically necessary.
—Jan Twardowski

To be clear, at the time, Vanguard was still a back-office company providing administrative services to the eleven Wellington funds. They were just adding onto that this new index fund venture on the side that didn't need to be managed. With all the necessary approvals and data checks, Vanguard filed for the First Index Investment Trust about a year after Samuelson's article appeared. Samuelson was over the moon. He loved it—maybe a little too much. In a 2005 speech to investment professionals in Boston, Samuelson said, "I rank Bogle's invention along with the invention of the wheel, the alphabet, Gutenberg printing, and wine and cheese: a mutual fund that never made Bogle rich but elevated the long-term returns of mutual-fund investors. Something new under the sun."

On the flip side, Bogle's mentor, Walter Morgan, didn't get the index fund concept at first. He basically thought it was a crazy idea. Even the index makers, such as Standard & Poor's, didn't think much of the idea. Today, the index licensing business does about $4 billion in revenue per year. But Bogle had to lead it there.

When I joined S&P, in 1982, the indexing department was about eight people—two of whom were graphic artists doing charts. It was a cost center. [Bogle] really introduced the idea that you could invest in indexes. There were a couple futile attempts before that on an institutional basis that didn't work in the early seventies. But he was crazy enough to create an index fund. He turned indexing from something you read about in the newspaper to something you could invest in. Bogle made indexing a business.

—David Blitzer

This Is Going to Take a Long Time

And like many world-changing innovations, it was a total flop in the marketplace when it was first launched. The company had hoped the index fund would attract $250 million in seed capital, but it only fetched $11.3 million. And some of that money was from friends and family such as Twardowski and Samuelson. Basically, no one wanted it. According to Bogle, the underwriters at one point suggested that they just give everyone their money back and forget about the whole thing.

I was scared shitless. I wrote these programs and they would give me actual money to run, but it wasn't very much money. It was eleven million. That's just not enough. I said we can't even buy round lots of all five hundred stocks.

—Jan Twardowski

In an attempt to drum up some assets for the fund, Bogle and his right-hand man, James Riepe, went out to try to sell this new index fund concept to brokers. It didn't go well.

First of all, Jack got to go to New York, Los Angeles, and Miami, and I went to Cleveland and Buffalo in the middle of the winter. They were very difficult meetings. We'd go and do our pitch, and we'd have questions and answers, and one of the first questions was, "Why would I put one of my clients into this? I'll never get any commissions, and this is just average. My clients are looking for more than average." We would say, "If you could shoot par on the golf course, would you call that average? This is par." That played pretty well, but it was still really tough.

—James Riepe

And that was pretty much the first decade. The flows were nonexistent to weak for years. Thinking about how clear the value proposition for an index fund is through today's eyes, many have wondered why it took so long to take root. And when it finally did, why did it grow so fast?

Vanguard Index Fund Assets

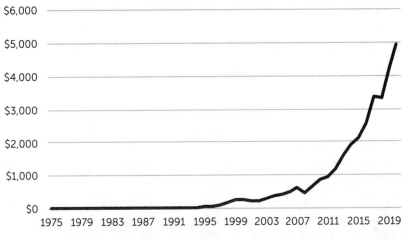

Vanguard's Index Fund (including ETFs) Assets $B

Vanguard

Right at the end of my two years at Salomon Brothers, I was selling Liar's Poker (in the late eighties) and my editor handed me Burton Malkiel's A Random Walk Down Wall Street, *and I can remember thinking, This is all true. And my question was: Why hadn't index funds already overrun the industry? You would have thought it would take a couple of years. It surprised me how slow it was.*

—**Michael Lewis**

My Offer Is This: Nothing

One of the main reasons it took so long is that Vanguard wouldn't pay for distribution—their funds didn't have loads or other sales commissions, which again put it outside much of the system, as it relied on people to find it. Bogle was basically channeling Michael Corleone in *The Godfather: Part II* replying to a bullying US senator looking for a bribe, effectively telling folks, "My offer is this: nothing." Brokers didn't take it well. Here's Bogle on the topic in a speech to the crew in 1991:

The mere whisper of no-load in the early 1970s was so appalling and contentious to broker-dealers that it had strong competitive implications in the marketplace. When Vanguard converted to no-load on February 9, 1977, not only did our dealer sales vanish—literally overnight—but Dreyfus felt compelled to run full-page advertisements with their lion roaring, "No Load? No Way!" (I'm not sure the accuracy of their ads has gotten much better over the years since then.)

And which he later expanded on in *Stay the Course*:

In our "road shows" in a dozen cities around the country, my second-in-command, James S. Riepe, and I both sensed that the brokerage firms' representatives did not seem particularly smitten with the idea. An index fund, after all, implied essentially that their profession—selecting well-managed funds for their clients—was a loser's game.

No one really even noticed [Vanguard] at first. There was no distribution. And there's no internet. So, to me, that was like the gutsiest or craziest move you could do. I don't think it shook up the industry or threatened everyone at the beginning very much because no one knew about it.

—Nicole Boyson

Without broker support, Bogle would have to rely on word of mouth and PR. That's why in speeches to the crew in the early days, he would highlight and rejoice at each new billion in assets, treating them like a battle won. Here is his opening line in a speech to the crew in 1982:

We are gathered here to celebrate a triumphant milestone for the Vanguard Group of Investment Companies: crossing the $5 billion mark in assets. As many of you know, these celebrations make me a bit apprehensive because as tough as it is to reach each milestone, it is an even greater challenge to remain above it and to go on to the next mark.

Losing Faith in the "Professionals"

Another reason for the slow start is that it took a few market events for people to reevaluate their options. Extreme circumstances—good or bad—can really change the marketplace for investments.

We got repeated bad market events one after the other that showed that the traditional propaganda that the active management put out—namely that we are here to protect you from down markets— never turned out to be true. The Vanguard 500 Index Fund really took off after the '87 crash. Then from '95 to '99 the S&P did so well—it went up like 25 percent a year, and active managers just couldn't keep up. Then you had two of the worst crashes of the past half century basically within six or seven years of each other. Then it was curtains for active managers. The evidence was too glaring for people to ignore, and that's when it became a tidal wave.

—Jason Zweig

In addition to investors' personal experience with underperforming funds, a number of scandals and mismanagement in the financial industry started to add up, which played into Vanguard's hands. Bogle's firm seemed Boy Scout–esque in comparison.

Part of the success of Vanguard has been a philosophically defendable position of low-cost passive indexing. But the other half has been the absolute rapacious incompetency of Wall Street and the parade of disasters. I look at the global financial crisis as the cherry on the sundae of Wall Street's history of calamity, fraud, and scandal. The drumbeat got louder and louder and culminated in Bernie Madoff, which didn't affect the average person, and the GFC, which did. It ended with Mom and Pop saying, "We're taking our ball home and leaving the playground." And by "ball" I mean money, and by "playground" I mean Wall Street, and by "home" I mean Vanguard and BlackRock. I don't need to pick stocks. I don't need to be involved in your endless schemes, fraud, overpriced commissions, conflicts of interest, and refusal to adhere to a fiduciary standard. So Mom and Pop said, "Go fuck yourself. I'm just putting money into indexes and leaving it there for twenty or thirty years." I don't think it is a coincidence that passive has blown up (in popularity) since 2008. The way to beat someone at their game is to not play their game.

—Barry Ritholtz

The Internet

Indexing also took a long time because information wasn't spread as fast as it is today. This is arguably why indexing really started growing after the internet went mainstream. There is a clear correlation and connection between the spread of the internet and the amount of assets in index funds. Michael Kitces, one of the most respected minds in the wealth-management world, argues that this correlation was also causation, and he credits the internet for why Vanguard went from oblivion to domination in such a short time frame. Kitces made the case in a 2016 blog post:

> *The reality is that before the internet, the average investor didn't have the tools to know that so many actively managed mutual funds underperformed their benchmarks, and how to select which were the few funds that were actually good. Instead, most investors could only look at quarterly statements, or the* Wall Street Journal's *pages of stock prices, and figure out that they had "made money" because the investment was up. But not actually whether it was up more or less than it should have been, given peer comparisons.*
>
> *With the rise of the internet, though, the tools suddenly became widely available. Investors could actually do real performance benchmarking and cost comparisons for the first time. The tools were finally available to shine a bright light on relative mutual fund performance, and easily identify the laggards. The technology was a transformative moment for real transparency on performance and putting it into an easily usable format.*

To be fair, there was information out there pre-internet in newspapers and services like Morningstar that helped to shed light on indexing and costs in the eighties and nineties—as well as Bogle's own books—but nothing can really compare with the internet's ability to spread information.

I was so intrigued by Kitces's internet theory that I sent it over to Bogle in an email and asked what he thought. Here is his full email reply. Enjoy:

> *Hi, Eric,*
>
> *I'm tempted to say "you're the expert" who can appraise this subject objectively, but let me give it a quick shot on a late Sunday afternoon. First, of course the internet (and the attendant acceleration of the information age) is one reason for the explosion, but only one reason among many others, and, I'd say, not at all the most important one. Here are some others which coalescing combined to produce the burgeoning acceptance of passive investing:*

1. *Actual investor experience. (Don't knock it!) They saw their active managers fail to meet their expectations and realized that broad market index funds held their own on the downside of 2007–2009 and more fully reaped the benefits of the upside that followed, and they voted with their feet (dollars).*

2. *Yes, the tools to evaluate fund performance helped, but they've been there a long time . . . although you had to look. I could fairly easily compare the average equity fund with the S&P 500 in my presentation to our board in 1975. Lipper goes all the way back to the go-go era in the mid-1960s, and those old Wiesenberger Investment Company manuals date easily to 1944. The data were all right there. And late-to-the-game Morningstar (circa 1988) brought a new level of sophisticated analysis to investors and (importantly) to financial advisors.*

3. *Educators adopted the new reality and gave it academic acceptance. College students and MBAs were taught the passive doctrine, without (as far as I know) a single exception. By the turn of the twentieth century to the twenty-first, "heresy had become dogma" (approximate title of a speech I gave at Washington State University two decades ago).*

4. *And while I'm at it, don't forget Vanguard. We were the outspoken missionary and preached the index gospel far and wide, unceasingly and without cavil. The press seemed as if it were our spokesman, and (not to be too self-serving) the hundreds (yes!) of speeches I gave all over the US must have opened scores of thousands of eyes to the likelihood that passive was "a better way." And my books, totally dominated by the concept of passive, low-cost, long-term indexing (don't forget those last two!), beginning in 1993, made numerous best-seller lists, with sales now approaching one million copies. (The cognoscenti tell me that means about 2.5 million readers.)*

5. *Finally, there is the trend line. The growth of passive in the past, say, decade is on trend but perhaps a bit lower. The meme spreads, and the internet fosters memes. But for the idea whose time has come, to repeat, it is the coalescing of multiple forces that counts.*

"Victory has a thousand fathers, but defeat is an orphan."

Best,
Jack

Efficient Market Hypothesis

One of the other factors associated with helping the rise of index investing is the Efficient Market Hypothesis (EMH), which basically states that the prices of securities are accurate and reflect all available information. After all, there are more than fifty analysts covering Amazon alone. What edge could anyone really have? It makes a lot of sense on a certain level. The theory won some academics the Nobel Prize.

While Bogle tends to get associated with the EMH—which arguably helped drive assets into index funds—he really had nothing to do with it, and it had nothing to do with why he started and championed the index fund. He hadn't even heard of it when he first started Vanguard. As he told Cliff Asness on his podcast in 2019, "When these Nobel laureates [Eugene Fama, Robert Shiller, and Lars Peter Hansen] got their prizes a few years back [2013], and they said they were the genesis of the index fund, I had never heard of them. They were totally unknown to me. The EMH—I had never heard of that. I was just a pragmatic indexer."

Further, while the EMH makes sense on one level, it is hard to believe at the same time. Anyone who has watched markets will be hard-pressed to agree they are entirely efficient. Clearly there are times when you just know the market is not pricing stocks anywhere near correctly as evidenced by manias such as internet stocks in the nineties or more recently by Tesla or the meme stock trend.

As such, Bogle was probably wise to steer clear of the EMH, given that it doesn't really pass the sniff test for most people. Instead, what he did was riff off EMH with the Cost Matters Hypothesis (CMH), which basically outlined the laws of costs and how they can kill your returns. CMH does pass peoples' sniff test and can be proved through math as well.

Jack had a piece in the Journal of Portfolio Management *that challenged the typical academic argument for indexing, which was that the market was reasonably efficient. That was certainly a good part of the argument I made. His argument was the reason for indexing was not EMH but rather CMH, the Cost Matters Hypothesis. And what he showed is, if you wanted to predict how any fund was going to do—active or passive—look at the expense ratio. Of all the pieces Jack wrote for journals, I think that was his finest.*

—Burt Malkiel

The Bogle Effect

How big would index funds be today if Jack Bogle the human being (and Vanguard) never existed? My estimate is that they would probably only have 5 percent of the assets they do today, which is eleven trillion. As such, indexing has ironically gotten far too much credit for the index fund revolution. Because it really isn't about the index fund. It's about how cheap they are. They would not have the power to do what they did if they were costly. It is all about the CMH, not the EMH. And so indexing arguably needed Vanguard more than Vanguard needed indexing—although the two were a match made in heaven.

An expensive index fund makes no sense at all. The whole advantage of indexing over active management is low cost. So an expensive index fund has no advantage over active management. I used to look at competitive index funds back then, and you'd see them anywhere from fifty basis points to 150 bps, and you realize what they were doing is offering it because they just had to be able to say they had an offer. If they had a client who was asking, they could say, "Oh yeah, we can put you into our index fund," and the client wouldn't realize they were paying some outrageous fee for it.

—Gus Sauter

The reason we can assume that index funds would be pricey today without Bogle is that's just how the industry is designed and incentivized. No one else had an incentive to lower fees. Perhaps a little price competition would have played out but nothing near to what we have today, when you can get index funds or ETFs tracking any asset class for under 0.05 percent.

If Bogle didn't exist—and I knew him for forty years—we would have passive investments, but they would be much, much more expensive.

—Ted Aronson

Just look at the second S&P 500 index fund to launch (from Wells Fargo in 1985). After all these years, the retail share class still has an expense ratio of 0.44 percent and a front-end load of 5.75 percent, and that is *with* Vanguard in the picture.

Not-So-Cheap US Equity Index Funds

Ticker	Name	Expense Ratio %	Category
RYSPX	RYDEX S&P 500 FUND-H	1.66	Blend
SBSPX	FRANK S&P 500 INDEX FUND-A	0.59	Blend
HSTIX	HOMESTEAD STOCK INDEX	0.59	Blend
MUXYX	VICTORY S&P 500 INDEX-Y	0.45	Blend
WFILX	WF S&P 500 INDEX FUND-A	0.44	Blend
GRISX	NATIONWD S&P 500 INX-INS SRV	0.42	Blend
PLFPX	PRINCIPAL L/C S&P 500-R5	0.41	Blend
MMIEX	MM S&P 500 INDEX FUND-SV	0.37	Blend
IIRLX	VOYA RUSSELL L/C INDX-INIT	0.36	Blend
VSTIX	VALIC I STOCK INDEX FUND	0.36	Blend
SPIDX	INVESCO S&P 500 INDEX-Y	0.32	Blend
WINDX	WILSHIRE 5000 INDEX PORT-INS	0.31	Blend
POMIX	T ROWE PRICE TOTAL EQTY MKT	0.3	Blend
MSPIX	MNSTY MCKY S&P 500 INDX-I	0.29	Blend
INGIX	VOYA US STOCK INDX PORT-INIT	0.27	Blend

Bloomberg

Price tags like this would have relegated index funds into some small niche or made them a novelty item pursued by fans of the EMH. And active funds' underperformance wouldn't have been as big a problem because buying their benchmarks directly (a dirt-cheap index fund) wouldn't have been an option.

It was Bogle's obsession with promoting the low cost that drove assets into index funds. Because an index fund with a 1 percent fee plus a load would look like a loser from the start. Why would I try to match an index and know that I'm going to underperform? The whole argument about indexing has always been that you can be average and match the index and still outperform 80 percent of active managers. But if you knew going in that you were going to miss the average by 1 percent, I just think psychologically people would have been turned off. It is all about the cost.

—Dan Wiener

This is why I'd argue that Bogle's label as the "father of the index fund" is slightly off. A more pitch-perfect title for him would be the "father of low-cost investing."

If I had to say something very concise about him and his message, I would say that it really never changed. He's had the same simple mantra ever since I can remember him saying anything, which is, "Costs matter," and everything else flowed from there. He was saying this from the index fund's infancy until quite literally the day he died.

—John C. Bogle Jr.

Buffett's Take

Warren Buffett also weighed in on Bogle's achievement during the 2017 Berkshire Hathaway annual meeting to which he invited Bogle and introduced him to the audience of forty thousand people:

Jack Bogle wasn't the only one talking about an index fund, but it wouldn't have happened without him. Paul Samuelson talked about it. Ben Graham even talked about it. But the truth is, it was not in the interest of the investment industry or Wall Street to have the development of an index fund because it brought down fees dramatically. Index funds overall have delivered for shareholders a result that has been better than Wall Street professionals as a whole.

So when Jack started, very few people—certainly not Wall Street—applauded him. He was the subject of some derision and a lot of attacks. And now we're talking about trillions when we get into index funds, and we're talking about a few basis points when we talk about fees. I estimate that Jack at a minimum has put tens and tens of billions into their pockets. And those numbers are going to be hundreds and hundreds of billions over time. It's Jack's eighty-eighth birthday on Monday, so I just say, happy birthday, Jack, and thank you on behalf of American investors. And I've got good news: you're eighty-eight years old and in only two years you will be eligible for an executive position at Berkshire. So hang in there, buddy.

I asked Buffett about that day and what it meant to him. "It was great to have [Jack] at the annual meeting a few years ago, and the crowd was absolutely delighted," Buffet replied. "He was already a hero to a great many in the audience, and a number got the chance to tell him so."

Buffett had spent his whole career in constant contradiction to the same forces that Bogle was fighting against, which is overpriced, entrenched active management that trades too much, achieves too little, and overcharges people. Buffett has ranted about high fees almost as much as Bogle did over the years. The other thing is, they are both financially very conservative figures. When markets are exuberant, they tell people it is not going to be this good forever. And when markets are bad, they tell people it's going to get better. Bogle always had that contrarian-speak. And I think Buffett recognized that and admired it.

—Jason Zweig

The Punk Rocker

It's one thing to have a disruptive product (the index fund) and a disruptive message (the CMH), but it's another to deliver it—to break through the noise and the system and hit people in the gut, heart, and mind. Had Bogle been mild-mannered or shy, it's likely that indexing would also only be a fraction of what it is today. But he wasn't. He was loud, relentless, abrasive, and fearless in his advocacy for low costs and indexing, a concept that put him at odds with basically the entire industry. Most of us like to avoid confrontation and awkwardness. He relished the tension and would consistently drop uncomfortable truth bombs onto an audience.

He is the first businessman that I ever truly looked at and thought, He doesn't give a ****. You could just see in any given meeting that John Bogle did not give a flying you-know-what what anybody else thought about what he had to say. He was right, he had a message, and he was going to convince you. And if you weren't convinced, you were an idiot. That was his worldview. He didn't do it with a sense of arrogance or condescension. He did it because he was a true believer, an evangelist. And the people who believed him were apostles. It had that kind of fervor to it.

—Dave Nadig

As Bogle himself wrote in *The Clash of the Cultures*: "I had always loved contrarian ideas that challenged the status quo and was often inspired to take the road less traveled."

Bogle may have looked like a latter-day Henry Fonda, but his message and style had more in common with punk rock. Just as punk was a reaction to disco and style over substance, launching low-cost index funds was a reaction to the financial industry's frothy status quo. Both were about being the opposite of what they saw around them. *Rolling Stone* magazine describes punk rock as "a negation, a call to stark, brutal simplicity." If that doesn't describe Bogle's life's work—and a cheap index fund—I don't know what does.

Coincidentally, Vanguard and punk rock were born roughly at the exact same time, in the early seventies. Vanguard became a reality just a few short weeks after the Ramones played their first show in a very dirty CBGB to about twenty confused but mesmerized people. Both were arguably a "let's get real" backlash to the self-indulgent and flaky sixties that collapsed both culturally and economically. As Johnny Ramone once put it to a journalist,

"What we did was take out everything we didn't like about rock and roll and use the rest, so there would be no blues influence, no long guitar solos, nothing that would get in the way of the songs."

Right about now you may be thinking, *C'mon, man, I think you've taken your pop-culture metaphors too far this time.* OK, fair. And sure, Bogle probably did a lot less heroin than Dee Dee Ramone, but there are too many similarities for me to leave this alone—especially the stripped-down "addition by subtraction" mantra and his unvarnished delivery that regularly antagonized audiences.

One example is when Bogle was once asked to be the keynote speaker at one of the first InsideETFs conferences, which is akin to the Comic-Con of ETFs and largely a celebration of how great ETFs are. Bogle used the opportunity to shred ETFs.

"Bogle came with a very anti-ETF speech," says Jim Wiandt. "He would just come and tell you why ETFs are shit and here's the data."

Bogle would do the same thing at mutual fund conferences—except instead of going after trading, he would go after fees.

He would routinely do it at our conference, too. His standard presentation was about how active management was ridiculous. And he would get up there and deliver it to a crowd that was filled with advisors and institutions that created active products, and he didn't really care. He would say, "Gentlemen, lower your fees!"
—Christine Benz

Another example was on the fiftieth anniversary of the S&P 500 Index. Bogle was invited to sit on a panel with folks from S&P and academia. It was supposed to be a casual little thing before drinks.

Instead, recalls David Blitzer, "Jack Bogle arrived with a copy of his latest book and fifteen to twenty pages marked with paper clips and this big yellow legal pad with pages and pages of notes. My guess is, he took the train up from Philly and spent the whole train ride writing notes.

"When we got into the discussion, everyone was being polite and talking markets a bit. But Bogle was serious. He launched into how ETFs are terrible, they are trading too much, they were wasting their money trading. The brokers were robbing them blind, and they should just buy an index fund and never touch it.

"This was serious stuff for him, and I think some of the panel was a little surprised. We thought this was a friendly chat where we all had cocktails and congratulated one another for fifty years. He was there for real business. I think that was his personality. He took this stuff very seriously."

And while this constant conflict drew attention to his mission and index funds, he had to deal with being shunned by peers. Here's Julie Segal describing Bogle in an article for *Institutional Investor*:

> *I remember an Investment Company Institute meeting—the annual gathering of the mutual fund industry—after Bogle stepped down as chairman of Vanguard in 1999. At the event, asset management CEOs told me that they tried their best to avoid him. No one would say it publicly, but Bogle and especially his message of how much costs ate into investors wasn't welcome. Vanguard was having its first great decade and investors were starting to embrace the index fund, even if it didn't seem much of a threat to active managers. Bogle told me he really didn't care about being snubbed by his peers and would just continue talking about costs until things changed. At the time, it was hard to imagine investors caring about fees—or asset management firms caring to cut them.*

Not surprisingly, the ICI didn't exactly roll out the red carpet for Bogle as the years went on. In our final interview, he seemed genuinely sad about this cold-shoulder treatment: "The ICI doesn't want me to come down there and speak to them," he said, "which I thought was really weird. Here I am the founder of the most successful company in the history of this industry, a former governor, a former attendant, and I mean former—at the general membership meeting every year."

On the flip side, Bogle would be continually asked to appear on financial TV despite his antitrading and antiactive talk. He would say trading was for losers and trying to beat the market was an exercise in futility—which was basically a condemnation of much of the content, guests, and viewers on the show. He was surprised that shows continued to invite him on: "They still ask me on CNBC. I'm like, why are you asking me? I think the answer is, because they can't find anybody else that day."

4
Explaining Bogle

"In all the nearly nine decades of my life, I've never done anything but battle."

Once you begin to really grasp the scale of the impact Bogle has made, you can't help but wonder: What made this guy tick? Why did he bother? Why not just take the same road as all the other industry titans, become superrich, and call it a day? I asked everyone I interviewed this question, and almost everyone's initial response was the same: "That's a good question."

He was just different. And I bet if you went and found his roommate from Blair Academy, he'd say, "Wow, this kid is different."
—Ted Aronson

It almost seems like he was miscast in time and place, like he would have been better suited as a preacher, a military leader, or a doctor in an earlier century but fate and circumstance intervened. On the other hand, he was arguably *perfectly* cast in the fund industry, which, while boring to most, sits at the ever-so-tempting intersection of people, their retirement savings, and a return-generating market.

So how exactly did Bogle happen?

The Great Depression

Bogle's family knew what it was like to be both well-off and poor—as a household and as a nation—thanks to the Great Depression. His family lost their house and inheritance via Bogle's grandfather following the Wall Street Crash of 1929, which was also the year he was born. This was clearly a huge factor in shaping him or anyone else from that era. Even though he was not able to serve in World War II due to issues with his heart, which his son says Bogle always regretted, his fabric and mentality were definitely of the Greatest Generation.

He's always been very conservative and frugal. I think it is mostly due to his upbringing, having been in a family that went from plenty of wealth to no wealth.

—John C. Bogle Jr.

As such, Bogle was one of those guys who worked constantly during high school and college, which was probably tiresome at the time but ultimately gave him the gift of a work ethic and likely kept him out of trouble. He knew early on he was not a rich kid. He was always working.

Perhaps his youthful years as a newspaper boy, a waiter, and a bowling-pin setter struggling his way through school made him aware of how most people live.

—Taylor Larimore

I realized only after knowing Jack for many years that he had been a scholarship kid at his school, and I was like, "That explains so much."

Because I always had the sense that he did have a little bit of a chip on his shoulder.

—Christine Benz

Bogle's work ethic was in contrast to that of his father, who had trouble holding down a job. At one point he was unable to afford the one-hundred-dollar payment toward tuition for his sons' school. Luckily, the headmaster let it go, but all this likely motivated Bogle as well, as each generation naturally wants to correct the flaws of the one before. Bogle once said he loved his father but "he just didn't have the strength. He did his best."

Despite working hard to make sure he'd never have financial problems like those of his father, he also didn't overdo the work side of life either. He married well by his own account, and together with his wife, Eve, raised six kids. Family and career is a tough balance to maintain, but he seems to have pulled it off.

The one thing I can best say about him as his son—and I think this surprises people—is he was a really good and attentive dad, as much as he could be, given how busy he was throughout his entire career. He would find time on the weekends to go out and throw a football or take me to a car show or play golf. He was home every evening pretty much by 6 p.m. We'd have a family dinner almost every night. He was around. I always admired him. He was my hero.

—John C. Bogle Jr.

His Great-Grandfather

While the Depression-era mindset provided a big environmental influence that formed young Bogle, there was also some genetics at work. It turns out that having a passion for taking on powerful money centers and challenging them to cut their fees runs in the Bogle family. Bogle's great-grandfather Philander Banister Armstrong tried to reform the fire insurance industry and then the life insurance industry. Bogle referred to him as his "spiritual progenitor." Armstrong once said, "Gentlemen, cut your costs!" in an 1868 speech, according to Bogle. It's almost *too* perfect.

Armstrong even wrote and published a book, *A License to Steal: Life Insurance, the Swindle of Swindles: How Our Laws Rob Our Own People of Billions*, in 1917, which strongly foreshadows the tone of Bogle's own books. It's basically a 250-page smackdown of the life insurance industry done with hard data and a fiery spirit. Here's the opening paragraph:

> *Can it be possible that life insurance, which is looked upon as a benef-icence, is really a swindler, that these giant corporations which boast of "the strength of Gibraltar" are monopolies, obnoxious to the common law and statutes; their boasted assets a menace to the republic, not consisting of profits in legitimate trade, but assessments wrongfully taken from their own members—a mark of infamy, not a badge of honor?*

The language looks antiquated through today's eyes, but the spirit is dead-on Bogle. Here's another section that seems like it could have come straight from one of Jack's books:

> *The Old Line Insurance system is not only dishonest but they know it to be a fraud. Net premiums are over three times too large to pay death losses in full and seven times too large for the benefits paid, and the real profits are concealed under "net premiums" and expenses amounting to criminal waste and by malicious falsifications in bookkeeping and in official reports.*

If this doesn't make the case for something "running in the family," I don't know what does. And while we are on the topic of ancestry, it is possi-ble he also got some of his nature from his Scottish roots. In fact, the name Bogle comes from a Scots word for "devil" or "goblin." Someone once called him Beta Bogle, the Data Devil. He took it as a compliment.

I had the pleasure of interviewing Jack a couple of times, and he was very proud of his Scottish ancestry. I remember him talking about wanting to save money. He famously didn't spend a lot of money on going first-class, and when there was a free lunch he would take it. He said that was down to his Scottish roots.

—Robin Powell

Princeton

Bogle would definitely not have been able to do what he did had it not been for Blair Academy and Princeton, both of which he attended via scholarship. He called himself a son of those schools. While both were crucial in forming him, it was Princeton where his fate—and that of the mutual fund industry—would be sealed. This is yet another part of his story that hinges on serendipity.

When Bogle was a junior at Princeton and looking for something to write his senior thesis on, he was tooling around in the campus library one day, leafing through the December 1949 issue of *Fortune* magazine where he stopped to read an article titled "Big Money in Boston" about the Massachusetts Investors Trust and the "peace of mind" it was selling small investors in this new financial product called an open-end fund. The magazine had no blurbs on the front indicating what the articles inside were about, so you had to be in a curious mood to page through it.

One wonders where Bogle would have ended up had he picked up a different magazine, such as *Time*, which in December 1949 featured a cover article on Conrad Hilton and his growing hotel business. Would Bogle have become a low-cost hotelier instead?

But he didn't pick up *Time*, he picked up *Fortune*. And he read the article. And it inspired him to spend a year and a half writing his thesis about the mutual fund industry, which he was certain would become huge. And while many would have seen this nascent mutual fund business as a great place to work and make a lot of money and have a career, Bogle's take on it in his thesis was idealistic and even prophetic. Here is a summary of the main points in his paper:

» Investment companies should operate in the most efficient, honest, and economical way possible.

» Future growth can be maximized by reducing sales charges and management fees.

» Funds can make no claim to superiority over the market averages.

» The principal role of the investment company should be to serve its shareholders.

» There is no reason [an investment company] should refrain from exerting its influence on corporate policy.

You can definitely see the seeds for Vanguard right there, although they would need to wait for the right circumstance in which to germinate. But the paper also served a more immediate purpose: it got him his first financial job, at Wellington.

The Sixties

The 1960s were hugely formative for Bogle, although not in the way they were for boomers who tuned in and dropped out but rather in a market cycle way. He experienced firsthand how it felt to sell his soul to appease a roaring bull market, only to have it all blow up in his face when the inevitable bear market came and left a permanent scar that would remind him never to take the bait again.

After that, he never got carried away by bull market exuberance, which can be intoxicating and make you think, *This time is different*—and forget that the euphoria is simply speculative return. He would stay laser-focused on the intrinsic value and investment return created by businesses and how prices will always revert to that. This was also when he would latch onto his signature phrases like "Stay the course" and "In the long run, reality rules" as advice for investors, but they could also apply to the way he would lead Vanguard during multiple market manias.

The first test of Bogle's conviction would come in the 1980s, which saw the S&P 500 return about 200 percent in the first six years of the decade, while interest rates hit 16 percent. Everyone was getting rich and snorting cocaine. The era was famously captured in the movie *Wall Street*, released in 1987, which was supposed to be a warning about the dangers of greed but turned into a model for many young traders. "So many people came up to me afterwards and told me they went to Wall Street because of that film," the director, Oliver Stone, told the *Daily Mail*. "Now they're billionaires."

While audiences—including impressionable young future Wall Street denizens—were in movie theaters across America watching Gordon Gekko give his now-famous "Greed is good" speech, Bogle was giving *his* annual speech to the Vanguard crew in Valley Forge, Pennsylvania. It was a study in contrasts. Here's a snippet:

Our 1987 operating expense ratio—a critical measure of the value we deliver to our shareholders—will improve by at least 10 percent from a 1986 ratio . . . Vanguard maintains a sound balance in an industry that seems to have lost it . . . the discipline not to jump on the bandwagon of speculation and excess [that] is all too rampant in the world financial system and in the US mutual fund industry today.

Bogle getting excited about lowering expense ratios amid the fraught eighties economy is amazing. No one really cared about costs that much back then. On the flip side, Bogle was focused on the same thing during the following bear market and then again when the nineties bull market kicked in. Basically, he had tunnel vision and total focus on one goal: lowering costs. And there's no doubt that his experience in the sixties reminded him not to waver from the cause.

I think he was just superclear in his mind about his basic idea, and he was going to say it again and again. And he never strayed from that. There was never a word about increasing costs, right till the very end. And he was incredibly lucid about it, always on the data.
—Jim Wiandt

Valley Forge

While Vanguard is mentally and spiritually far removed from the actual Wall Street machine, it is physically far removed as well, headquartered in Valley Forge, Pennsylvania, a historically significant but typical suburban-type area about twenty miles outside of Philly. The offices are tucked away in a complex that is barely visible from the main road. Without GPS or good directions, you probably wouldn't even notice or find it. It has a similar vibe to the rebel base on Yavin 4 in *Return of the Jedi.*

The history of Valley Forge fit Bogle's self-conception perfectly. In September 1777, George Washington fled Philadelphia after the British had taken the city. His 12,000-man army ended up spending the winter in Valley Forge. They remained there for six months, where the army lost two thousand soldiers to disease and malnutrition. As General Lafayette put it, "They were in want of everything." But they stuck it out, retrained, regrouped, and got a spiritual and manpower boost from a new French alliance. Washington left in much better shape in June 1778. And the rest, as they say, is history.

Bogle was all over the symbolism. He loved that connection to the American Revolution. And when Vanguard moved its offices to nearby Malvern, he kept using the Valley Forge address. Here he is in *Character Counts* summarizing the themes in his speeches in the early nineties:

> *Like our new campus, both were close to Valley Forge National Park, and we continued to use our Valley Forge postal address. Just as America went through her first challenge at Valley Forge in the winter of 1777–1778, our land and institutions were once again being challenged, and it was up to our own institution to respond.*

Beyond the Valley Forge connection, there was also a broader Philadelphia connection, which again is largely outside of the financial power centers in America. But Bogle loved the place and had lived in the region since age sixteen, when his family moved there in 1946.

He would write in his books about how someone was "from Boston" or was "a Philadelphia guy" in an us-versus-them way. This bias was cemented during his fight with his partners at Wellington, who were from Boston. Here he is in *Stay the Course* using geography to define his friends and enemies:

> *Six board members, most based in Philadelphia with long service, were invited onto the board by Mr. Morgan. Three other directors, all from Boston, had been nominated by my former partners . . . it seemed clear that when it came time for a vote, the six Philadelphians leaned toward my position to mutualize. The three Bostonians leaned toward the Doran/ Thorndike position to have the status quo prevail, to terminate me as CEO, and to get on with the business.*

At the time there was talk of moving Wellington up to Boston. But Bogle was not having it. In *Enough*, he wrote:

The partners intended to move all of Wellington to Boston—I wasn't about to let that happen. I loved Philadelphia, my adopted city that had been so good to me. I had established roots here . . . the birthplace of Wellington in 1928 and Vanguard in 1974.

Being out in suburban Philly was also a good way to retain talent, given its low cost of living and sprawling suburbs. People would settle there and have families, so it was harder to get poached away for more money to a place like New York or Boston.

It's a community of true believers. And I'm not saying people don't make money there, but they make less than they would at BlackRock or State Street or Fidelity. They are in Malvern, PA, and they have their family, and they stay there. And that's part of their [Vanguard's] trick of holding people. It's almost a religious culture.

—Jim Wiandt

Beyond the geographical stickiness, many at Vanguard appreciated the *psychic income*, or the mental satisfaction that comes from knowing you are doing good work for society. This is the term many use for people who take jobs at nonprofits or in government.

Jack didn't maximize his own personal wealth. And maybe some of us didn't either, but I think we all had a large portion of psychological compensation. We really believed in what we were doing, and I felt it the first week I was there. I had worked for five other companies, and the first week I was at Vanguard, I realized this is a company I want to work for the rest of my career.

—Gus Sauter

Vanguard is sort of a cult. But with good reason.

—Nicole Boyson

Speaking of the Philly area and value systems, many people I interviewed also pointed to the fact that Bogle embodied a lot of Quaker values à la William Penn. His big ideas of simplicity (buying and holding an index fund) and prioritizing one's life in the right way, along with concern for society at large, are hallmarks of Quakerism. Here's Bogle saying as much—although with some caveats—at an actual Quaker business gathering in Philadelphia in 2017:

> *I have come to realize that my design for Vanguard reflects many of the basic Quaker values that William Penn fostered: simplicity, efficiency, service to others, and the conviction, in the words of George Fox, that the truth is the way. I confess that I am not so strong on some of the other Quaker values. In particular, consensus, patience, silence, and humility [pauses for audience laughter] . . . but William Penn and his fellow Quakers have been and are a constant inspiration for me and it finds its way into Vanguard.*

The Eighteenth Century

Not only was Bogle physically and spiritually distant from modern-day Wall Street, he was also chronologically distant. He was arguably born two hundred years too late. As I noted earlier, Bogle was behind what was essentially the investors' declaration of independence in 1974, but he would have definitely fit right in with the Founding Fathers and probably been first in line to sign the *actual* Declaration of Independence, two centuries earlier.

His eighteenth-century soul was reflected in his office, which featured paintings of ships and military heroes. It just had a different feel, almost more like a history museum than an asset manager.

He had Lord Nelson paintings in his office—and a painting of himself as Lord Nelson—and he was very fond of quoting from the Constitution. He was a big booster of the National Constitution Center at Independence Mall in Philadelphia.

—Erin Arvedlund

In *The Little Book of Common Sense Investing*, Bogle compares himself with the ultimate eighteenth-century man, Benjamin Franklin. In one section, he put Franklin's quotes before his own to show how they shared similar philosophies on topics such as saving for the future, the importance of self-control, taking risks, understanding what's important, the markets, safety, forecasting, and steadfastness. "Yes, I freely concede that eighteenth-century Franklin had a far better way with words than twenty-first-century Bogle," he writes. "But our near-parallel maxims suggest that the principles of sensible saving and investing are time-tested, perhaps even eternal."

He was fascinated by the eighteenth century and its values and commitment to "old-fashion liberal humanitarianism that was the hallmark of the Age of Reason and a balance between man and machine." He longed for this era in some of his books, specifically *Enough*:

With Wikipedia at our fingertips and Google waiting online to serve us, we are surrounded by information but increasingly cut off from knowledge. Facts are everywhere but wisdom—that was rife in the age of our nation's Founding Fathers—is in short supply . . . As the first decade of the twenty-first century comes to a close, Franklin's noble eighteenth-century values stand in bold contrast to the bitter patent wars of today or the obscene salary demands of the executives of our giant corporations and the enormous compensation paid to hedge fund managers (often whether they win or lose or even survive).

He also tended to speak in an eighteenth-century tone and made everything seem so important and monumental—quoting poetry or sacred texts—both in his books and speeches, and even at casual events.

He was a brilliant orator, larger than life. I once saw him at his seventieth birthday party, and I thought it was extemporaneous, but he ended up reading some Lord Tennyson poem that went on for like, five minutes. I thought he was Napoleon up there. I said to his son John, "Can you believe it?" He looks at me and says, "Ted, can you imagine him at dinner every night?"

—Ted Aronson

His Heart

Bogle's heart was at once a scary problem and a massive advantage. Death was always lingering in Bogle's life, and it had the effect of giving him a jolt of life—a *carpe diem* attitude and an ongoing awareness of how precious every moment is.

If you are going to look at what drove him and what made him, I think you have to talk about health. He was told he would never live to be forty. He was told he would never live to be fifty, sixty, seventy. There's no question that when he woke up every day wondering, "Is this my last day?" that he was fueled to accomplish something.

—Jim Norris

Here's Bogle in *Stay the Course*:

I had my first heart attack when I was thirty years old. I went to the Cleveland Clinic, which was the only place you could get a pacemaker in 1967. I got worse and worse since the heart attack. So at age thirty-six or thirty-seven, they stick a pacemaker in me. And it made the heart more erratic. One doctor said, "You really shouldn't count on living past forty." Another doctor said, "Why don't you get a place out in Cape Cod and stop working and enjoy the few years you have left? Don't work anymore." If I had taken the second doctor's advice the first doctor would have been right.

Even though death from heart disease was much more common in the sixties, it was still rare for someone that young. I can't imagine having a heart attack at age thirty. But Bogle did, thanks to a genetic heart disease known as arrhythmogenic right ventricular dysplasia (ARVD), which resulted in his wife, Eve, having to take him to a hospital about *ten times,* where doctors would electrically shock his heart back into its normal rhythm.

No one wanted to play squash with him. He'd bring the defibrillator onto the court. Could you imagine playing and he passes out and you have to shock him back? It's like the movies, and it's true.

—Ted Aronson

I had just become the mutual funds editor at Forbes in 1992 and so naturally one of my first trips was to go down to Vanguard to meet with Bogle. I remember two main things from that interview. The first was, I had this very powerful feeling that I'd never see him again. I thought he was going to die in a few months, and that was around the time I drafted my first obit for him. He looked like hell. The second was, he had this insane prediction that someday index funds would be bigger than actively managed funds, and I distinctly remember when he told me, I just burst out laughing. That was the most ridiculous thing I ever heard. With human beings, hope springs eternal, and active management was hope in a bottle. And people are always going to want to do better than average. So I was definitely wrong on one count, and I guess I'll soon be wrong on the other count.

—Jason Zweig

The reason he "looked like hell" in the early nineties is that half of his heart wasn't functioning at all. At age sixty-five he would need a heart transplant. He waited in Philadelphia's Hahnemann University Hospital for 128 days, connected around the clock to an intravenous line feeding him heart-stimulating drugs. In *Character Counts*, he recalls his mentality at that time:

> *Strangely, despite the traumatic circumstances, I never thought I would die. I never thought I would live, either. It just didn't seem sensible to think about the outcome . . . I reassured our crew members that despite the imminent danger that my heart would cease to beat, I too had no fear. Indeed, in the hospital each night my final prayer was, "Not my will, but thy will be done."*

But eventually, in February 1996, he got the heart of a twenty-six-year-old male. Two weeks later, he was back home. He would last thirty more years, albeit he had to lay off booze and take his meds, which he did.

He seemed like he had nine lives. I remember meeting him face-to-face for the first time, and he had just gotten the transplant, and he was like, "It's great. I feel terrific. I have the heart of a thirty-year-old. I feel like I got my life back." But there were always rumors about how he was sick or back in the hospital. It was always hovering in the background.

—Erin Arvedlund

Every time he was about to die, he didn't, and he kept going, total Energizer bunny. One time, about twenty years ago, after his heart transplant, I took a train with him up to New York. We went to some magazine event, and he was giving a speech. Then we headed back that night to Philly, and I'm beat, I'm ready to fall asleep, and Jack goes bounding up the stairs—even though there was an escalator—like a track runner. I took the escalator, and I said to him at the top, "Aren't you a little tired?" And he said that when he got the heart transplant, they couldn't connect the nerve that tells you you're tired, "so that was nothing." I looked at him like he was the Bionic Man. The energy this dude had was unbelievable.

—Ted Aronson

Bogle was very appreciative of the doctors who helped him throughout his life, whom he called his guardian angels. His doctors credit Bogle's iron will for his longevity as well. But there's just no denying the spark that a new heart gave him to finish his mission.

One thing about Jack is, he was very often talking about his heart after having the heart transplant and saying, "I'm on this earth to do good work for as long as I can."

—Lee Kranefuss

The Bible

Bogle had an active spiritual life that no doubt informed and guided him. He attended Sunday church services regularly and, in his book *Don't Count on It! Reflections on Investment Illusions, Capitalism, "Mutual" Funds, Indexing, Entrepreneurship, Idealism, and Heroes*, he credits his church's preachers for his "gaining enlightenment, inspiration, and faith." But he didn't just go through the motions; he also really absorbed the words in the Bible and quoted from it regularly. It is easily the most referenced book in his writings. You can tell he was nourished by it. Here he is describing his view on faith in a 2017 interview with Signe Wilkinson:

> *What is real and what do you have to take on faith? It's very hard for me to believe the body can be resurrected. The soul maybe. Why not? Since we don't know exactly what the soul is. But the body! I'm looking out this window, and I'm not seeing a whole lot of things moving up to heaven. So I'm a pretty realistic person. That conflicts with organized religion, but it doesn't conflict with my faith. There's something bigger and more important than we are sitting out there. We happen to call it God. That's good enough for me.*

He did not let his skepticism of the literal keep him from the richness of the figurative. If you have ever read the Bible, you know how powerful and inspiring it is. It's also full of amazing stories of underdogs challenging the powers that be—with some help from God along the way. I could see how the Bible had fanned the flames of Bogle's mission. After all, he was the guy who spent his life flipping over merchant tables in the temples day in and day out, figuratively speaking. In *The Clash of the Cultures*, Bogle alludes to that exact section:

> *If we want to encourage and maximize the retirement savings of our citizens, we must drive the money changers—or at least most of them—out of the temples of finance. If we investors collectively own the market but individually compete to beat our fellow market participants, we lose. But if we abandon our inevitably futile attempts to obtain an edge over other market participants and simply hold our share of the market portfolio, we win.*

He loved to reference the famous Psalm 118:22 verse, which says, "The stone which the builders rejected has become the chief cornerstone." This was repeated multiple times in the Christian scriptures by Jesus's disciples to describe him. That's how Bogle viewed Vanguard and, to a degree, himself. Why not? He and his idea were ignored and even mocked for years, only to have his firm become the biggest fund company the world has ever seen two times over.

Bogle also subscribed to the axiom that God helps those who help themselves, along with the idea that once you take the first step, God will have your back, citing all those serendipitous twists of fate in his life that led to the birth of Vanguard and his mission. Here he is in *Enough*:

> *Whenever I have committed myself with boldness, Providence has followed, whether it was stumbling on that* Fortune *magazine article on the mutual fund industry way back when I was searching for a topic for my senior thesis . . . or being fired by my Wellington partners . . . or receiving a new heart . . . or any of the other acres of diamonds that were always providentially there, waiting to be discovered but requiring commitment to capitalize on their value.*

Going to church regularly may have also influenced Bogle's evangelism regarding Vanguard and low costs. He delivered many a sermon—to anyone who would listen—about his mission.

Although there's a fine line between inspiring and moralizing, Bogle basically lived on that line. There was Saint Jack and there was fire-and-brimstone Jack—the latter of which could definitely rub people the wrong way, even those close to him. His former trusted assistant James Riepe (one of two people who helped him launch Vanguard and the first index fund and who went on to become vice chairman of T. Rowe Price, an active mutual fund company) once bought Bogle a priest's collar and presented it to him at one of the famous annual dinners that Bogle hosted for all his former assistants.

*Jack was always pretty well convinced that whatever he thought was
the right thing was in fact the right thing. When he would disagree on
something, he would routinely toss his wallet on the table as a "bet"
as to who was right. With respect to indexing, this attitude ultimately
generated the self-righteousness label . . . We [his older former assis-
tants] thought he had started to get over the top a little bit, so I went
and bought a clerical collar and we presented it to him at one of
those dinners. We said, "If you are going to be this self-righteous,
you probably ought to have the right uniform." He loved that.*

—James Riepe

Ego

Despite his man-of-the-people image and "enough" ideology, almost everyone I spoke with mentioned Bogle's massive ego, or sense of self-importance.
While a crucial ingredient in the Bogle DNA—as you need one to do big
things—it can also be a sign of deep insecurity and leave one a little empty
at times, like a hole that can never be filled. Most of the people who saw him
up close saw this dichotomy between the saint and the egomaniac.

*I don't think anyone who has achieved what he has achieved doesn't
have an ego. In fact, I used to joke with him, "You know, Jack, your
ego is like a furnace. You have to keep shoveling coal into it to keep
that thing burning. He would just laugh and say, "You're probably
right about that."*

—Jim Norris

*For someone who was as well-known as he was, certainly in the
investment world, he always had a little insecurity about his own
position and his own accomplishments in life. It's almost like he had*

this insatiable need to be reminded that he's done a lot of really good things. He liked to be in the public eye. He liked when people would walk up to him in the street and say something like, "Geez, I want to thank you so much. It's because of Vanguard that my kids are now through college or I've got plenty of money in retirement." He never tired of hearing those things. It was one of the quirks of his personality we couldn't really understand.

—John C. Bogle Jr.

The guy had an ego three times bigger than that statue of him standing outside the headquarters.

—Dan Wiener

The statue is arguably the ultimate evidence that Bogle's ego was not small. Although to his credit, Bogle acknowledged the arrogance of it. He knew how it looked to have a statue outside of your own office while you still worked there. He said the idea for it was put forth right before his heart transplant, as people were not sure how much longer he'd be around. As he wrote in *Character Counts*:

On the one hand, we all think of a statue as a memory of the departed, a memorial. I wasn't ready for that then, and I'm surely not ready now! But at the time the possibility of a sculpture of me first arose, I was comforted by seeing a photograph of a sculpture of a very-much-alive Arnold Palmer, soon to be delivered to the Augusta National Golf Course. And since my future was uncertain, I thought, "Why not?"

Understanding Jack

A good way to end this section and the chapter is this fun "Understanding Jack" memo written by some of his former assistants, namely Jim Norris (and shared with me by Jan Twardowski), as a translation dictionary of what he says versus what he means. Enjoy:

Over the years, all of us have come to appreciate and cherish those aspects of Jack's personality that I shall broadly define as "Bogleisms." Some of these Bogleisms are mannerisms; for instance, Jack's characteristic way of dipping his head and waving his hand in salute as he passes by. Some are merely phrases that have become his trademark, such as "The hell you say!" But without question, my favorite aspect of my relationship with Jack has been the process of coming to terms with the quintessential Bogleism: reconciling "what Jack says" with "what Jack means." In no particular order, here are some of my favorites:

Whenever Jack Says:	What He Means Is:
"I know it's not your fault."	"It's your fault."
"Whose responsibility is it to . . . ?"	"Isn't it your responsibility to . . . ?"
"I need this whenever you get a chance."	"I meant to ask you to do this yesterday, so now I need it in five minutes."
"Could you have somebody . . . ?"	"Could *you* . . . ?"
"Wiser heads than mine will have to decide."	"Someone else will have to make the decision, but I'll be sure to change it to the right decision."
"You decide."	"Do what I would do."
"I'm sure it's my own fault."	"Well, it sure isn't my fault."
"Don't spend too much time on it."	"Stay as late as you need to, but make sure it's right."
"Something doesn't look right here."	"You screwed the whole thing up."
"Have you double-checked these numbers?"	"There's an error."

"I hope you didn't stay too late."	"I don't care if you stayed late, as long as it's finished."
"I need it by 3:00."	"I need it by 1:00."
"Well, don't take my word for it!"	"Back into the number."
"Do I have to do everything around here?"	"You're not holding up your end."
"I think the number is something like 264."	"I just read in *Barron's* that the number is 264."
"Could you take a whack at this?"	"I'll rewrite your version later."
"Have you read the Windsor Annual?"	"There's an error in the Windsor Annual."
"Do you have time to review this letter?"	"Drop what you're doing and review this letter."
"Pick me up around seven-ish."	"Pick me up at seven and not one second later."

5

The Fall (and Rise) of Active

"When we talk money rather than basis points measured in hundredths of 1 percent, we get a far better picture of the staggering profit in fund management."

We just spent a lot of time looking at the disrupter. Now let's look at the disrupted: active mutual funds. Most people think the problem with active mutuals is that they chronically underperform. That's largely true, but it's arguably just a symptom of a much deeper problem and one that was largely self-inflicted.

The root of the problem with active mutual funds was that they didn't share any economies of scale, which is to say, they neglected to pass on savings in costs as a result of getting bigger. As markets went up and up during the past few decades—doubling and tripling their assets and revenue—irrespective of whether they worked harder or delivered outperformance or brought in any new clients, by and large active funds didn't really share any of this extra free revenue with their investors. This was a huge missed opportunity. This isn't to judge them per se—as most of us probably would have done the same—but rather to offer up some real talk so we can understand how they were so utterly disrupted by Vanguard. It is also a warning to other parts of the industry that are at risk of suffering the same fate.

Here are Bogle's thoughts on this in *The Clash of the Cultures*:

Despite the fund industry's quantum growth (from $35 billion in 1965 to $10 trillion in 2011), the costs incurred by fund investors grew rapidly. The expense ratio of the average equity fund, weighted by fund assets, rose from 0.50 percent of assets on the tiny $5 billion asset base of 1960 to 0.99 percent for the giant $6 trillion equity fund sector as 2012 began—a stunning increase of almost 100 percent. In dollar terms, the cost of investing in equity mutual funds rose an astonishing 17 percent annually, from $5 million in 1951 to $60 billion in 2011.

Dollar Fees

Fast-forward to 2020 and those fees in dollar terms (a number you rarely hear about from anyone but Bogle) are even higher at about $140 billion. And that's an *annual* number, although if Bogle had never existed it would probably be somewhere in the neighborhood of $250 billion to $300 billion (about the revenue of the entire auto industry). These numbers are generated by—and in contrast to—the innocent-looking fee rates, which are in percentage form. The difference between fee rates and the dollar fees they generate is easily one of the most underexplored and misunderstood stories in finance.

The reason dollar fees are so important is because that is how an asset manager gets paid. That's actual money. And the way they grow is twofold: One is new money coming in via new cash coming in ("inflows"). The other is by the market going up. This second form—market appreciation assets— is where the vast majority of their increase in assets and revenue is coming from (regardless of whether they outperformed or attracted any new clients). And the stock market has doubled in size twelve times since the early nineties when these funds became popular. This sent their assets, revenue, and profit margins into the stratosphere.

I used to give a lot of talks at ICI meetings and Morningstar, and at every meeting I'd say, "You people are crazy. You are running the most profitable industry in the world. You make a higher net margin than computer software. You have no fixed costs. What is wrong with you? Why are you making 38 percent net after tax profit margins just because you can? What do you think is going to happen when stocks stop going up? You are going to have to give some of it back or your customers are going to abandon you. Just give some of it back now, when you can afford to, instead of waiting until it will hurt when you do it." And people would throw tomatoes at me. They didn't want to hear that. And I understand why—it's human nature.

—Jason Zweig

3-Year Average Operating Margin %

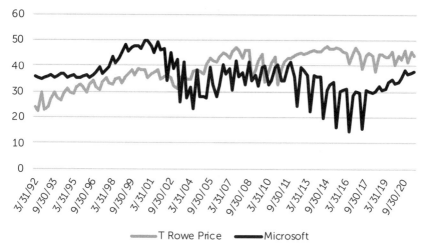

T Rowe Price   Microsoft

Bloomberg

The beauty of this business model is that these expense ratios tend to look like these innocuous little percentages. I think you might ask your average consumer and they may think, What difference does it make if I pay 1.5 percent versus 0.5 percent? *Those are small numbers. No one is writing a check or has a sense of what their annual expenses are. One thing I think Bogle did so well is express each of those levies as tolls that investors pay that dig into the investors' take-home return.*

—Christine Benz

Now, this isn't to say that charging a 1 percent fee or making a profit is bad or that active investing is bad. That isn't the problem that Bogle and indexing exploited. After all, asset managers starting out have to keep the lights on and hire some people. The sin is keeping that 1 percent fee in place when the fund gets massive. There is a point at which the cost of running the fund is utterly dwarfed by the revenue earned. That's when the fee could have been lowered significantly to 0.50 percent or even 0.25 percent, and the fund would likely still be taking in much more in dollar fees than the 1 percent it charged when it was starting out. As Bogle explains in *The Clash of the Cultures*, "A 1 percent fee for a $100 million fund may seem reasonable [in dollar terms], but even one-quarter of 1 percent for a $30 billion fund—$75 million per year—may be excessive."

In the example Bogle gave, the fee rate was unchanged but the dollar fees went up seventy-five times. Does it cost seventy-five times more to run the $30 billion fund versus when they had $100 million? Maybe a little more, but nowhere near seventy-five times more. Multiply this by thousands of funds and trillions of dollars, and you have an industry earning billions and billions in extra revenue just because the market went up, which made it wildly wealthy but also very vulnerable to the Bogle Effect.

Bogle tried, largely in vain, to get more transparency around dollar fees. In *The Clash of the Cultures*, he says, "The focus on rates over dollars for fees goes back to the 1920s, when rates were reasonable and dollars modest . . . But in the modern era of $30 billion and $100 billion funds, the dollar fees are enormous . . . I couldn't even persuade the justices of the Supreme Court that the distinction between actual fees paid and fee rates was critical to evaluating advisory fee contracts."

While Bogle was unable to convince the Supreme Court, he *was* able to convince investors—not by getting them to think about dollar fees per se, but by simply providing an actionable contrast that a cheap index fund had to a fee-laden, underperforming active fund. But that contrast was made clear largely as a result of active mutual funds not sharing their dollar fees. Active funds just didn't notice how stark it was until it was too late.

The Steve Jobs Rule

The story of getting too rich and comfortable at the top only to be disrupted is not exclusive to the asset management industry. It happens all the time. Capitalism can be brutal. It was famously summed up by the late, great Steve Jobs when he said, "If you don't cannibalize yourself, someone else will."

Apple has taught us all about cannibalization, which the financial industry has a real hard time with. Apple puts out an iPod for $500 and it has ten megabytes, and then the next year Apple says, "We're now going to give you thirty megabytes for $400." And then one hundred megabytes for $200. And then it's a gigabyte [one thousand megabytes] for $100, and then nobody can catch them. Could you imagine the average financial company saying, "We know this is 1.5 percent and it's underperformed, but now we're going to give it to you at 0.75 percent"? It just doesn't happen.
—Barry Ritholtz

The unwillingness to self-cannibalize famously played out in the music industry in the 2000s, which was documented fabulously in the 2015 book *How Music Got Free* by Stephen Witt and in the documentary *All Things Must Pass: The Rise and Fall of Tower Records* that same year. In the music industry, everyone was blinded by the money and never passed on economies of scale. In 1998, manufacturing costs had fallen to less than one dollar per CD, and yet the average price record companies were selling them for remained steady at $16.50.

David Geffen, the cofounder of Asylum Records and founder of Geffen Records, summed it up well in the *All Things Must Pass* documentary: "What they should have done was lower the CD prices."

Besides being expensive, CDs were also subject to "forced bundling," meaning you had to buy all thirteen or fourteen songs in one shot, even if half of them were meh (which was largely the case outside of a few classic albums). Of course the industry didn't want to embrace the MP3 or the internet, which gave consumers cheaper and more flexible options. And then it was disrupted by them both.

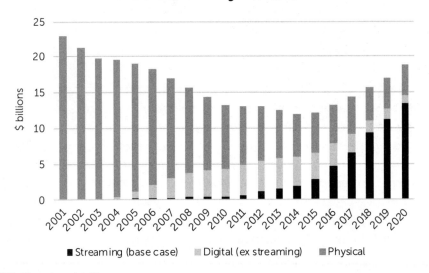

Music Industry Revenue

IFPI, Bloomberg Intelligence

And consumers had absolutely no loyalty to or love for the record companies—or musicians, for that matter—given how exploited they had been for decades, and were more than happy to go on pirating music like crazy. And then, when they would ultimately go back to paying for music, they would spend far less money. Basically, the MP3 slashed music industry revenue from $23 billion a year in 2000 to $13 billion a year in 2010, according to IFPI.

The Bull Market Subsidy

However, there is one *big* difference between asset management and the music business (or any other business, for that matter). Almost every industry out there has to rely on sales made for revenue and survival, whereas in the asset management industry, your revenue can grow simply because the market went up, as I mentioned earlier. We call this unusual phenomenon the Bull Market Subsidy because it really is like being subsidized. Even if asset managers lose customers, they can still make more money.

What makes the asset management business amazing is that you can lose 7 percent of all your clients and all your assets every single year and double every twenty years in size. In what other industry can you lose clients at that rate? You'd be out of business in five years. You're done. But the market bails out the industry forever. You can just keep going.

—Jim Norris

Active vs. Passive Market Share of Total Fund Assets

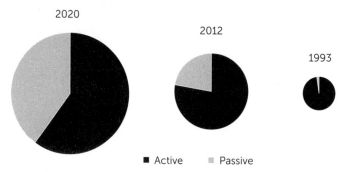

ICI, Bloomberg, EconomPic

A good way to visualize this is with pie charts. While active mutual funds' slice of the pie is shrinking via flows (which is what most of the media focuses on), the entire pie keeps growing. Active's slice can shrink so long as the pie itself keeps growing. And the pie grows not because the asset management expanded the business to new customers but because stocks and bonds simply have much higher prices today. And the asset managers get a percentage of that pie. If the pie grows faster than your slice shrinks relative to others, you can make more money despite losing market share.

For example, the market share of passive funds increased from 2 percent in 1993 to 43 percent in 2020. In another industry, that would mean active's business would be nearly cut in half. But instead, active's assets still grew from $1.5 trillion in 1993 to $13.3 trillion in 2020.

Here's where this really becomes mind-numbing. Try to wrap your head around this one: In 2010, active equity mutual funds had about $3 trillion in assets. Then, during the next ten years, they saw $2.3 trillion in outflows, yet they ended up with more than $5.5 trillion, nearly *double the assets and double the revenue.* So today, every time the stock market goes up 1 percent, it raises the total assets of active funds by (roughly) $70 billion and their revenue by $410 million.

Active Equity Mutual Funds Outflows and Assets Since 2010

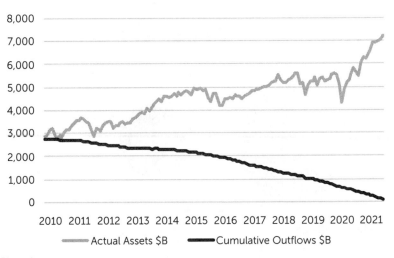

ICI, Bloomberg

This is why a prolonged bear market—or 2008-style downturn—is easily the biggest risk for Wall Street, as the asset mirage will crumble without any real customer base to fall back on because much of it has been eaten away by the Bogle Effect during the last twenty years. In short, the Bull Market Subsidy will turn into a Bear Market Tax. This on top of any existing investors in the funds leaving in a panic. It will get ugly. There will be blood.

While this scenario is inevitable, it may not happen for a long time, especially as the Federal Reserve seems intent on backstopping declines in the market. Active mutual funds hold much of the boomers' assets and retirement savings (and boomers are in the highest rungs of power in both the government and on Wall Street), so there's an argument to be made that the Fed views mutual funds—and the overall stock market—as the new "too big to fail." At *some* point, though, the hollowing out of active mutual funds' customer base will catch up with them.

And it didn't need to be like this. These firms could have lowered fees a lot—and without even having to cannibalize themselves—by just sharing some of the excess dollar fees.

I think active shops did partly contribute to the success of the index fund by not being more willing to share economies of scale. I've long thought that it's not that active managers are that stupid at all, it is simply that most are hobbled by untenable costs relative to index products. I do think the industry would have done itself a service by lowering fees, and it still would have remained a plenty profitable industry.

—Christine Benz

Lower Fees Equal Better Performance

Sharing some of these economies of scale would not only have built trust and goodwill, it would also have had the residual effect of helping those damning performance numbers that we looked at in chapter 3. Those miniscule "beat rates," or funds that outperform the benchmark, would have been healthier. Add better performance numbers to the trust and goodwill built from lowering fees for your customers over the years, and it's very likely that Vanguard (and passive in general) would be a fraction of its size today. In other words, Bogle had picked a really good foil.

How did the industry miss this so badly? Why didn't it try to be more competitive on the fee front? Active mutual fund managers had to know it would have helped their odds of beating benchmarks. They intimately know that every basis point in fees is like having to begin one foot farther back behind the starting line.

Moreover, most of these asset managers do nothing but study companies and industries. Surely, they've seen many cases—like the music or tech
industry—where companies fall behind because of disruption, cost, and
cannibalization. You'd think they'd apply it to themselves. Why didn't they?

Bogle's explanation for this comes back to the "two masters" problem.
He wrote in *Character Counts*:

> *If a fund manager were interested in maximizing its own profits—
> inevitably at the expense of the owners of the mutual funds it manages—
> it would charge the highest fee that traffic would bear unless absolutely
> forced to charge lower fees, either by the marketplace or government regu-
> lation. But if a firm's goal were to maximize the profits of its fund share-
> holders, it would charge the lowest fees possible, and minimizing fund
> costs would be the highest and most obvious priority.*

While it may seem like I'm disparaging active managers and mutual
funds here, I am only trying to give it to you straight. There are many nice,
honorable, highly intelligent, well-intentioned people at mutual fund companies. I'm friends with some of them. Many are Bloomberg clients. I feed
downstream from them. But I'm also an analyst covering this area, so I need
to understand the root cause of this massive trend.

And if we're honest, would any of us have done it differently? You see
your fee revenue double in five years. Would you use that extra gravy to
lower the prices of the funds? Or would you keep it to increase your salary,
increase executive bonuses, upgrade the office, sponsor a sports stadium, and
maybe expand the company? It's hard for any of us to say we'd share it with
the investors, especially if the overriding norm was to keep it. This is why
Bogle is so interesting and worthy of study.

It Comes Down to One Word

And just to be clear: this isn't an active-passive dichotomy either. In fact,
Bogle was not really antiactive. After all, Vanguard has $1.3 trillion in active
mutual fund assets, which makes it the third-biggest *active* fund company.

It likely will be the second soon and possibly first when all is said and done. Moreover, Bogle's own son is an active manager. And he was very encouraging of him.

He said there is a place for active management, and that's why he kept the active funds at Vanguard. He never really was against my active management. It was almost the opposite—"Give it a try, maybe you will be able to do it." And whenever I would complain that we had a bad quarter or year, he would say, "You know, it's a hard business." But he wasn't saying it to rub it in or say, "I told you so." He was simply saying, "You will have ups and downs. Maybe you'll have success. The odds are against it, but who am I to say my son can't add value?" And he has never said active management can't add value. He has said active management on average can't add value.

—John C. Bogle Jr.

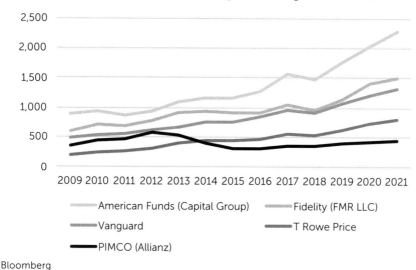

Top 5 Active Fund Companies by Assets ($B)

Bloomberg

For Bogle, all this wasn't as much about active versus passive as it was about one's role as a fiduciary. He distilled it all down to one word in *Character Counts*:

Stewardship: The one great idea that explains what Vanguard is, who it is, and what it does. Serving the shareholder first; acting as trustee in a fiduciary capacity. Mutual funds of the investor, by the investor, for the investor. If you reflect on this concept, you quickly come to realize that it is from this one great idea that everything flows.

The fiduciary mindset is integrity on steroids. You need to put your customers first, your employees right next to them, and everything will work out.

—Sheryl Garrett

Vanguard's Active Funds

One of the most surprising things I found when researching this book was just how proudly Bogle spoke about some of Vanguard's active funds—particularly in his last book, *Stay the Course*. And yet, he was always quick to credit much of their success to their conservative approaches and low fees, which were courtesy of Vanguard's mutual ownership structure. Their mutual structure–induced low fees basically let them bring a gun to a knife fight. Again, the mutual ownership structure is the source of their success and they'd likely be the biggest active shop two times over had they not been so into promoting indexing.

For example, Vanguard's active funds have an asset-weighted average expense ratio of just 0.20 percent, a good three to four times less than the 0.66 percent for active mutual funds, and seven times cheaper than the 1.4 percent for hedge funds and private equity.

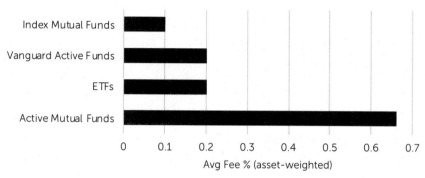

Average Fee (Asset-Weighted) Comparison

Bloomberg

Ironically, the fund Bogle seemed to be the proudest of wasn't the Vanguard 500 Index Fund or the Vanguard Total Stock Market Index Fund but rather the actively managed Wellington Fund, which today is called the Vanguard Wellington Fund. In his last book, he dedicated a whole chapter to it, referring to it as "Vanguard's Alpha and Omega." He spends far more time explaining this fund's history and performance than he does any of the other index funds (except for maybe Vanguard's first), even though it is but a small fraction of their size. Not only is the Wellington Fund like his first-born son, it also almost died in his care but he was able to save it. They went through a lot together. Bogle writes:

> *Sometimes in life, we make the greatest forward progress by going backward. This is just what we did when we decided to take Wellington back to its roots . . . Wellington Fund now enjoys a truly awesome annual edge of ten-plus basis points (versus its peers)—solely because of its low costs— and the advantage of one full percentage point a year in extra return. Yes, costs matter.*

Today, the fund has about $120 billion in assets, which is by far the most among the half dozen or so original mutual funds that were launched in the 1920s—most of which are dead or barely alive today. This is an important point. The fact that Wellington is basically the last man left standing in a hundred-year race speaks volumes for the longevity Vanguard is likely to have as well.

Another good example of the pride Bogle had in his active funds is the Vanguard PRIMECAP Fund, which was launched in 1984 and charges about half of what the average active fund does. It has nearly doubled the returns of the S&P 500 Index and the Russell 1000 Growth Index (although it has lagged recently as growth stocks have outperformed).

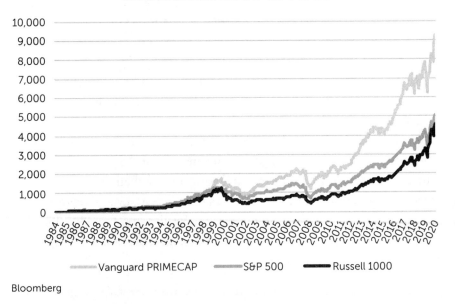

Vanguard PRIMECAP vs. S&P 500 and Russell 1000 Growth

Bloomberg

Again, he gives much of the credit to the low costs and being a good fiduciary. As he explains in *Stay the Course*:

> *The fund's low cost proved to be an advantage that has had a major impact on the fund's success. PRIMECAP's expense ratio of 0.33 percent (down from 0.75 percent in 1990) in 2017 is a full percentage point below the 1.33 percent ratio of its peer large-cap growth funds. Vanguard's cost advantage, back then, accounted for 40 percent of the annual 3.3 percentage point edge that the fund's lifetime annual return of 13.8 percent reflects over its peer funds (10.5 percent). Almost one-half of the fund's*

expenses reflect Vanguard's operations efficiencies and economies, the other one-half is due to the relatively low ratio of advisory fees to the fund's assets. The magic of low costs and long-term compounding writ large!

Boglemetrics

When it came to Vanguard's active funds, Bogle knew where every basis point of cost came from and was hell-bent on cutting out whatever he could, as that would give the fund a better chance at success. It is not dissimilar to the sabermetrics that were featured in the book and movie *Moneyball*, in which a baseball manager found success by valuing traditionally boring stats like on-base percentage and slugging percentage over the more popular stats like batting average and home runs. While most obsess over the manager's degrees and their investing formulas, Bogle was laser focused on the costs and the volatility—which tend to be much better predictors of total return. If Bogle were a baseball manager, all his players would share the trait of low risk and low cost. His team would be boring as hell, but it would win a lot of games.

To that point, about half of Vanguard's active funds beat their respective Vanguard index funds during the past ten years, which is about double the industry average, according to Jeffrey DeMaso of Advisor Investments, a Vanguard watchdog. This largely proves the point that, had these other active fund companies shared economies of scale in the form of lower fees, they'd have done much better performance-wise, versus their benchmarks, and would have been much less vulnerable to disruption.

A totally separate study by Morningstar, which had nothing to do with Bogle, found that there was a very clear inverse correlation between fees and beat rates. It found that expense ratios had predictive power. In every category it tracked, the funds with the lowest cost had a much higher beat rate during the past ten years than the funds with higher cost. For example, in the US Large Blend category, 23.4 percent of the lowest-cost funds outperformed their benchmark. While that is still low, it was quadruple the 4 percent beat rate of the highest-cost funds. The moral of the story is that there is clearly a correlation between cost and one's inability to beat a benchmark.

Active Funds' Success Rates by Category and Cost

Active Funds' Success Rate by Category (%)

Category	1-Year	3-Year	5-Year	10-Year	15-Year	20-Year	10-Year (Lowest Cost)	10-Year (Highest Cost)
U.S. Large Blend	44.8	27.4	26.4	11.0	9.9	10.3	23.4	4.0
U.S. Large Value	48.8	29.3	31.3	18.8	19.2	16.3	27.9	5.8
U.S. Large Growth	25.6	42.8	32.1	11.9	5.1	8.6	24.7	5.8
U.S. Mid Blend	46.1	32.4	26.5	14.3	6.7	8.0	22.7	4.5
U.S. Mid Value	43.1	48.8	39.0	9.7	27.1	—	13.6	4.5
U.S. Mid Growth	17.3	58.9	51.1	42.9	26.0	9.8	57.9	35.9
U.S. Small Blend	37.6	34.0	22.7	13.3	9.2	12.5	13.9	11.1
U.S. Small Value	27.6	26.5	21.4	12.1	20.2	17.7	13.6	17.4
U.S. Small Growth	40.3	68.8	56.0	42.9	29.7	15.5	42.9	46.5
Foreign Large Blend	60.8	46.4	42.0	33.5	27.0	17.8	51.4	19.4
Foreign Large Value	50.5	39.8	35.5	32.1	12.0	—	40.9	23.8
Foreign Small-Mid Blend	58.6	34.4	28.6	38.1	—	—	50.0	25.0
World Large-Blend	49.0	25.9	24.3	22.2	—	—	22.2	11.1
Diversified Emerging Markets	65.5	57.5	47.4	50.0	33.3	—	60.0	37.5
Europe Stock	75.0	54.5	35.0	33.3	40.9	14.0	50.0	25.0
U.S. Real Estate	20.3	70.8	57.4	45.2	27.0	37.7	58.3	38.5
Global Real Estate	70.0	67.9	52.4	54.0	—	—	50.0	50.0
Intermediate Core Bond	84.8	42.9	52.9	27.8	16.0	10.6	46.7	12.9
Corporate Bond	82.0	63.0	71.4	64.5	—	—	—	16.7
High-Yield Bond	68.8	55.4	55.4	46.7	—	—	74.1	19.4

Morningstar

The Rise of Active

OK, let's take a deep breath here and regroup. We just explored at length how the high-cost active mutual fund (a massive industry) is in trouble and will likely shrink in the coming decades. But that doesn't mean active itself is dead—far from it. Vanguard's successful active mutual funds are proof of that. Some other low-cost active funds have done OK, too.

But beyond the thrifty survivors of the old world, there are a bunch of relatively new ways active management is evolving and changing in an effort to stay alive and in business in the coming Vanguardian future. Vanguard's growing occupation at the center of investor portfolios has forced the whole active industry to adapt and work around it. The good news for active managers is that at the end of the day there will always be at least some investors who want to try to "do better" than the market, despite the odds. Like the title of the classic Monty Python movie, there will always be a search for the holy grail when it comes to investing.

Ironically, many of these forms of new active are actually index funds, albeit designed in a way to make active bets. Some are more volatile than others. Some are cheaper than others. Some were even pioneered by Bogle and Vanguard. But despite influencing much of these new forms of active, Bogle was also very critical of most of it, including Vanguard's own funds.

Smart-Beta

Smart-beta is basically when an active manager takes a strategy or process, converts it into a rules-based index, and then launches an index fund or an ETF tracking said index, typically for a relatively low fee. It's also referred to as *quantitative investing* or *strategic beta*. In the end, though, it's basically active AI—kind of like trying to put Peter Lynch's brain into R2-D2.

Some smart-beta ETFs try to outperform by tracking the various characteristics of stocks—such as momentum, low volatility, and quality—or capturing market inefficiencies using fundamental metrics. They have trillions in overall assets—much of which is in hedge funds and mutual funds—but most recently they have blossomed in the ETF market, where they have grown to more than $1 trillion in assets in the past fifteen years.

Vanguard actually pioneered these types of funds, launching growth- and value-index funds all the way back in 1992. These two funds basically divide large cap stocks into two sections: *growth* (stocks that are anticipated to grow at a significant rate) and *value* (stocks that appear to trade at a lower price relative to their fundamentals). This was a blunt and basic way of doing it, but it was innovative at the time, and it showed the potential to apply various designs and filters to an index. And to this day, Vanguard's growth and value funds are the two biggest smart-beta funds (and ETFs) in the world, with more than $100 billion each.

People don't give Vanguard credit for that. But those value and growth funds are huge. I think the quants kind of thumb their nose at them because they are very simple in the metrics they use to break down value and growth. But they are big in smart-beta.
—Ben Carlson

Bogle explained his rationale behind launching the growth and value funds in one of our interviews:

And you should know, by the way, this great hero with which you are meeting here this morning started the oldest and largest smart-beta funds to this day—the value- and growth-index funds. But why did I do that? Because I thought investors would be well served by accumulating money in a growth fund, which is going to be very tax efficient because more of the return is capital growth, not income, and the fund shouldn't have a lot of capital gains. And when they get to retirement, they would switch over to a value-index fund, which would give a much higher percentage of their return in dividends. Perfect. What happened? They both did 9 percent from that time to date. However, the investors in both funds earned 4.5 percent. They were in the wrong one at the wrong time, time and time again. So what does this say about strategic beta?

The differences in returns between growth and value indexes in the short term versus their *lack* of difference in the long term is an important truism of investing and funds and reminds me of that scene from *Almost Famous* when the rock critic Lester Bangs—the late Philip Seymour Hoffman in one of his best roles—tells a young music reporter not to worry about the kids at his high school hating him because he'll "meet them all again on their long journey to the middle."

Vanguard Value vs. Growth vs. S&P 500 (1993–2019)

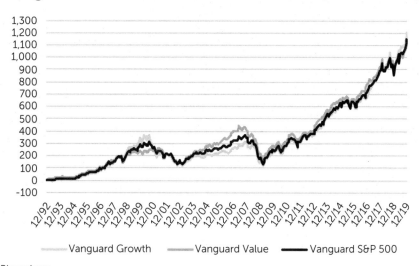

Bloomberg

As such, in the 2010s, value was hated while growth was popular. But by the time you read this, that may well be reversed. And while these "regimes" tend to feel permanent, they are subject to the same forces of mean reversion, or their "long journey to the middle." This fact arguably helps validate Bogle's "Just buy the whole market and wait fifty years" message.

Interestingly, value and growth weren't even Bogle's first foray into quantitative strategies. In 1986, he launched the Vanguard Quantitative Portfolios Fund, which utilized quantitative techniques and charged an advisor fee of a mere 0.24 percent—a shockingly low fee for that era. While Bogle would end up pointing out its futility, he would also take credit for pioneering it.

Well, he always took credit for starting it or thinking of it because of the value fund and then the growth fund. But then he was always skeptical of what that whole movement eventually became and whether there was any likelihood that investors would be able to add value to their portfolios with factors. He was always a real skeptic of investors' timing abilities.

—Christine Benz

In my interviews with Bogle, I would try to make investment cases for some of these new styles of active funds, but he would shoot each one down with calm precision, like a veteran skeet shooter, with statements like: "The past is not prologue. People think it's the right thing because it worked in the past. But let's even say that you are right and there is a permanent bias in favor of an undervalued section of the market. Say, value versus growth, then people will bid up the prices of value stocks and bid down the prices of growth stocks, and it will be gone. So if you're right, you're still wrong."

The insurmountable problem he had with quantitative strategies was that he found them all so futile compared with buying and holding a dirt-cheap total market index fund for a lifetime. He just didn't believe, although he did his best not to judge those who did. "They're all such nice guys, too," he said. "They truly believe they have found the holy grail. But the problem with that is, there is no holy grail."

Despite Bogle's skepticism, Vanguard is the biggest smart-beta fund company on the planet by assets and is regularly expanding its smart-beta ETF lineup in this category. Most recently, it added some more actively managed, equally weighted quant ETFs, which offered up more concentrated (unusual for Vanguard) exposures of value and momentum. I wrote about these for Bloomberg when they came out, and Bogle must have appreciated our take as he commented on our piece in *Stay the Course*:

The funds offer a choice among the quality factor, momentum factor, minimum volatility factor, value factor, liquidity factor, and a multifactor fund combines these various factors into a single fund. We shall have to wait and see how they fare for their investors and carefully asses their contribution to Vanguard's growth. I've avoided public comment on them, but the media seems to have guessed how I felt. Bloomberg's headline read: "Add the Hot Sauce, Hold the Bogle."

High Conviction Active

Speaking of hot sauce, as low-cost index funds utterly dominate in the new world—and in the center of portfolios—there's a growing market for the complete and total opposite: high conviction, highly concentrated, "swing for the fences" Babe Ruth–style active investing, or as I affectionately call it, shiny objects. These funds—which could be traditional discretionary active, or index based—use a limited number of stocks in an effort to increase their "pop" potential, albeit their volatility, too.

A popular recent example of this style is the ARK ETFs founded by Cathie Wood, which took the ETF world by storm by laying down some jaw-dropping performance numbers between 2015 and 2020. The suite of theme-oriented "innovation" ETFs grew to more than $50 billion—an unreal feat considering that ARK ETFs are selling stock-picking for a relatively pricey fee from an indie issuer with little distribution. Being any one of those three things can make your life a living hell in the ETF market. ARK was all three and became a massive success. Further, that growth happened at a time when active equity mutual funds saw about $800 billion in outflows. But ARK was able to buck the trend with a combination of performance, transparency, and audacity—a possible blueprint for how to survive as a stock picker in the future.

Wood has made some bold calls. The most famous of these came in 2017 when she went on CNBC and Bloomberg and said Tesla would hit $4,000 in five years. The price was $400 at the time. The stock proceeded to slide about 25 percent in the year after that call, yet she stuck to her guns and kept buying more despite mounting mockery and jeering on social media. And then Tesla's stock started going up parabolically, and it hit her target in 2021—with about a year to spare. In other words, marketing is a big part of the blueprint, too, as there are many high-conviction active managers who starve for assets.

Average Number of Holdings for New ETF Launches

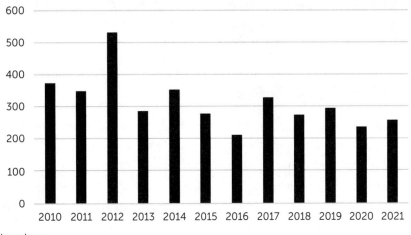

Bloomberg

As such, during the past few years, the average number of holdings in new ETFs has dropped. No surprise, Bogle was not a fan of these types of high conviction strategies. He outlines a series of examples of these "live by the sword, die by the sword" funds, including the Janus Twenty, in his books and describes how they have been like shooting stars throughout the years. Remember, he learned about them firsthand through Wellington's acquisition of the Ivest Fund, which flew high only to crash and burn in the early seventies. That is why Bogle was determined to make all of Vanguard's active strategies much more conservative, even if it meant lagging behind his peers during speculative periods. As he wrote in *The Clash of the Cultures*:

> *Experience shows that fund speculators who hopped on the bandwagon of "hot" performance have lost tens of billions of dollars by their counterproductive behavior. Logic and common sense tell us that the same patterns will recur in the future . . . Paraphrasing economist Herbert Stein: "If something can't go on forever, it will stop."*

Wood argues that mean reversion may not apply to her strategies. "When the world is not changing rapidly, mean reversion makes sense," she says. "But when the world is not only changing rapidly but there's also a convergence of technologies and platforms, it is very difficult for traditional research departments to even understand because they are so siloed and specialized. I think it will be very difficult in this new world for reversion-to-mean strategies."

The Portfolios, They Are a-Changin'

Regardless of where you land on this debate, these shiny object–type funds—as well as new developments like cryptocurrencies—will likely have some staying power and a safe home in the Vanguardian future. Because as low-cost index funds replace high cost, benchmark-hugging active mutual funds in the core of the portfolio, investors will naturally look for something very different to add to their plain vanilla portfolio to spice it up, à la putting hot sauce on an otherwise dull, albeit healthy, meal. And people will pay a little more for hot sauce.

This is very different from decades past where your active fund (conservative or shiny) was likely a core holding. And when it lagged, you got nervous and sold it. But now, cheap vanilla-flavored index funds are in the core. This has changed things. In short, the Bogle Effect is one of the reasons why Cathie Wood was able to get so popular. ARK doesn't compete with Vanguard, it complements it.

The flow data shows this as well. The cash coming into funds today resembles a barbell with about 80 percent of the cash going into boring but dirt-cheap plain vanilla funds, while most of the rest goes into the polar opposite—higher-cost funds built to pop. Because that's how portfolios look now. One could argue that the money going into these high-flying, more risky strategies is a behavioral hack to keep yourself entertained and stimulated so you don't go and touch the vanilla core of the portfolio, which needs time to compound.

3-Year Flows into ETFs ($B)

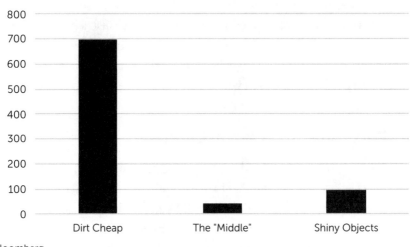

Bloomberg

It also keeps the overall cost of investors' portfolios low while allowing active managers to still get paid. As long as the core of the portfolio is dirt cheap, investors would be more willing to use a fund that has a higher fee, as it won't raise the overall cost of the portfolio too much. Thus, supporting-role active funds have a better chance to make a living. That said, even these funds will likely see cost pressure during the next decade as well.

Alternatively, active funds that insist on being the core of an investor's portfolio, the star of the show, are in trouble, as they have to compete with Vanguard and BlackRock on fees—which is a near impossible battle to win, as I demonstrated many times previously in this book. That is why high-cost, benchmark-hugging active mutual funds are currently in a no-man's-land— soon to be on the endangered species list.

The middle is already hollowing, and it's going to continue to hollow out. Most investors by the numbers are in underperforming active funds that charge too much. That's the middle.

—Dave Nadig

I think that middle is—I don't want to say collapsing, but there will be a grinding down. I certainly wouldn't want to be there. How do you differentiate yourselves these days? I think you need to be out there.
—Cathie Wood

Despite this lack of interest, many legacy mutual fund companies have tried to launch ETFs using their popular strategies, such as the Fidelity Magellan ETF, and they have been largely ignored despite their brand names and deep marketing budgets. They are neither cheap nor shiny. Even though they are in the desired wrapper (the ETF), the dog still has to want to eat the food inside.

That is why some mutual fund managers have taken the path to converting their mutual fund into an ETF. The first few conversions happened in 2021 and were successful. While converting a mutual fund into an ETF still doesn't solve the problem of lack of organic demand, it can be more appealing because the active managers get to enter the ETF industry with their track record, their assets, and some dignity. Our team estimates that $1 trillion worth of active mutual funds will convert during the next ten years.

One quick note here regarding flows and the middle. There are a couple of firms that have been able to be successful without being cheap or shiny. And the reason is because of their old-school sales and distribution tactics, which lean on personal relationships and wining and dining intermediaries. As a Twitter user put it, they "waterboard advisors with cabernet and force-feed them filet mignon." This is why we like to say on our team that there are three Cs to ETF success: cheap, creative, or cabernet. You pretty much have to be one of those three things to make it these days.

Themes

Another form of active that has taken off—largely in the shiny-object lane— is *thematic ETFs*. Of course, theme investing isn't totally new per se, but it has blossomed recently in the ETF structure. As I write this, theme ETFs have around $200 billion in assets, which is more than any sector category. What used to be dismissed as silly is now big-time.

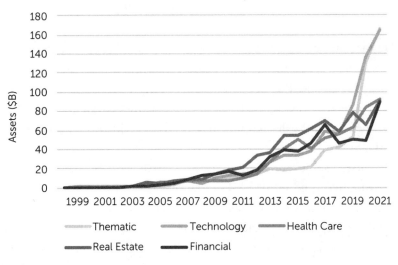

Theme ETF Assets vs. Sectors

Bloomberg

The reason for this goes back to how portfolios have begun to resemble barbells. These ETFs cross sectors, are typically concentrated, and are made up of small caps and some international stocks, so they have very little overlap with popular indexes. Thus, they can serve as a complement to a cheap passive core. They also have updated and reimagined what can feel like stale sector groupings (tech, discretionary, health care, etc.). Is Tesla more than a car company? Is Amazon only a retailer? What isn't tech these days? Theme ETFs will ignore these long-established sectors and group the stocks that may cross multiple sectors with names like innovation, cybersecurity, infrastructure, blockchain, etc.

When I look at, say, a genomics ETF, it is going to have a bunch of stuff that crosses traditional sectors. The problem is, how do we classify companies? Themes make sense. Sectors don't.

—Dave Nadig

While there have been some wacky themes over the years—such as whiskey, fishing, and professional-sports sponsors—those tend to come and go quickly, while the more legitimate ones survive.

We don't even have to guess what Bogle thought of themes. Not a fan would be a massive understatement. Over the years, he would refer to theme ETFs as "fruitcakes," "nutcases," and "the lunatic fringe." But once again, Bogle was dumping on an area he helped pioneer. Bogle launched a flurry of theme funds back in the eighties, although he was never really comfortable with them. Here he is in *Stay the Course*:

> *I was anxious—too anxious—to compete with arch-rival Fidelity's hyped array of eight sector funds, including Defense and Aerospace, Leisure & Entertainment, and Technology. I decided we needed to meet the challenge so we formed Vanguard Specialized Portfolios. I should have known better . . . It occurs to me that most of the mistakes I've made during my long career came on those occasions I put on a marketing hat.*

While most of Bogle's theme funds are no longer around, the Vanguard Health Care Fund (VGHCX) is, and it's actually one of the best-performing mutual funds of all time. Even Bogle admits that. But it just wasn't his style. It didn't sit right with him. He just didn't think you could win long term.

I really tried to make the case for theme and industry ETFs in one of my interviews with Bogle, presenting what-if scenarios and situations, and even trying to appeal to his concern over cost. "Say you are a sophisticated investor or even an advisor and you have your broad exposure already covered," I prompted. "Instead of using an active manager, what about using a smart-beta ETF or going into a niche area such as semiconductors where you have some opinion or like the story. This is better than paying 1 percent to an active manager, no?"

"It's better to speculate on markets [using a basket of stocks] than individual stocks," Bogle replied. "OK? I'll concede that. That's my first opinion. But my second opinion is, anybody that's a speculator is a damn fool. Did I make that clear? I mean, you can't win. And there's someone on the opposite side of every speculation."

While we probably won't see Vanguard launch any theme ETFs in the near future, their influence is still present as other issuers have "Vanguarded" certain theme categories by undercutting a hot product in cost. One example is when BlackRock launched a robotics ETF for 0.47 percent—nearly half the most popular product on the market. More recently, the Defiance 5G Next Gen Connectivity (FIVG), the first 5G ETF, launched at 0.30 percent—a staggeringly low fee for the first mover in a new theme. This was perhaps a way to spray BlackRock repellent on the ETF, to fend off any thoughts of undercutting it after it grew big. FIVG has more than $1 billion in assets today. Again, the Bogle Effect can be found nearly everywhere you look.

ESG

ESG (Environmental, Social, Governance) is another way in which active has reinvented itself. While most don't tend to think of ESG as active management per se, it is definitely active because it veers away from market beta and popular benchmarks. As I write this, there is over $100 billion in ESG funds, but some estimate that will grow into the trillions in the next decade.

Some of the metrics used for the *E* include a company's waste management, utilization of raw materials, and use of renewables. Some of the metrics used for the *S* include diversity, community relations, and safety. And some of the metrics used for the *G* include board diversity and independence, as well as transparency and accountability. These funds can also go by other names such as SRI (Socially Responsible Investing) or impact investing. And the way they are bundled can vary from excluding the "bad" stocks (oil and guns) to going after the "good" stocks (progressive companies).

While many are super optimistic about ESG's role in the future of portfolios, it will face some serious hurdles. First, ESG is being pitched as "saving the world" by lining up one's investments with one's values, when it is really just an active strategy. Many will balk at replacing their cheap beta ETF or index fund with ESG, or perhaps they will implement it and then have regrets when it goes through a period of underperformance. Second, ESG tries to make objective something that is very subjective and personal. You may be fine with guns and alcohol but your ESG ETF isn't. Or you may think Meta Platforms (previously called Facebook) is the Devil but your ESG ETF doesn't. I encourage anyone to look through a couple of ESG ETFs; I guarantee you will be surprised by what is and what isn't in them. And finally, many stocks that get excluded—such as oil companies or Amazon and Netflix—are likely to be companies that ESG investors are loyal custom-ers of. What is the point of not investing in a company when you are adding to its profits? These are the inconvenient questions that will continue to arise and challenge the hype of ESG.

Bogle was largely pro-ESG, albeit on a spiritual and conceptual level rather than investment level. While he thought corporations should be judged more closely on ESG metrics, he recognized the difficulty of mea-suring it properly since using one-size-fits-all data screens can sometimes throw the baby out with the bathwater—and vice versa. In a *Bloomberg Markets* interview in 2016, he said:

> *I'm very much on the ESG bandwagon. I believe companies should be way more sensitive to these issues. I don't know exactly how to measure any of it, though. And what do you do about a company that has good social values but bad environmental values? Or Berkshire Hathaway, with its governance model? They're well-governed, so no simple thing gives you an answer to a complex situation. So while I like the idea of ESG, it's still pretty fuzzy. And if you don't run a business, you won't do any good for anyone at all—it can't be at the expense of doing business well.*

US ESG ETF Assets

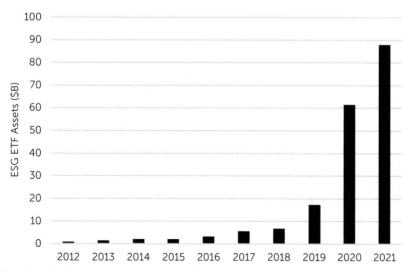

Bloomberg Intelligence

ETF Picking

You've heard of stock picking. One new form of active is ETF picking—or the attempt to produce alpha by actively trading passive ETFs. Again, it's an ironic by-product of the Bogle Effect.

The technical name for these ETF pickers is *ETF strategists*. And they are like master chefs who use ETFs as ingredients. They go deep into the toolbox, too. They are like active investors who think more like economists than stock analysts. They are more concerned about economic indicators, interest rates, inflation gauges, and geopolitics than they are about individual company fundamentals.

And what they make are *ETF model portfolios*. There are over a thousand of these portfolios to choose from, and they have in the neighborhood of $300 billion in assets, according to Morningstar. This used to be the domain of smaller players (e.g., Stadion, RiverFront, Astor), but the trend was co-opted by the big firms (e.g., Vanguard, Charles Schwab, BlackRock), which tend to charge much less—although the big players are typically going to make less-tactical models and more plain vanilla ones, while the smaller players are likely going to be much more active. For example, Astoria Advisors has an Inflation Sensitive portfolio full of different ETFs that are designed to benefit most from an inflationary environment.

On one hand, Bogle hated all the trading in ETFs and wasn't a fan of these models. On the other hand, some of the models use plain vanilla ETFs and don't trade a lot. In fact, Vanguard has model ETF portfolios that it sells to advisors. And some advisors pick the ETFs on their own, which makes this an arguably much larger phenomenon and shows how all passive funds tend to be used actively at least to some degree.

That is why advisors, it has been argued, are the new active managers of the financial world. As they replaced clients' active mutual funds with index funds and ETFs, they now are in control of the outcomes of a portfolio. Their decisions on what ETFs to buy and what weights to give them is the biggest and most impactful "active" decision for their clients. As Michael Kitces put it, they have "disintermediated the active mutual fund manager." We will explore their world—which is starting to face similar fee pressures to that of the active mutual funds they disintermediated—later in the book.

Astoria's Inflation Sensitive Thematic Model ETF Portfolio, 2021

Ticker	Name	Weight
XLI	Industrial Select Sector SPDR Fund	14%
XLB	Materials Select Sector SPDR Fund	12%
ITB	iShares U.S. Home Construction ETF	12%
VTIP	Vanguard Short-Term Inflation-Protected Securities ETF	10%
KBWB	Invesco KBW Bank ETF	10%
MOO	VanEck Vectors Agribusiness ETF	9%
GLDM	SPDR Gold MiniShares Trust	8%
GDX	VanEck Vectors Gold Miners ETF	6%
SLV	iShares Silver Trust	5%
PICK	iShares MSCI Global Materials & Mining Producers ETF	4%
COPX	Global X Copper Miners ETF	4%
XLE	Energy Select SPDR Fund	3%
XME	SPDR S&P Metals & Mining ETF	3%

Astoria Advisors

Direct Indexing

Another way that active fund shops are looking to resell active in a world gone passive is through direct indexing, or custom indexing, which is sort of like Build-A-Bear but for your portfolio. The idea is you build your own index fund or ETF, albeit with customized tweaks.

One of the big pitches for direct indexing is that you can lessen your tax burden. The idea is, by owning one hundred or five hundred stocks as opposed to one ETF or index fund, it creates more opportunities to harvest losses (tax loss harvesting) to use against your gains to minimize your tax hit. Even in a year when SPY is up (which means there are no losses to harvest), many of the stocks in it could be down for the year. Direct indexing proponents estimate this "tax alpha" is worth 1 percent to 2 percent a year, although it is a variable number and likely to diminish over the long term.

The other pitch is customization. Remember the subjectivity problem I just mentioned when it comes to trying to index ESG investing? Well, direct indexing attempts to solve that by letting the investors pick out any stocks from the index that they don't want. Makes sense, but now you are an active manager, at least partially, and I just spent many pages of this book writing about how even professional active managers struggle to beat the index.

When I hear "customization," I hear active. So we are essentially turning back the clock and saying that we are going to provide actively managed, separate accounts for investors. That goes against every trend that we've seen during the past decade-plus. The trend has been toward simple, lower-cost, index-based investing. Direct indexing goes against that trend. And I haven't seen any evidence that it's what investors want or that it provides a better investment outcome. Once you let people tweak the index, that's active management. Not only that, we don't even know what the cost and the spreads are going to be. There's a reason why Citadel is buying Robinhood's order flow.

—Nate Geraci

Direct indexing (DI) also isn't really a new concept. They do this a lot in the institutional world; they're just called separately managed accounts (SMAs). Direct indexing is mostly just a new marketing term for SMAs as they get democratized and become available to more investors thanks to technological innovation and the advent of free stock trading.

It's a clever term. And I think the tax-management aspect is valuable for a certain segment of clients. Actually, even before our acquisition of [DI firm] Aperio, we were the biggest direct indexer in the world because we run thousands of indices in SMAs and many of them are customized versions that we've been screening for clients based on their needs and we've been doing that for decades.

—Salim Ramji

One of the reasons direct indexing is likely to find a growing audience is that some of the biggest passive players, such as Vanguard, BlackRock, and Schwab, now have a DI solution. We've seen how much they've grown in ETFs so it is only natural they will grow here, too.

I think it is going to grow tremendously. We will make software where just with the click of a button you will own everything in the S&P 500. Naysayers to DI say it's too many stocks, it's too time consuming, it's too hard to keep track of, there will be too much tax reporting, etc. That's all stuff technology automates. Give computers another five to ten years' worth of compounding and that's going to be readily solved.

—Michael Kitces

That said, DI is unlikely to kill ETFs or even mutual funds, as some have suggested. One of the main challenges for it is that it is more expensive (DI is typically 25 bps to 40 bps), more complex, and more active. This has it trying to reverse the mass movement to cheap, simple, and passive.

I don't believe direct indexing will ever overtake ETFs. Number one, direct indexing is not indexing, it is active management. You are going to start saying, "I don't want to own this. I don't want to own that." And if you really care about tax-loss harvesting, you can tax-loss harvest with ETFs. This idea that direct indexing is going to rule the world and be bigger than ETFs is, in my mind, total rubbish.

—Deborah Fuhr

More than 100 million people use our indexing capabilities. Not all of them want customization. For many, life is already too complicated.

—Salim Ramji

Bond Funds

Bond funds, yet another investment product pioneered by Bogle, have largely sidestepped the exodus out of active—at least for now. While they aren't exactly hauling in the cash like passive, they are holding their own. For example, between 2013 and 2021, active fixed income mutual funds took in about $700 billion versus $1.7 trillion in outflows for their stock picking siblings. There's even been a steady supply of active fixed-income ETFs launching. Basically, advisors tend to be much more apt to give their money to a bond manager than a stock picker. Why is that?

There are a few reasons. First, the bond market is just so much bigger and more opaque. There are an estimated two million bonds in the US versus about 3,800 stocks. Also, bonds have a maturity date, so there is a time component that complicates the math—making it seem more like chess than checkers. This is why the current state of and future outlook for interest rates and the Fed is so huge and commands so much attention in the financial media. If rates go up, then all the bonds you are holding will lose value because they have lower yield—and vice versa.

Second, bond managers have much easier benchmarks to beat than do stock pickers. While stock benchmarks tend to be weighted by market cap, so there's some momentum baked into them, bond benchmarks tend to be weighted by the debt outstanding, so there is some molasses baked into them. The most popular benchmark for active bond managers to track is the Bloomberg Aggregate Bond Index, which is made up of about 70 percent government bonds and 30 percent corporate bonds, and it doesn't hold any high-yield or international debt (which many active funds will use).

Whereas the average investor feels they can make informed decisions about the stock market either with individual stocks or by choosing well-diversified index-based strategies, many investors don't trust themselves with bonds. They don't understand interest-rate sensitivity and credit risk, and they are more comfortable outsourcing that and paying an active manager to do the SEC selection and macro calls for them. The performance also plays a role. The AGG [aggregate] has been beaten by active managers that have benefited by taking on credit and interest-rate risk. There's just nothing like the S&P 500 or the Russell 2000 within the fixed-income world.

—Todd Rosenbluth

While there is arguably more math required to do bond analysis, much of the outperformance rates are simply due to the fact that the portfolio managers take on more credit risk by dipping into junk bonds or international bonds. We call this *yield doping*, and while it can help with performance, it can also spell trouble if and when there are sell-offs. In these sell-offs, many active bond mutual funds tend to start underperforming their much more conservative benchmarks and see outflows.

Pimco Income Fund vs. Vanguard Active Bond Fund vs. AGG During March 2020 Sell-Off

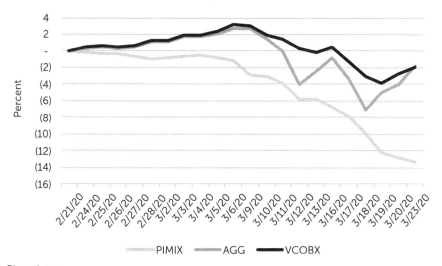

Bloomberg

Yield doping is why a prolonged sell-off could result in an exodus out of active bonds à la active equity funds. Further, if investors started using more accurate benchmarks to judge bond funds, that could also destroy their mystique as well and lead to an exodus. For example, the Bloomberg U.S.

Universal Index is arguably a better benchmark for many bond funds as it includes a dose of high-yield and international debt. When you replace the 'AGG' with the Universal, the beat rate of those active bond funds gets cut in half and is more on par with the stock pickers.

So while active isn't dead by any means, the Bogle Effect has wreaked havoc on it and forced it to adapt, by either getting cheaper or creative. And much of this active evolution and fee cutting is happening in the world of ETFs—one of Bogle's not-so-favorite topics—which we explore next.

6

Bogle and ETFs: It's Complicated

"An ETF is just another form of a mutual fund, a bastardized form, for lack of a better word."

Exchange-traded funds (ETFs) essentially take Bogle's index mutual fund idea and add intraday trading to it. And they are a smash hit. They take in a few billion dollars every day and now have about $7 trillion in assets in the US alone. Investors love that they can get diversified exposure to anything their heart desires for a relatively low fee and in a tax-efficient wrapper that trades on an exchange just like a stock.

ETFs track everything: stocks, bonds, international markets, commodities, futures, digital assets, active strategies, cash, packaged trades, you name it. While the bulk of the assets are in plain-vanilla exposures, there are some exotic products as well. The level of innovation in and experimentation with ETFs is off the charts, making them the Silicon Valley of the investing world, for better or worse.

Top 15 ETFs by Assets, October 31, 2021

Name	Ticker	Total Assets $MM	Expense Ratio	Avg Bid Ask Spread
SPDR S&P 500 ETF Trust	SPY US	409,796	+0.09%	+0.00%
iShares Core S&P 500 ETF	IVV US	304,415	+0.03%	+0.00%
Vanguard Total Stock Market ETF	VTI US	280,029	+0.03%	+0.01%
Vanguard S&P 500 ETF	VOO US	262,976	+0.03%	+0.00%
Invesco QQQ Trust Series 1	QQQ US	194,549	+0.20%	+0.00%
Vanguard FTSE Developed Markets ETF	VEA US	106,229	+0.05%	+0.02%
iShares Core MSCI EAFE ETF	IEFA US	102,544	+0.07%	+0.01%
iShares Core U.S. Aggregate Bond ETF	AGG US	88,414	+0.04%	+0.01%
Vanguard Value ETF	VTV US	88,176.2	+0.04%	+0.01%
Vanguard Growth ETF	VUG US	86,632.2	+0.04%	+0.01%
Vanguard Total Bond Market ETF	BND US	82,130.7	+0.04%	+0.01%
Vanguard FTSE Emerging Markets ETF	VWO US	82,054.7	+0.10%	+0.02%
iShares Core MSCI Emerging Markets ETF	IEMG US	81,092.7	+0.11%	+0.02%
iShares Russell 1000 Growth ETF	IWF US	75,699.1	+0.19%	+0.01%
iShares Core S&P Small-Cap ETF	IJR US	71,493.6	+0.06%	+0.01%

Bloomberg

While ETFs were first launched in the early nineties, they didn't really break through into the mainstream until after the global financial crisis of 2008. Just as the 1987 crash helped to get index funds going, the 2008 debacle was the year that ETFs really expanded their base. Traders loved how they provided liquidity during that chaotic time, when liquidity was sometimes scarce. Meanwhile, long-term investors were disappointed once again that their active mutual funds largely didn't do any better than the market, and so many of them started migrating over to ETFs. Since then, ETFs have been growing by $1 trillion every few years.

US ETF Assets

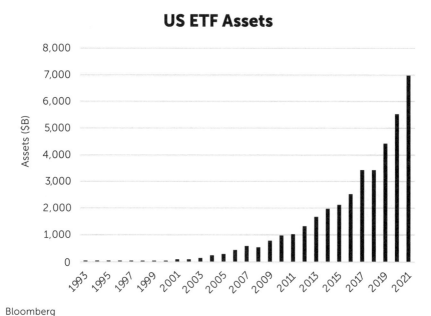

Bloomberg

Bogle Instrumental in ETF Success

Today, ETFs have more in assets than do index mutual funds, and they did it in about half the time. Although, to be fair, they got to stand on the shoulders of a giant, given Bogle's trailblazing work to make indexing and low-cost popular in the decades before the ETF existed. Bogle's contribution to ETFs is wildly underrated. The inventor of the ETF, Nate Most, actually went to meet Bogle in the early nineties to see if his idea for a fund that trades all day could be based on the Vanguard 500 mutual fund. Bogle declined, as the idea of people trading his precious traditional index funds was an abomination to him. But he became friendly with Most and provided him with some helpful critiques on the product design.

ETF vs. Index Mutual Fund Assets

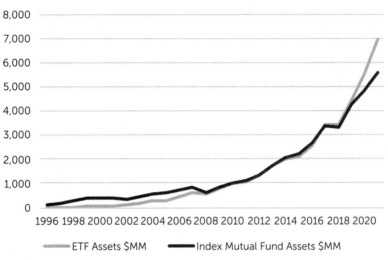

Bloomberg, ICI

"Nate Most walked into my office when I was running [Vanguard],"
Bogle recalled in an interview. "Nicest guy. He came in and he wanted us to
partner. He wanted to use our S&P 500 index fund for his [ETF]. First, I
said his idea had three flaws. Here they are . . . But second, even if you fix
them, I'm just not interested. The idea of trading all day long in real time is
just anathema to me.

"So we left as friends, and by the time he got off the train in New York,
he fixed the three errors and then went up to State Street and sold it. Guess
how much regret I have about that decision, and guess how many people I
talked to before making it? Zero and zero."

Bogle's influence went further, though, as the expense ratio that Most
decided to give SPY was 0.20 percent, which was the same as the Vanguard
500 Index Fund. Most wanted it to be on a level playing field with that fund,
which he considered the standard. Low cost was absolutely critical in helping the ETF—which was originally designed for traders and institutions—
spread to the advisor and retail world, where about 85 percent of their assets
today are from. Had Most priced SPY at 0.90 percent (the going rate for an
active mutual fund at the time), it is likely that ETFs would have remained
on the fringes of the investment world.

Purdey Shotgun

Bogle famously slammed ETFs many times over the years in his very colorful Bogleian style, despite his positive influence on them. Some of the highlights include "ETFs are like handing a match to an arsonist" and his assertion that they were "the greatest marketing innovation of the twenty-first century." He once compared them to the Purdey shotgun, which "is great for big-game hunting in Africa. It's also an excellent weapon for suicide." He suggested that ETFs should come with warning labels such as HANDLE WITH CARE or CAUTION: PERFORMANCE CHASING AT WORK. He even titled a chapter in one of his books "The Invasion of the ETF." You get the idea.

And yet, here we are today with Vanguard as the second-biggest ETF issuer and on a trajectory to be *the biggest* in five to ten years. ETFs are the biggest growth area inside Vanguard. The firm launched them in 2001, about five years after Bogle retired from Vanguard's board and about ten years after Bogle declined Nate Most's offer to give him first dibs on launching an ETF. This was a big part of the friction that had developed between Bogle and Vanguard, which we will explore more later in the book.

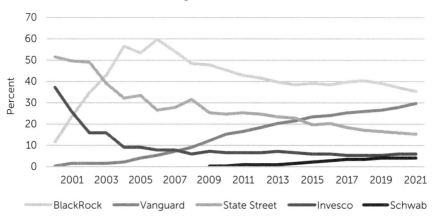

ETF Issuers by Asset Market Share

Bloomberg

I imagine that for Bogle, seeing ETFs explode in popularity was akin to being a father whose firstborn daughter married the tatted-up bad boy. This wasn't the kind of guy he wanted in the (indexing) family, but it's not his choice and now he has to deal with him. In trying to find the words to express this feeling, Bogle went full hyperbolic, referencing a 1971 hit song by Melanie, "Look What They've Done to My Song, Ma," which he then answers with, "They've tied it up in a plastic bag and turned it upside down, Ma; that's what they've done to my song."

Protecting the Index Fund

Why did Vanguard launch ETFs despite Bogle's misgivings? The main person behind the push was then-CIO Gus Sauter, whom Bogle "loved like a son," according to people who knew them both. Sauter revered Bogle as well. But Sauter believed that launching ETFs was a good idea.

"I was worried," Sauter explained in an interview. "What if we get a sell-off—and invariably we will—like a 1987 crash–style sell-off? So I started thinking, *What if we had another class of shares that people could trade?* The people who were not long-term-oriented to begin with would migrate to those shares. They could sell them at any time throughout the day and leave the rest of the fund unimpacted. And I thought about it for nine months before I ever proposed it to [then CEO] Jack Brennan because I wanted to make sure that I thought everything through. I finally came to the realization that I couldn't find any way that it wouldn't help our funds. It helps the resiliency. It also got rid of the problem of bad money trying to sneak into the funds. If it was bad money, it went through the ETF channel, and it had no negative impact on the fund. So it seemed like a win-win for us to do that."

I was a bit shocked by Sauter's admission. I had always heard that Vanguard launched ETFs as a growth play—to increase distribution to advisors via brokerage platforms. This seemed to have been Bogle's interpretation as well.

"I can understand why they were doing it," he said. "Some of the directors were on the record as saying we had to do it to get into a broker market, to have someone distributing our stuff again. But our original premise was to build a better mousetrap and the world will [beat] a path to your door. And all of a sudden we were out there hunting mice. And so, it didn't warm my heart."

Bogle actually found out about Vanguard's plans to launch ETFs by reading about it in a newspaper while on vacation. Needless to say, he was less than thrilled.

"We didn't want to let it get out to the public," Sauter recalls. "So it was very hush-hush around Vanguard. Jack went to Lake Placid every August, and [the news] leaked out that month, so Jack literally found out about it by reading the *Wall Street Journal*. When he came back, he saw me near the cafeteria from the second floor, and I was at the bottom of the stairs. There were probably thirty people in the foyer, and he yells, 'Gus, what the hell is going on around here?!' And I said, 'Jack, good to see you.' That wasn't a fun day."

And while launching ETFs did ultimately do wonders for distribution, the move also fulfilled Sauter's original goal of protecting the index fund investors from short-term traders, as well as helping to minimize capital gains distributions. The current portfolio manager of the Vanguard Total Stock Market Index Fund, Gerald O'Reilly, talked about the company's usage of ETFs on the Bloomberg *Trillions* podcast:

> We sometimes get calls from institutions looking to bring money to Vanguard, and they'll tell us up front, "Hey, we just fired a manager. We just want equity exposure." In the mutual fund, we would not be huge fans of taking in that money if we knew it was going to leave a month from now or three weeks from now. But obviously if you have an ETF, they are going to be paying their own freight on the way in and the way out.

The idea that Vanguard needs to be prepared for an investor exodus during a market downturn was something Bogle thought about a lot while he was running Vanguard. Ultimately, ETFs also solved his issues with turning down money. Now the short-term money has a place to go. In a mutual fund, the existing investors have to pay for others' activity. But in an ETF, since it is bought and sold on an exchange, the trading costs and any tax consequences are on the investor. In other words, ETFs *externalize* costs. People love this quality, and why not? It is simply more fair for people to pay based on their own actions instead of the actions of others.

Vanguard for All

But even if protection of the index mutual fund was the main motive, it was overshadowed by the distribution coup for Vanguard, as it allowed brokers, advisors, and retail investors to easily access Vanguard's low-cost passive strategies. Vanguard had traditionally asked you to come to Vanguard, and now, to a greater extent, Vanguard could come to you. This was big.

ETFs have to be given at least 50 percent of the credit for putting indexing on the map. They made indexing accessible to a huge number of people and brokers who didn't have access.
—Rick Ferri

Vanguard's launching of ETFs added another voice of reason and investor protection to the market that was selling the right things, so I appreciated that. Now Jack was very opposed to ETFs, but it was more that he thought they would get misused than [any] outright issues. That was all just part of being vigilantly protective of people.
—Lee Kranefuss

To be sure, ETFs did increase Vanguard's distribution, although it didn't happen overnight, as they still were up against some of the same issues of not paying for distribution, namely from the Wall Street broker-dealers.

"Back in the early days, I went around with our salespeople to talk with some of the major wirehouses [full-service broker-dealers]," says Gus Sauter on the *Bogleheads* podcast, "and one of the very largest wirehouses was all excited. 'You mean we can buy Vanguard funds?' Because their clients had been asking for Vanguard funds, and they hadn't provided them.

"I said, 'Yeah, absolutely you can buy Vanguard funds now in this format, and we'd love for you to do that.'

"They said, 'Great, how are you going to pay us?'

"And I said, 'We're not going to pay you. You are going to have to figure that out with your clients. We're not paying you, but you do have access now to the funds in the format you want them in.'"

Eventually, though, Vanguard got onto most of the advisory platforms because of demand from advisors who were going through their shift to fee-based models and were on the hunt for dirt-cheap exposures. They also got onto retail brokerage platforms and could eventually be traded commission-free. Fast-forward to today, and ETFs now account for the majority of Vanguard's flows and are the indexing tool of choice for many advisors looking to create a low-cost portfolio for clients.

Vanguard's ETFs vs. Index Mutual Fund Assets ($B)

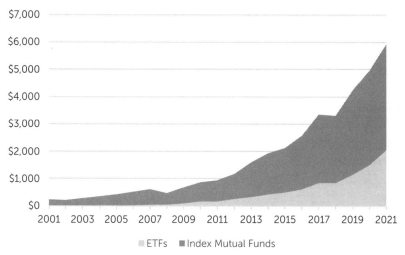

Bloomberg, Vanguard

The Tax Edge

One of the main reasons advisors, in particular, love ETFs—even more than index mutual funds—is their tax efficiency. Due to the way shares are created and destroyed—by swapping shares of the ETF for shares of the stocks in the basket—advisors are largely able to avoid triggering any capital gains distributions. This was simply a happy accident when Nate Most and his team created the ETF. But it turned into one of the ETF's biggest advantages.

In 2020, for example, roughly half of all mutual funds distributed capital gains, while only 5 percent of ETFs did, according to data from Morningstar and State Street. This comes in handy for advisors with clients in taxable accounts. Any advisor with wealthy clients will tell you that most of them hate paying taxes more than they love positive returns. As one advisor told me, "Help them save on taxes, and they will be a client for life."

ETFs' 2020 Cap Gains Report Card

Morningstar US Category Group	# of ETFs	# of ETFs Estimating Capital Gains Distributions	% of ETFs Estimating Capital Gains Distributions	# of ETFs Estimating Cap Gains >1% of NAV	% of ETFs Estimating Cap Gains >1% of NAV
US Equity	302	4	1.3	0	0
Sector Equity	277	3	1.1	1	0.4
International Equity	317	5	1.6	2	0.6
Allocation	29	2	6.9	1	3.4
Taxable Bond	252	52	20.6	7	2.8
Municipal Bond	48	4	8.3	0	0.0
Commodities	22	0	0.0	0	0.0
Alternatives	145	0	0.0	0	0.0
Total	1,392	70	5.0	11	0.8

Morningstar

Just to be clear, though, ETFs don't sidestep taxes. They just allow you to defer them. Basically, you are only taxed when you sell the ETF, as opposed to a mutual fund, in which you can be taxed when *others* leave the fund because it means the fund portfolio manager will have to sell some of the holdings to cash them out, and that typically triggers a capital gains distribution. This means the people in a mutual fund are innocently impacted by those who leave. This is why, in my opinion, ETFs aren't some loophole, per se, but arguably the fairer way to do tax investors.

Even Bogle acknowledged this tax benefit of the ETF structure in one of our interviews—although with a caveat as usual. "Our index fund hadn't paid a capital gain in twenty, maybe thirty years," he said. "So they are highly tax efficient. The ETFs, if you hold them, are conceivably more tax efficient. But you don't hold them, you trade them. And all that trading creates, if you are lucky, capital gains."

Vanguard is in a unique position to take great advantage of this tax efficiency issue. It has a special patent in which its ETF is a share class of the bigger mutual fund. As such, the mutual fund can actually use the ETF to increase the tax efficiency of the mutual fund.

At Vanguard, the mutual funds lend the ETFs economies of scale— especially at the beginning, when the mutual fund asset base was so much larger than the ETF asset base, because the ETFs could not have had the pricing they did without the mutual fund as a backup. What does the ETF do for the mutual fund? The ETF brings the tax efficiency. So I see [them] as complementary.
—Elisabeth Kashner

While Bogle wasn't a fan of ETFs, he was acutely aware of how taxes could corrode returns. Bogle frequently used the low turnover of the index fund—and its relative tax efficiency—to strengthen his case against active funds. He wrote in *The Little Book of Common Sense Investing*:

The average actively managed equity fund earned an annual after-tax return of 6.6 percent, compared with an 8.6 percent for the index investor. Compounded, an initial 1991 investment of $10,000 generated a profit of $39,700 after taxes for the active funds, less than 60 percent of the $68,300 of accumulated growth in the index fund.

Agree to Disagree

Despite the fact that ETFs helped to bring Bogle's low-cost passive philosophy to the masses and protected the index fund from short-term traders and capital gains distributions, Bogle just couldn't get comfortable with them. Further, they weren't his idea. He continued to warn about ETFs even as some of his closest friends and colleagues supported them.

You have to bear in mind that ETFs were not his thing. They did not come from him. I pleaded my case [for ETFs] for years, explaining the tax efficiencies and the benefits of lowering costs. ETFs are a better structure. They just are.

—Jim Wiandt

All those benefits were simply overwhelmed by Bogle's two main problems with ETFs: trading and marketing. Let's deconstruct these two issues.

Issue #1: Trading

Bogle fought against trading as much as he fought against high fees. And as a group, ETFs trade *a lot*. In 2020 alone, ETFs traded $32 trillion worth of shares despite having only $5 trillion in assets at the time. On any given day, ETFs tend to make up 20 to 25 percent of all equity trading on the stock exchanges, although the percentage is higher in sell-offs—and in stress—as people lean on them to adjust their portfolios.

Unlike 90 percent of other critiques and worries about ETFs, over-trading is a legitimate concern, because we know investors can be their own worst enemies, and any tool that makes bad behavior easier could be detrimental. So it made sense to worry about this, especially for someone like Bogle.

To make his point, Bogle would quote turnover numbers as proof that ETFs are being traded a lot. Turnover is the percentage of the fund's assets that trade each year. For example, say an ETF has $1 billion in assets and sees $5 billion worth of shares traded in 2020. You'd say its annual turnover was 500 percent. Here's Bogle dropping some of these turnover numbers in one of our interviews:

> *Trading has always been a big part of our market, but not always this much. When I came into the business, the turnover on the Big Board [NYSE] was 25 percent a year. Even before ETFs started, it was probably up to 150 percent. It is now 250 percent. The average turnover for an*

ETF is 400 percent a year. And SPY is 3,000 percent. And here you're talking to a guy who thinks 3 percent turnover is pushing the envelope.

While those numbers are accurate, there is a case to be made that they are much too blunt to draw conclusions from. The problem is, there is no way to break down *who* and *where* the volume is coming from. It is possible that there are one hundred investors sitting in the ETF doing nothing while three massive institutional investors are moving in and out. You just don't know because volume is an aggregate number that you can't break down, and so one big trade can really skew the numbers.

The trading is also anonymous. We have no connection to who is doing the trading. And ETFs are unique in that a wide variety of investors use them, ranging from the world's biggest hedge funds and endowments to advisors and my mom. They are truly the one vehicle in which everyone plays in the same sandbox and gets charged the same fee.

You aren't going to find anyone who has more love and respect for Jack Bogle than me, but what I think he didn't quite grasp is that ETFs were different because you had so many different kinds of players in there—people shorting the market, hedge funds. There's all this various activity going on. It wasn't like Mom and Pop buying and selling ETFs all day.

—Jim Wiandt

Roughly speaking, we found that about 50 percent [of ETF investors] were institutional and 50 percent were individual. But if you look at the trading, 95 percent was institutional. In addition to their value as a long-term investment vehicle, ETFs are used widely by trading desks, hedge funds, and other fund managers who need to equitize cash, and those people really appreciated the liquidity. Those people are the ones who did a lot of the trading every day. ETFs are one of the few times you can get users with wildly divergent needs into the same vehicle without it coming back to haunt you in some way.

—Lee Kranefuss

A good way to think about an ETF is like a hotel, where many people are chilling in their rooms, yet the lobby is bustling. The bustling lobby can overshadow all the quietness going on in the rooms. And, further, one doesn't impact the other.

I brought this up in our interviews, and to Bogle's credit he did acknowledge the bluntness of the data. But still, he estimated that only one-sixth of ETF investors are buy-and-hold investors. Most experts—including myself—would argue that is way too low and the real number is more likely to be at least half. Still, there was some supporting data showing that ETF users tended to trade more than mutual fund investors.

For example, one study out of Europe looked at outcomes for about seven thousand investors in a large German brokerage between 2005 and 2010 and found that ETFs generally hurt their overall returns simply because they were more apt to trade them. Further, Fidelity reported that their client accounts showed the average holding period for an ETF was two years versus four for a mutual fund.

I agree with Bogle's view on ETFs. And I tell [people] to go to open-end mutual funds and not ETFs, purely for behavioral reasons. Because if you have an ETF, it trades throughout the day. It has a ticker. You watch it. If you have an open-end mutual fund, the NAV prices once a day, and you don't pay attention to it. I have this theory about how more information is actually bad for investing. The more data you have is bad. It's kind of sad that the open-end mutual fund industry is dying, because I think it is the better structure for most investors.
—Jared Dillian

As he watched ETFs grow and grow and grow, Bogle tried his best to fight back against the sentimental tide to make the case for index mutual funds. He even tried in vain to get the acronym TIFs (traditional index funds) to catch on as a way to separate his cherished, broadly diversified index mutual funds from what he saw as wild-and-crazy ETFs. "We have to make a distinction between traditional index funds," he said, "which I have given the acronym TIFs, which nobody follows. I lead but nobody follows."

The good thing is, investors have a choice. You can get near-free exposure in both a Bogle-approved index mutual fund or in an ETF. And if you are the type of person who is vulnerable to temptation, an index mutual fund is probably the better choice—although most ETF users would say that trading is not an issue for them.

We are not tempted to trade using ETFs. We are not day-trading our clients' accounts. The biggest reason we use ETFs over index mutual funds is for taxes. Are we trading the ETFs on a daily basis? No. The other thing we like about ETFs is that when we do buy one at, say, 1 PM, we know what price we are going to get. If the market moves, the mutual fund doesn't price till 4 PM and change. We've had a few things where we've gone from mutual funds to ETFs and there's a timing mismatch, and all of a sudden, the market moves and we are short, so we had to correct that. Kind of nice when you are all in the same product.

—Ken Nutall

If you have two investments and one allows you to buy and sell during the day (ETFs) and the other allows you to buy and sell at the end of each day (mutual funds), why would you not want that optionality? But from a behavioral standpoint, I don't think it makes any difference if you trade intraday or once a day.

—Nate Geraci

Issue #2: Marketing

The other thing Bogle did not like was the wild product proliferation and seemingly endless mutations on the concept of an index—what Rick Ferri refers to as "special purpose indexes," or "SPINdexing." Bogle loved to show people the *Wall Street Journal* page that listed all the (hundreds of) ETF quotes and say something like, "What the hell is going on here?" He just thought the industry had taken the simplicity of broad index funds and gone crazy with it. It weighed on him regularly. He wrote in his book *Enough*:

I'm afraid that the new jazzed-up iterations (largely ETFs) of the simple index fund that I spawned all those years ago are helping to lead the way. No wonder I wake up some mornings feeling like Dr. Frankenstein. What have I created?

Jack and I were totally aligned on that. We were deliberate in our development of indexing. We didn't just throw funds out there that we didn't think were good tools for investors. It wasn't about trying to see what you could throw against the wall to see what sticks.

—Gus Sauter

There are too many products. Just the fact that we have seven or eight different cannabis ETFs. The industry has been sliced so narrowly, yet there's so much competition where you have five or six firms going after the same narrow slice of the investment market. Whereas the investor would probably be better off buying broadly diversified, low-cost, index-based strategies and rebalancing periodically, instead of swinging for the fences with every theme that one can invest in.

—Todd Rosenbluth

Bogle saved his most colorful savagery for niche and exotic ETFs. I've compiled a medley. Enjoy:

» "There may be forty broad-market ETFs, but that leaves you 1,460 that are in many respects fruitcakes, nutcases, the lunatic fringe."

» "It's become a marketing business. Now we have one that is short retail and long electronic marketing. Then we got the Republican and Democrat ETFs, and the Whiskey & Spirits ETF, and where it ends nobody knows."

» "Can you believe that we now have a HealthShares Emerging Cancer ETF? It should have been called Curing Emerging Cancer or something . . ."

» "Now we have a cloud computing ETF, which almost sounds like the weather is computing the ETF . . ."

» "ETFs that bet on down markets are asinine . . ."

» "Bet on the market with 300 percent leverage—what sense that makes is beyond my comprehension . . ."

When Bogle was on our ETF podcast, we asked him what his favorite ETF ticker was (the standard, lighthearted last question that we ask every guest). He paused for about three seconds and said, "C-R-Z-Y," which I thought perfectly summed up his feelings on ETFs as well as showed sharp wit for an eighty-seven-year-old.

To be fair, though, Vanguard has had its share of niche fund launches over the years—mostly under Bogle's watch, too (e.g., the Vanguard Service Economy Fund and the Vanguard Precious Metal and Mining Fund)— although Bogle would later go on to trash those funds as well as himself for launching them. That's the thing about Bogle: he is equal opportunity in his savagery.

Some ETF proponents have moved a little closer to Bogle's position on this issue, worrying that the industry has gotten away from its core value-add of low-cost, liquid, and tax-efficient exposures and into more gimmicky and exotic "products."

I do think the ETF industry has lost the thread a little bit. It's largely all bullshit. Most people are going to be better served by broad diversification and low cost, and no one is saying that anymore, not even Vanguard. I feel like somebody should be taking up the mantle because it is so on the money.

—Jim Wiandt

As I discussed in the last chapter, one of the reasons ETFs have become so colorful is because of how popular Vanguard has gotten. These issuers simply can't compete with a three-basis-points index fund, so their only hope is to try to complement it with unique and trendy strategies. Thus, however ironic it is, many of the most C-R-Z-Y ETFs are arguably by-products of the Bogle Effect.

Gremlins

Bogle's two critiques on trading and marketing are some of the reasons I frequently compare ETFs to *Gremlins*, the 1984 movie in which a dad buys his son this cute, big-eared, big-eyed pet in a box from an antique store in Chinatown. The adorable little creature, however, comes with three rules: Keep it away from sunlight. Don't spill water on it. And never, ever feed it after midnight because it will turn into a vicious monster and terrorize your house and probably the whole town.

ETFs are a bit like that. You'll be OK if you just mind a few rules of thumb, such as limiting your trading, staying away from products you don't understand, and most importantly, not buying one based solely on the name or the ticker but rather only after looking at the holdings, index design, and cost.

What's inside the ETF and what the ETF is called can be very different, and two ETFs that sound the same will often perform quite differently because they own different securities.

—Todd Rosenbluth

There are simply so many ETFs, and they have democratized pretty much everything under the sun—from Vietnamese equities and bank loans to vegan-friendly stocks and oil futures. And literally hundreds of new ones launch every year.

To help people with the avalanche of funds coming at them, as well as allay some of Bogle's concerns, we at Bloomberg created the Bloomberg Intelligence ETF Traffic Light System, which is intended to give advance information of any potential nasty surprises to investors. The system is modeled after movie ratings, which is a simple and effective way to allow for innovation while protecting the innocent.

Instead of looking at factors like violence, drug use, language, and nudity, we look at leverage amount, hidden fees, low volume, derivative usage, alternative tax treatment, and so on. This is where Vanguard and BlackRock—normally fierce competitors—are largely on the same page.

I think there are too many things that are called ETFs. We came up with our own naming proposal. You have your traffic light. Regardless of what the standard is, we are both getting at the same point, which is, what's inside actually matters, such as leveraged and inverse products that don't share the same features as broad-based, diversified, transparent ETFs. And you shouldn't masquerade as something you are not . . . Everyone can buy whatever they want, but they should be aware of what they are buying.

—Salim Ramji

Making Peace (Sort Of)

Bogle would have appreciated the efforts to help investors navigate the ETF world, even if it didn't totally solve his overall problems with them. And as someone who met with him multiple times in the later years of his life, I saw him progressively warm up a bit to ETFs. He saw that Vanguard's ETFs were not nearly as traded as those of other issuers, so he took some reassurance in that. Sauter was also finally able to explain to Bogle many years later that his motive wasn't asset growth but rather to protect the current index fund investors.

"The one time we sat down and talked about it was a little get-together he organized at Princeton in 2014 with about five or six people," Sauter recalls. "I told him then and there that the reason I wanted to do ETFs was not to attract assets but to help defend the index funds and the concerns of money flowing in and out of the funds. I think that was the first time he really accepted it. That was a good twelve or fourteen years [after the fact]."

I think Bogle did begin to see that some investors were indeed using ETFs as long-term building blocks and taking advantage of their superior tax efficiency. So I think he was softening a little bit.

—Christine Benz

In his last interview with me, Bogle said, "ETFs are fine as long as you don't trade them. You should stay with the classy ones, the diversified ones: the total stock market, the S&P, total international, total bond, or total balanced is even easier."

That was probably as close to coming to peace with ETFs as he ever got. That said, he couldn't just leave that nice olive-branch comment there, and so he followed it up with a "but." He just couldn't help it.

"This is a marketing product," said Bogle. "This is a product to bring in money. And does it serve investors well? We don't really know that."

7

The Great Cost Migration

*"Vanguard's focus on cost put big pressure on this industry.
There's no question about it."*

While much of the attention in the media is focused on the sea-change shifts from active to passive, from mutual fund to ETF, and even from broker to advisor, the common thread through all of it is the move from high cost to low cost. This is the mother of all trends—the heart of the Bogle Effect.

The problem with some of those other aforementioned trends is, there is a lot of nuance. For example, while there's no denying the active-to-passive trend, many index funds are really active in nature. Even the S&P 500 is active to a degree, given that it only invests in large caps and has criteria for inclusion and a human committee to boot. On the flip side, many active funds have index tendencies and hug the benchmark. It's not black-and-white. The same applies to the mutual funds-to-ETFs trend. While active mutual funds have largely seen outflows, index mutual funds generally take in cash, and many active bond mutual funds take in cash.

What's not nuanced, however, is the trend of money moving from high cost to low cost. Cash is almost entirely traveling south today. I refer to this as "the Great Cost Migration," which may sound like the title of a *Peanuts* special (e.g., *Charlie Brown and the Great Cost Migration*) but it is as distilled as I could get it. And, yes, *The Great Cost Migration* was also the title I almost gave this book.

It is *great*. We are talking about tens of trillions of dollars in play here. And it is almost 100 percent about *cost*. What a fund charges is the first thing most people look at today. Expense ratio has largely replaced the past-performance chart as the main criterion in fund selection. And it is a *migration*. This is not some temporary visit—those investors and their money are never going back. They are proud and permanent residents of Cheapville.

Bogle compared it to an awakening on the *Bogleheads* podcast: "People have started to realize that cost is almost everything. Performance comes and goes but costs go on forever . . . and when clients get aware of that and wake up, the industry will wake up."

These clients (whom I refer to as "the retail host organism") aren't just awake, they're pissed off. And they are hell-bent on keeping as much of their money as possible now. The data shows this awakening clear as day. For example, if you group together all the various types of funds (mutual, ETFs, closed-end), throw them onto one giant spreadsheet, divide them into deciles by their expense ratios, and then run the three-year flows, you will find a chart that cascades down left to right.

That correlation between expense ratio and flows is found when you isolate each type of fund as well. You see it in the flow data for active funds, index mutual funds, and ETFs. Morningstar has a great chart they update regularly that shows the average fee for active and passive funds in which they both equal weight and asset weight the averages. You can literally see the gravity pulling all of them down. It's one of those charts I'm jealous of. It captures the Bogle Effect really well.

Fund Fees Are Falling

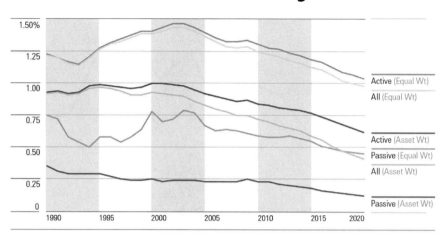

Morningstar

There are other ways to show this trend as well. At Bloomberg, we created a chart we call the Cost Obsession Thermometer, which looks at what percentage of flows into index funds and ETFs (which take in 500 billion to one trillion dollars a year) go to funds charging 0.20 percent or less. In 2018, it reached a peak of 99 percent (with 70 percent of it going to funds that charge 0.10 percent or less), although it has come down a bit since thanks to a soaring market that has birthed many young, trading-happy retail investors as well as passive investors looking to add a little spice to their otherwise cheap beta portfolios as we discussed in the last chapter. The thermometer tends to rise when markets are flat or down and drop a little when markets are up and investors are seeking a little adventure. Either way, it is likely to remain elevated for a long time.

The Cost Obsession Thermometer

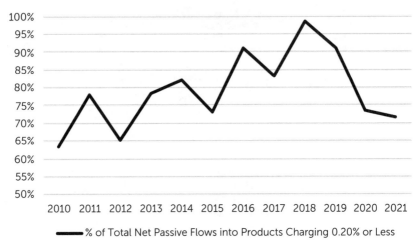

———% of Total Net Passive Flows into Products Charging 0.20% or Less

Bloomberg, ICI

Cost Is King

This new era of cost obsession isn't only in the hard data, it's also in the anecdotal data. Just talk to an advisor or even a retail investor and they'll likely tell you they look at fees first and won't buy anything that charges more than 0.20 percent. This trend also shows up in survey after survey, which show that investors rank "low expense ratio" as their *number one* criterion when selecting an ETF. It's so intense that even index fund advocates have tried to warn investors that cost isn't everything and that they need to remember to look under the hood.

When I see those surveys, I want to shout from the rooftops that costs matter much less than what's inside the portfolio. Each index provider has different criteria as to what makes it into the portfolio, and year after year you will see performance differences that are much, much greater than the fee differential.

—Todd Rosenbluth

Similarly, Bogle's former assistant turned competitor, James Riepe, told the *Philadelphia Inquirer* that Bogle went too far sometimes: "Are costs important in investing? Yes. But should you make choices based only on cost? No, not necessarily. With Jack, everything tends to be portrayed as black or white. I happen to think the world is often a little more gray."

On one hand, investors can be too fixated on cost if it trumps exposure, but on the other, it's understandable given how many have had the experience of getting burned by picking funds based on a past-performance chart. To quote Billy Joel, it's a "matter of trust." Investors generally don't trust the charts anymore, but they do trust the fee.

Some even boast about how little they are paying, which is now replacing the boasting about how good one's fund manager is that peaked in the nineties. Canada's *Globe and Mail* newspaper did a piece in 2018 about how "fee shaming" was becoming common, which included this quote:

People talk at dinner parties, and they say things like, "Oh man, you're paying 2.5 percent? I'm only paying [a lower percent] for my ETF."
—Shannon Lee Simmons, New School of Finance

While I personally have never witnessed fee shaming at a dinner party (although I have two young kids, so a *dinner party* these days means pizza or Chick-fil-A), when I do talk to people about their personal investments, most will say they have gone almost completely passive and are unwilling to pay up for a fund anymore. And while there will always be some speculating on the latest investment craze, by and large, hearts and minds have changed.

401(k) Plans Go Passive

This Great Cost Migration is happening inside defined contribution plans as well, where the employer matches employee pretax contributions up to a point. These plans used to be dominated by higher-fee active funds but have since seen a marked shift toward index funds. In fact, today, the majority (52 percent) of the equity assets inside 401(k) plans are in index funds—up from 38 percent ten years ago, according to *Pension & Investments*.

Many of these 401(k) investors will get their low-cost index fund exposure via target date funds, or *life-cycle funds*, which have exploded in popularity and now have about $2.8 trillion in assets, according to Morningstar. These funds hold other index funds in percentages that are in line with an investor's time horizon and risk tolerance—slowly morphing into a more conservative allocation as the year-end approaches. For example, the Vanguard Target Retirement 2055 Fund (VFFVX) is currently a very aggressive allocation.

US-Defined Contribution Assets Under Management from P&I's Money Manager Survey ($B)

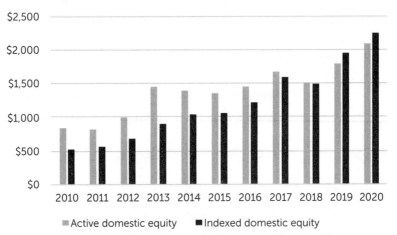

Pensions & Investments

As I write this, VFFVX has 54 percent invested in the Vanguard Total Stock Market Index Fund, 36 percent in the Vanguard Total International Stock Index Fund, and the remaining 9 percent in two of its bond index funds for an all-in fee of 0.15 percent. Vanguard has a little over $1 trillion in target date fund assets.

As we know, Bogle was critical of many of the innovations in the fund world, even many that he himself spearheaded, but one that he really liked was target date funds—albeit with the major warning that investors would still need to look under the hood to make sure the fund is using low-cost index funds, since some use pricey active funds or are double charging. In *The Little Book of Common Sense Investing*, Bogle says, "Target date funds can be an excellent choice, not only for investors who are just getting started with their investment programs, but also for investors who decide to adopt a simple strategy for funding their retirement."

Another way that defined contribution plans will get cheap index exposure is via Collective Investment Trusts (CITs), which have about $4 trillion in assets, according to Cerulli Associates. A CIT is basically a fund but only available to institutional investors and employee-sponsored retirement plans. The reason they are taking off is that they have negotiable fees, which tend to be dirt cheap. The vast majority of the assets in CITs are in passive funds, so they, too, are part of the Great Cost Migration, albeit a less-talked-about one because the data is hard to get. I refer to them as the dark matter of the fund universe.

The Power of One . . . Basis Point

One of the by-products of the Great Cost Migration is the never-ending ETF fee war. Because investors favor cheapness, issuers keep cutting fees. They don't like it, but they have to adapt to the demand side of the equation. Investors' obsession with fees is so strong that we've seen billions get redirected after an issuer cuts its fee by just one basis point (which is one-hundredth of 1 percent, or 0.01 percent).

A good case study to show the Power of One (basis point) comes from the ongoing fee war between Vanguard and BlackRock and their two S&P 500 ETFs, VOO and IVV, which collectively have close to half a trillion dollars in assets. These two are like the Godzilla and King Kong of ETFs trading blows. For example, in October 2016, after having trailed VOO in flows by about $15 billion during the prior two years, BlackRock cut the IVV fee from 0.07 percent to 0.04 percent, which made it one basis point cheaper than VOO. During the next two years, it took in $50 billion, while VOO saw "only" $31 billion. Then, in June 2019, VOO cut its fee to 0.03 percent, or one basis point cheaper than IVV. In the next twelve months, VOO took in $27 billion to IVV's $4 billion. Then, in

June 2020, IVV cut its fee to tie VOO at 0.03 percent, and they've been about even since.

While there are other variables and crosscurrents at play, the fee cuts clearly had a huge impact on the flows into these two funds. But the good news for both is that by battling it out to these low extremes, each became more and more attractive to people sitting in high-cost active mutual funds.

Getting money into IVV is less about competing with other S&P 500 ETFs, and more about people wanting to replace more expensive active funds or simplify their portfolios away from the stocks they collected over the years.

—Salim Ramji

Some model portfolios—which hold five to ten ETFs and are very popular among advisors—are programmed to only put money into the cheapest product in the category, which has resulted in some extreme cases.

Splitting a Basis Point

One issuer actually went as far as to split a basis point in an effort to undercut the competition. In 2018, the GraniteShares Gold Trust (BAR), which had recently been undercut by one basis point by the SPDR Gold MiniShares (GLDM), announced in a formal press release that it would cut its fee to 0.1749 percent, making it half a basis point lower than the 0.18 percent fee for GLDM. By making the new fee 49/100th of a basis point, it would round down to 0.17 percent, thus rising to the top of a model portfolio's ascending order search by expense ratio.

While there have been hundreds of fee cuts over the years, this one to me was symbolic and always stuck in my memory because of the precision of the cut and the fact that it happened in a category that Vanguard doesn't even compete in. There really are no more VFZs (Vanguard-free zones, or safe places for asset managers to keep fees high and not worry). Now, issuers have to worry about a competitor "pulling a Vanguard" and undercutting everyone else.

Fidelity Zero

Perhaps the ultimate example of pulling a Vanguard came in August 2018 when Fidelity stunned the financial world by announcing zero-fee index mutual funds. Now, to be sure, they already offered very cheap index mutual funds, but this made a splash because it was the first time any fund manager of that size and stature went to zero. And the fact that it was the king of active funds added to the buzz and spoke volumes about the Great Cost Migration—and the Bogle Effect.

Here you have Fidelity taking the fight to Vanguard right on its home turf of index mutual funds, where it has approximately 75 percent market share. And Fidelity had success doing it. The zero-fee suite of funds crossed the $20 billion mark in about three years—adding to the hundreds of billions it takes in via other ultralow-cost index mutual funds. Fidelity's goal was to be cheaper than Vanguard in all categories, which it made very clear in a July 2019 press release:

> As is the case with Fidelity's 53 existing stock and bond index funds and 11 sector ETFs, the new funds have lower expense ratios than their comparable funds at Vanguard. The five new funds are available to individual investors, third-party financial advisors, and workplace retirement plans.

Fidelity pointing out that it is cheaper than Vanguard shows just how much the world has turned. Here's Bogle taking a victory lap about it in *Stay the Course*:

> Fidelity chairman Edward C. Johnson III doubted Fidelity would soon follow Vanguard's lead (in 1988, however, he would do exactly that). "I can't believe," he told the press, "that the great mass of investors are going

*to be satisfied with just receiving average returns. The name of the game is
to be the best." (Today, index funds represent fully 30 percent of all equity
fund assets managed by Fidelity.)*

While Bogle ended up winning the idea war, I think you have to give
Fidelity some credit for swallowing its pride and adapting. Some firms
didn't. And now they have nothing to offset their outflows with. And if
Bogle really did want to see a world in which Vanguard's share class would
start to erode, ironically it is Fidelity—and a few others—who is helping to
make that happen. It is a legit passive player with about $1 trillion in index
fund assets.

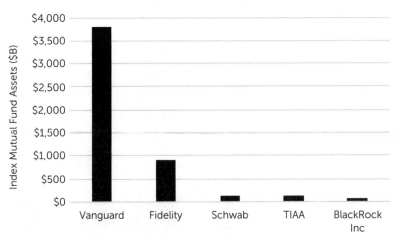

Index Mutual Fund Assets by Issuer (ex-ETFs)

Bloomberg

Bogle was thrilled to be the instigator of this shift. He told the crew in
1991 he was proud of the disruption Vanguard was causing:

*I am unabashedly proud of our achievement in putting our competitors'
expense ratios utterly to shame . . . Vanguard has been the agent of creative destruction. Many of our major competitors have been the victims.
We are among a handful of firms that have been not the destroyed but
the destroyers.*

Bogle's big contribution was indexing and being incredibly aggressive about cutting costs and prices and pushing the cost down. If you think back twenty to thirty years, the idea that you could buy an S&P 500 fund for 4 to 5 bps would have been crazy. And that's what you can do this afternoon. Investors owe more to Bogle than anyone else.
—David Blitzer

Manifest Destiny

Dave Nadig of ETF Trends calls all this "the manifest destiny of ETFs," and states, "There shall be an ETF for every asset class, and it shall be virtually free to own." That's basically where we are today. You can basically find free or near-free ETFs in every asset class.

The ETF industry veteran-turned-crypto CIO Matt Hougan tracks something he calls the World's Cheapest ETF Portfolio, which tracks six asset classes and used to cost 0.14 percent a year a decade ago but is now down to an all-in fee of just 0.02 percent. If you invested $10,000 in it, the annual fee would be $2—less than a slice of pizza in Penn Station.

The World's Cheapest ETF Portfolio

Asset Class	Weight	Fund Name	Ticker	Expense Ratio
US Equity	40%	BNY Mellon US Large Cap Core Equity ETF	BKLC	0.00%
Developed Markets Equity	30%	BNY Mellon International Equity ETF	BKIE	0.04%
Emerging Markets Equity	5%	Vanguard FTSE Emerging Markets ETF	VWO	0.10%
Fixed Income	15%	BNY Mellon Core Bond ETF	BKAG	0.00%
REITs	5%	Schwab US REIT ETF	SCHH	0.07%
Commodities	5%	GraniteShares Bloomberg Commodity Broad Strategy No K-1 ETF	COMB	0.12%

Matt Hougan

All-In Total Fee of the World's Cheapest ETF Portfolio

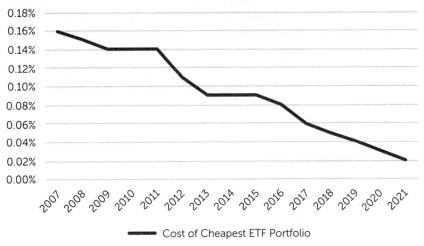

Matt Hougan

The ETF Terrordome

As it has to appeal to such a cost-obsessed base of investors, I refer to the ETF market as the ETF Terrordome, a term inspired by the great Public Enemy song "Welcome to the Terrordome." It is heaven for investors—which is why most of the new cash ends up here—but hellish for issuers.

Further, ETFs are heavily preferred by younger investors. Most surveys conducted by firms such as Schwab and BlackRock show how age and the percentage of your portfolio that is in ETFs is inversely correlated. Thus, asset managers that attempt to sidestep the ETF Terrordome risk fading into oblivion and becoming irrelevant as aging baby boomers cash out of their mutual funds or pass on their investments to their kids.

Asset managers are waking up to this reality, so there has been a torrent of new ETF launches hitting the market. In the United States, one new ETF is launched every day on average, and globally, it is three to four a day. Morningstar's ETF analyst Ben Johnson refers to the never-ending stream of ETF launches as "the spaghetti cannon" since there's so much being thrown at the wall to see what sticks. There is definitely some truth to that—although, to be fair, a lot of fundamental research goes into new ETF ideas. They usually are built on some thesis backed by data. But while the bar for entry into ETFs is low, the barrier for success is much higher. Some hit it big, while many linger in obscurity, and one in every four gets liquidated.

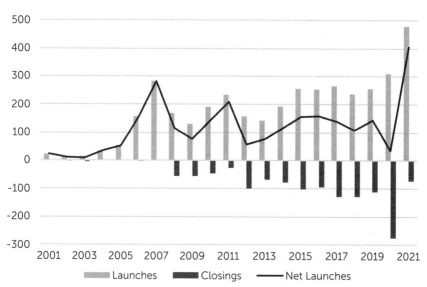

ETF Launches and Closures

Launches   Closings   Net Launches

Bloomberg

The ETF Terrordome humbles even the biggest mutual fund names with the deepest pockets on a regular basis. No longer can they pay off brokers to put their clients into their funds. They are on a level playing field for the first time, left to their own devices, trying to appeal to cost-obsessed, Bogle-influenced advisors and retail investors. It's akin to going from the country club to the jungle. Vanguard thrives in the Terrordome because the firm created it. It's a never-ending home game for them.

But for everyone else, the transition is reminiscent of the 2000 movie *Cast Away*, in which Tom Hanks morphs from a pudgy middle manager for FedEx into a 140-pound, spearfishing, fire-making badass. It takes a few years, but it can happen. And it is important that it does because the ETF Terrordome isn't some isolated place; it is the future of the whole industry. The dome will expand to cover almost everything in the next few decades. Anyone under it who can't hack it will probably go out of business or be acquired.

Xerox Moments

The ETF market is so unappealing from an asset manager's point of view that many big mutual fund firms passed up on golden opportunities to be early in the ETF business, either through a launch that was never followed up—like Fidelity—or people who pushed for the move internally but were denied—like Nuveen. I call these Xerox moments, which alludes to the printer and copier company that had developed the first personal computer, mouse, and graphical user interface but didn't really see the value in them at the time. Bill Gates and Steve Jobs did, and the rest is history.

A lot of other active mutual funds sat and watched the ETF industry boom but never jumped in because they were largely afraid to cannibalize themselves. Only recently, after the incredible growth in ETF assets, have many of them tried to evolve into this Vanguardian future either through launching nontransparent ETFs or converting their existing mutual fund into an ETF. Neither of those methods, however, solves the root problem of trying to sell higher-fee active management that hugs a benchmark.

No Victims (Yet)

What happens to the financial industry if no one wants to pay for their investments anymore? It's safe to say it is going to get smaller. If all the money in the fund business earned the same annual revenue as Vanguard does—which it is quickly on its way to doing—the fund industry would go from about $140 billion in annual revenue to $20 billion—an 85 percent decline. It probably won't get that bad, though. My guess is, it'll end up at a 50 percent decline. Either way, that is why I almost named this book *The Man Who Shrunk Wall Street*.

But this shrinkage will only come *after* a bear market, when there is nothing to offset outflows and hide organic growth problems. Bogle constantly acknowledged the pain he was inflicting on the industry, but at the same time he could see that there hadn't been that much damage (yet). Here's how he put it in a 2017 speech at the CFA annual conference: "So far, the index revolution has claimed no victims."

I think the fund families that have not entered and don't have a clear plan for entering the ETF market are planning on riding it out and hoping that the stock market continues to climb higher, which has inflated the asset base and helped them offset any outflows.
—Todd Rosenbluth

Active managers will argue that a bear market is actually when they will shine again, when people will want a human hand. They'll say passive is only popular now because it's been easy to make money thanks to a very accommodative monetary policy from the Federal Reserve. An index fund is all you need to own now. But you just wait, you'll appreciate us some day.

This argument is logical, and I'd make it, too, if I were an active manager. The problem is, the evidence shows the exact opposite. First, investors tend to flee faster out of active when the market is cratering, and second, active funds tend to display the same level of underperformance during down markets as they do in up ones.

The Triple Whammy

Let's break down why exactly active mutual funds are likely to see a ton of outflows whenever the market has a prolonged decline, which is exactly what happened during the last three brutal periods in the market (2008, 2018, and 2020). Active mutual funds saw their worst periods of outflows. I refer to the three reasons for this as a "triple whammy."

Flows for Active Mutual Funds, Index Funds, and ETFs ($B)

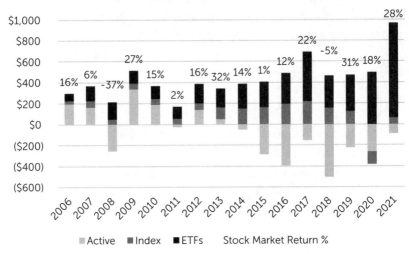

ICI, Bloomberg

First, they get hit with outflows from panicking investors who are typically older and don't want to risk losing their gains given that they need them for retirement soon. They are also less loyal because most of them were likely put into the fund not because it was necessarily a good fund but because a broker got a commission. Passive funds, on the flip side, tend to have more loyal, better behaved, younger investors with time on their side.

Second, a down market will free many investors from active funds who were trapped there during a bull market because they didn't want the tax hit of realizing capital gains. A bear market would give them losses to use against those gains. I estimate a few trillion is probably in this situation.

Active Mutual Fund Flows ($B)

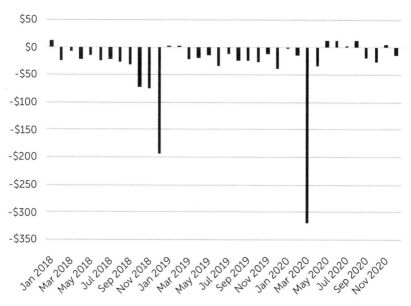

ICI

Third, there is still that baseline of outflows going from high cost to low cost that is immune to market conditions. Like three rivers coming together to form a confluence, these three factors will cause an exodus out of active mutual funds like we've never seen before. Although we did get a sneak preview of it in March 2020, when active mutual funds saw $320 billion of outflows in *one month*. If the Federal Reserve hadn't stepped in, these active funds would have likely seen well over a trillion in outflows in 2020, if not more.

The combination of a sustained bear market plus the growing influence of index funds will drive some active managers out of the business.

—Christine Benz

The Briar Patch

Contrary to what many out there think or hope, index funds, ETFs, and Vanguard will likely take in cash during the next bear market. Not as much cash as in the good times, but they will likely stay in the green, which means low-cost funds will eat up market share *fast*. Basically, a bear market is passive's briar patch, given their relative strength in organic flows.

People would make the argument, "Well, wait till the market goes down—the active managers will know how to keep their funds from going down as much, and people will flee out of the index funds." And it was the exact opposite. The index fund investors stayed with the funds. So what I found is that our index fund investors are the savviest investors we have or that anybody has. And part of the rationale there is that indexing was so counterintuitive as an investment strategy that you had to be sophisticated to understand why it was a good thing to do.

—Gus Sauter

Perhaps the best example of this was in 2008 when the S&P 500 ended up losing about 37 percent. But you would never know it by looking at Vanguard's flow data, as it took in cash *every single month*—including in October, when the market was down 17 percent in that month alone.

Vanguard's Monthly Flows During 2008 ($B)

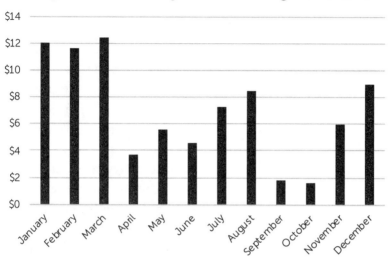

Vanguard, Bloomberg

Despite a steady dose of headlines such as "Market Rout Leaves US Reeling" and "Mounting Fears Shake World Markets," Vanguard ended up taking in a total of about $90 billion in 2008, while the rest of the industry combined saw about $120 billion in outflows. This is a pattern we have seen in every sell-off since. For example, in 2018, when stocks had several rough patches and the S&P 500 ended the year down 4 percent, Vanguard took in more than $200 billion, while the rest of the industry saw a combined net $200 billion in outflows. Many of Vanguard's funds even took in cash during the March 2020 rout.

Relative Predictability

I asked Bogle in our interviews why Vanguard's investors seemed so good at not flinching and staying the course during tough market declines relative to their peers, and he credited the predictability of the index fund as well as the lack of intermediaries. "We've always had a much lower redemption rate than the industry," he said. "Why is that? Because people come here [seeking us out] and also because—and this is a really important point—from the day Vanguard began, we talked about it in a staff meeting, and I said we have to create funds that have relative predictability."

This idea of predictability is important because it's in contrast with active funds, where it is unknown whether they will outperform during a down market. On average, most can't, although some do. If you look at any sell-off period, you'll typically find that two-thirds of managers underperform their benchmarks—about the same as in most other one-year periods or market conditions, according to the SPIVA scorecard. While some do better, one can rarely predict this ahead of time.

If we take a sample set of just the twenty largest active equity mutual funds during 2008, thirteen trailed their benchmarks and were unable to use their active management to buffer the collapse in the market. Further, as a group, those twenty funds underperformed, on average, by 1.43 percent, which is right around what the average fund cost is with expense ratios and trading costs. To be fair, these are largely more expensive class A shares, but even if you use the cheaper institutional share classes, you'll see much the same results.

Top 20 Active Equity Mutual Funds' Performance In 2008

Ticker	Name	Assets in 2007 ($MM)	2008 Fund Return	Benchmark	Difference
AGTHX	American Grw FD of Amer-A	193,453	-39.071	-36.999	-2.07
AEPGX	American Europacific Grth-A	124,010	-40.527	-42.999	2.47
CWGIX	Capital Wrld Grth & Inc-A	113,908	-38.377	-40.303	1.93
AIVSX	The Investment Co Amer-A	89,250	-34.735	-36.999	2.26
AWSHX	American Wash Mut Inv-A	82,424	-33.102	-36.999	3.9
FCNTX	Fidelity Contrafund	80,864	-37.164	-36.999	-0.16

Ticker	Name	Assets in 2007 ($MM)	2008 Fund Return	Benchmark	Difference
DODGX	Dodge & Cox Stock Fund	63,291	-43.309	-36.999	-6.31
ANWPX	American New Perspectiv-A	61,218	-37.834	-40.303	2.47
FDIVX	Fidelity Diversified Intl FD	56,765	-45.206	-42.999	-2.21
DODFX	Dodge & Cox Intl Stock Fund	53,479	-46.686	-42.999	-3.69
ANCFX	Fundamental Investors-A	50,370	-39.696	-36.999	-2.7
VWNFX	Vanguard Windsor II-Inv	49,770	-36.7	-36.868	0.17
NYVTX	Davis New York Venture FD-A	49,335	-40.026	-36.999	-3.03
FMAGX	Fidelity Magellan Fund	44,822	-49.399	-36.999	-12.4
FDGRX	Fidelity Growth Company Fund	37,073	-40.897	-38.459	-2.44
TEPLX	Templeton Growth Fund-A	36,917	-43.47	-40.303	-3.17
FLPSX	Fidelity Low Priced Stock FD	35,231	-36.173	-33.812	-2.36
VPMCX	Vanguard PrimeCap Fund-Inv	33,395	-32. 408	-36.999	4.59
AMCPX	AMCAP Fund-A	27,302	-37.678	-36.999	-0.68
PRGFX	T Rowe PR Growth Stock	26,070	-42.256	-36.999	-5.26
	Average		-39.7	-38.3	-1.4

Bloomberg

One reason why most active mutual funds were unable to do any better than the market in 2008 is that they must adhere to investment objectives. Outperforming the S&P 500 Index is difficult for a large-cap fund that's typically required to invest at least 80 percent of its assets in its designated strategy. But even if fund managers could move all the assets to cash based on warning signals from the market, it is nearly impossible to time without suffering a cash drag during a rebound and would likely result in under-performance anyway. Let's say that a fund manager had gone all or par-tially into cash in March 2020; it would have missed the massive rebound after the Fed introduced its liquidity program to backstop the bond market. The root of the problem, of course, is the inconvenient truth that no one—regardless of how many degrees or how much experience they have—knows what the future holds.

Consolidation Coming

Thus, a bear market combined with the ongoing Bogle Effect will likely result in a lot of consolidation in the fund industry—where there are still more than seven hundred companies. Firms will join forces to try to achieve scale, which will allow them to lower fees more. It can also allow them to broaden their distribution. We're already seeing it happen. Smart companies realize that their active mutual funds are cash cows today but will be less so during and after the triple whammy.

The consolidation will likely leave the fund industry resembling other industries, such as the airlines, media, or banks, where dozens of companies ended up merging. In aviation today, there are four to five massive players who control 80 percent of the business, while a smattering of niche air-lines that make a living offering specialty strategies (à la Hawaiian Airlines) account for the other 20 percent.

The banking industry could provide a good guide as to what asset man-agement consolidation could look like. Here's a mind-blowing chart show-ing the mass consolidation that took place in the banking sector since the 1990s. It resembles March Madness brackets where the industry is left with its own Final Four:

The Consolidation of Banks Between 1990 and 2010

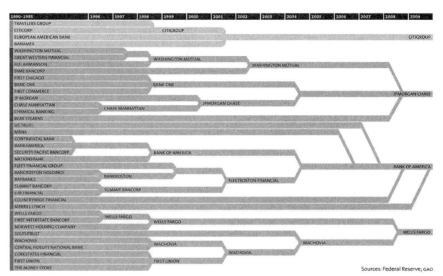

Visual Capitalist

While we are on the topic of banks, Vanguard may have had a little to do with that industry's consolidation as well. In Bogle's early 1980s speeches to the crew, he talked a lot about how the banks were peeved at Vanguard, which had introduced low-cost money market funds that gave a better yield than the banks offered in interest. Vanguard was basically stealing business from the banks. He told the crew in 1980 that "there is a big industry out there—our nation's banking industry—that wants to get 'its' money back."

That is why many banks in the nineties began offering mutual funds in an effort to get some of that money back. Here's vintage Bogle on this in a 1993 speech:

Mutual funds have now surpassed banks as the investment choice for America's households . . . The banks, not being stupid, have watched our industry's growth, first with curiosity and skepticism and then with envy and panic. They are now in the game, having started by selling the mutual funds of many of our competitors (but only if they receive a sales commission for doing so!). They are just beginning to start their own mutual funds.

In addition to merging with other fund companies, many asset managers have sought to acquire the end client by buying an advisor network or an online trading platform. Buying a client base to invest in your own funds (which I've affectionately dubbed BYOA, or Bring Your Own Assets) is definitely one way to keep assets up, although it doesn't really solve the long-term problem of lack of organic demand.

Milk It

But even if these companies consolidate and are able to lower fees in their funds and offset outflows from their higher-margin funds, it won't help all that much because they'll be making almost no revenue from the low-cost funds. So even success could result in failure, at least from a revenue point of view. I asked Bogle what he thought active fund companies should do to navigate around the brutal situation Vanguard has put them in, and in his grandfatherly assassin way, he advised them to essentially do nothing—don't bother changing at this point. It's too late. Just milk the juicy profits and the Bull Market Subsidy while it lasts.

"Could active mutual funds survive if they get cheaper?" I wondered.

"The answer to that is probably no," Bogle replied. "They could go to 50 basis points and nobody would give a damn. At 50 basis points, you are [eliminating] 100 percent of your entire profit margin. So what's the point of going to a place that is not going to do you any good?"

"What should they do then?"

"Sit on the cash cow."

"But the assets will eventually leave, no?"

"But it's going in drips and drips, and they will have taken out an awful lot of money on the way down."

Mass Mutualization?

While Bogle denied that lowering fees or consolidating would do much good, he did say there was one thing that active fund companies could do—and may be forced to do—when the reckoning comes. And that is a "mass mutualization" of the industry, where many big fund firms will be forced to convert to Vanguard's mutual ownership structure in order to survive.

"I am telling the world that in the coming era," he said during our last interview, "there will be mass mutualization of the firms in the business."

"You mean that asset managers will switch over to Vanguard's mutualization structure?" I asked.

"They will mutualize."

"Really? Why? Because they have to?"

"Well, there are a whole lot of reasons. One is, there's a competitor out there [Vanguard] that's eating their lunch, and they know perfectly why it's eating their lunch. And so far, they have not wanted to get competitive again. They'd have to slash their fees. But they could never slash them enough to get down to what a mutual can do. They like the active management business, but everybody knows it's a business that in the aggregate detracts from value created by corporations. That's just a fact.

"So they know they're riding a bad horse. So I think the pressure will be there. I also think that public policy will enter this. But it also could come from a set of strong directors saying, 'Look, you have fed at the trough for fifty years. That's long enough. Let's mutualize.'"

This is a bold claim by Bogle, considering the lack of motive economically to mutualize. He's basically predicting that things will get so bad for these companies that they will get *that* desperate—although he did add that many of the smaller firms would probably not need to because "they're probably local, doing things with their friends, and are conscious of lower cost."

This theory of mass mutualization along with Bogle's feelings about ETFs were the two things even his closest colleagues largely disagreed with him about. And the big reason is that mass mutualization discounts the extremely unusual circumstances in which Vanguard came to be. That was a one-in-a-million situation, a freak accident. There's simply no incentive otherwise to mutualize.

The only way an existing fund business could mutualize is to give up all its revenue, or have the mutual funds buy it out. So the economics just didn't work for people, and if you wanted to start a mutualized fund company, who is going to give you the capital to do it? Jack used to love to go around and say the whole industry should be this way and say, "I don't understand why they all haven't changed,"

*but Wellington only changed because of the bifurcation. Otherwise,
why would the management company ever do it?*

—James Riepe

---

*I would be surprised to see [mass mutualization] happen. I remem-
ber, twenty years ago when I was still part of our group of fund
researchers, that we talked about this. We had concluded that in so
many ways this mutualized structure is right for consumers—Bogle
is right. Should we make that something that is part of our platform
and hold it out as a best practice? And ultimately, we concluded it
just wasn't realistic. This business is too profitable as it is to suggest
that companies adopt this structure. I would be really surprised [if
companies mass mutualize]. I think there is an element of wishful
thinking to it.*

—Christine Benz

Even though no one was really on board with Bogle's prediction, it is
hard to discount a guy who was thirty years ahead of his time with his low-
cost and index fund vision. Perhaps he will be proven right again. Only time
will tell.

The Putnam Case

Bogle once tried to get Putnam, one of Vanguard's biggest competitors, to
mutualize. He nearly succeeded. Putnam was a firm on the decline in the
2000s after enjoying a nice run in decades prior. At the time, it had just
recently been embroiled in the time-zone trading scandal, in which nine
of its portfolio managers were found to have been trading against the very
funds they were managing. Basically, if any firm needed to be baptized in
the clean waters of mutualization, it was Putnam. Bogle knew this and had
lunch with the supposed "independent director" of Putnam, only to learn
later that he had served as the CEO of Putnam's parent company, Marsh
& McLennan (now Marsh McLennan), which was not disclosed in regulatory documents. Marsh & McLennan would lose out if Putnam went
mutual, making its stake worthless. Bogle was trying to appeal to someone

he thought was the independent director of Putnam's board, but clearly he wasn't independent and was thinking of Marsh & McLennan's bottom line. Thus, Bogle eventually got the message. As he put it: "No dice."

That case study makes it hard to think of any scenario in which mutualizing would be the chosen path. Perhaps subconsciously Bogle just made his prediction to remind everyone out there of their sins—and how good he was—once again.

"The whole structure of this industry is crazy," he said. "And yet, when we create the greatest structure ever known to the mind of man, if I may understate it slightly, and call it Vanguard, which means 'leader in a new trend,' and we're forty-two years old and have yet to find our first follower, that tells you something about the vested interest of this industry."

The BlackRock Way

Another possible path forward in this bleak future for fund companies is to get creative and aggressively diversify into other areas. This is somewhat what BlackRock has done. It has its long-established business line of dirt-cheap ETFs and index funds but it is also in the tech business, an institutional business, and an alternatives business, and it is very aggressively expanding overseas, where the Great Cost Migration hasn't kicked in as hard yet. In short, its diverse sources of revenue allow it to go toe-to-toe with Vanguard in the ETF and passive arenas. Basically, something has to subsidize your funds' business if you want to survive and thrive long term.

We compete in multiple geographies. And we also compete in very different product lines. In our core, we compete with Vanguard. In factor investing, our biggest competitor is Dimensional. In fixed income, our biggest competition is the bond market. In sustainable, a lot of our competition is European. And in areas like thematic investing, we compete with active managers through both index and active ETFs. Vanguard is a formidable competitor. We have many formidable competitors, but we are different because of our diversification across segments and geographies.

—Salim Ramji

Advisors Are Next

As I pointed out at the beginning of the chapter, the Great Cost Migration and the reformation it is bringing is not relegated to just the funds world, either. It is happening in the $25 trillion world of financial advisors as well. While they punished active funds for not sharing economies of scale by moving their clients' money toward lower-fee passive funds, they may be repeating the same mistake by clinging to their 1 percent fee. Some asset managers have referred to this as "protecting the point" in a nod to the hypocrisy of advisors publicly slamming and divesting from high-cost mutual funds yet charging the same, if not more. Advisors tend to counter with the fact that they do a lot for their clients in terms of planning, taxes, and behavioral coaching and so they are worth the 1 percent. It is an ongoing and heated debate.

If somebody else is charging you a high fee, that's terrible and you need to stop that, but if I'm charging you a high fee, well, that's OK because it's me.

—Rick Ferri

Dollar Fees All Over Again

Just as Bogle liked to look at mutual fund fees in dollar terms, the same could be applied here. Let's say you are an advisor making 1 percent a year, and you managed $10 billion in assets in 2015. That's $100 million in fee revenue. But the stock and bond market has doubled since then. You now make $200 million for doing the same exact job and without adding any new customers. You basically get paid double for doing the same amount of work—just like those active mutual funds that we looked at in chapter five. This is the beauty of getting paid as a percent of assets.

*The industry is ready for disruption. And I think that people are going
to go down kicking and screaming. There is some entitlement to that
1 percent. But just because you are a financial advisor doesn't mean
you get to be rich. It's like being a cop in Boston entitled to a whole
bunch of overtime because that is the way it is set up.*

—Nicole Boyson

Don Phillips, the former CEO of Morningstar, was on the *Bogleheads*
podcast and relayed a story about getting paid as a percentage of assets that
always stuck with me and seems prescient right now.

"From the advisor's standpoint, it is delightful," said Phillips. "If you
can get paid in basis points, what a wonderful way to make money. I remember one of the first money managers I ever saw speak was a guy named Tom
Ebright, who ran money for Chuck Royce. I remember him saying, 'I get up
in the middle of the night and I go to the bathroom and I'm making money.
I'm getting paid. I get paid around the clock, all the time. That meter is
ticking on the AUM fees.'"

Cullen Roche, an advisor in San Diego who prides himself on charging
very low fees, was on *ETF IQ*, and he put it this way: "When you walk into
an advisor's office once a year for your annual update, if you have a million
dollars, you are walking in there with a $10,000 briefcase. That's a lot of
money for most people. Most people don't pay their doctors or accountants
that much. So I do think there's going to be increasing pressure."

This pressure is coming from many places. One is robo-advisors, such
as Betterment and Wealthfront, which digitize and automate much of the
process of managing your portfolio, helping with taxes, and even planning.
Robos will do much of what a full-service advisor will do but for a fee of
0.25 percent. Robos tend to be big users of Vanguard ETFs, as well as Bogle
disciples. In fact, Jon Stein, the founder of Betterment, said in a blog post
after Bogle passed away that his firm wouldn't exist without Bogle:

Jack has had as much influence on my professional life as anyone. Better-
ment would not exist without the example he set. I don't say this lightly. I
mean it seriously: none of the impact we've had on the financial industry—
and I hope we're just getting started—would have happened without him.

That said, robo-advisors are small relative to the giant pot of money out
there. But they have shown that there is a thirst to pay much less for advice
and planning. And some of the bigger asset managers have jumped in with
their own low-fee advisory services.

Vanguard's Next Target

One of those asset managers is Vanguard itself, which launched its own
advisory arm a few years back. It charges between 0.05 percent and 0.30
percent, depending on the asset levels, for planning and advice. Vanguard
CEO, Tim Buckley, basically put advisors on notice when he said this to *The
Globe and Mail* in 2019:

We've been really pleased with the price competition we have introduced
in the mutual fund sphere. We liked that we have had that much of an
impact. But the area that really needs to come down is in advice.

Fee Schedule for Vanguard's
Personal Advisory Service

Fee (%)	Client Assets
0.3	< $5 million
0.2	$5–10 million
0.1	$10–25 million
0.05	> $25 million

Vanguard

Vanguard's advisory service already has about $260 billion in assets—
about ten times what Betterment has—although the majority is existing
Vanguard fund clients. It also has an army of over one thousand certified

financial planners. This is the real threat, and it shows how Vanguard's mutual ownership structure is not limited to just one arena. It can go anywhere.

Assets in Vanguard's Personal Advisory Service

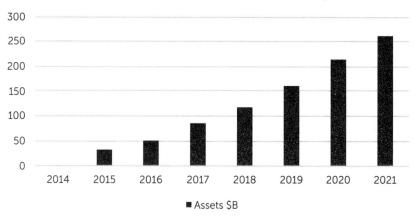

Vanguard

Michael Kitces, who arguably knows more than anyone about the history of and current trends in the advisory world, thinks that Vanguard and the Bogle Effect could disrupt up to 75 percent of the industry. The remaining 25 percent is likely to hang on to that 1 percent fee by catering to very high-end clients who require a lot of work or offering specialized services. Some may also have a regional connection.

It is entirely possible that an advisor could be worth 1 percent if they are doing very high-end stuff that requires a lot of expertise— like working with businesses they need to sell and more complex things—and being on the ball about it. But if they are doing what we [Betterment] do, they probably shouldn't be getting paid 1 percent.
—Dan Egan

The reason Kitces thinks the numbers could be this high is because there are currently three hundred thousand "advisors," but two-thirds of them are actually brokers, and even some of the remaining third aren't true CFP advisors (the ones that do full planning and are arguably less disruptable).

"I think [Vanguard] will have success," says Kitces, "but I think Buckley slightly overstates the case. And I mean that with the utmost respect to Buckley and Vanguard. When he says *advisors*, I think he's talking about what the rest of the brokerage industry called financial advisors, which were actually the brokers. They give no advice. They have no training.

"Vanguard's Personal Advisor Services [PAS] still hasn't nuked the rest of the advisory community," he continues. "What it does do, though, is force the rest of the advisory community into niches, specializations, regionally dominant players. So I expect to see a similar thing happen with Vanguard, where it may end up serving the bottom 70 percent or 80 percent, and the independent advisory community will end up forming a whole bunch of niches and specializations for people with higher income, higher assets, and more complexity. The rise of family doctors did not put neurosurgeons out of business."

Assuming that 75 percent of the $25 trillion under advisory assets ends up paying half of what they are paying now, that's about $100 billion a year in investor savings. While not all of it is directly attributable to Bogle and Vanguard, it could ultimately be added to the trillion a year in savings I discussed in the first chapter.

I think VPAS has been successful at gathering assets, and the more they gather, the market has to really take that seriously. Does that mean all advisory prices are coming down to VPAS level? That seems unlikely, because there are going to be clients with special needs— whether those needs are more emotional or more practical—that VPAS won't be able to serve.

—Elisabeth Kashner

Cheap or Niche

This would echo what is going on in the fund business, which is also headed toward a model in which a few massive companies manage around 80 percent of the assets and compete on fees, while the rest is overseen by niche managers and local players.

I think that the next frontier of Bogle's legacy is advisor fees and the delivery of advice to mainstream consumers in a really cost-effective way. I think some of that is happening internally at Vanguard. Other firms like Betterment have tried to deliver a product along those lines. So I think that's going to be where the innovation is during the next couple of decades.

—Christine Benz

In *The Little Book of Common Sense Investing*, Bogle was relatively nuanced when speaking about advisors, as opposed to his more absolute language regarding asset managers. He thought there were good advisors and bad ones and they were good at some things but potentially not as good at others:

I'm skeptical of the ability of advisors as a group to help you select equity funds that can produce superior returns for your portfolio. (Some do. Most do not.) Professional investment advisors are best at providing valuable services, including asset allocation guidance, information on tax considerations, and advice on how much to save while you work and how much to spend when you retire. Experienced advisors can help you avoid the potholes along the investing highway. At their best, these important services can enhance the implementation of your investment program and improve your returns.

It's not like advisors are just sitting out there saying, "Let's charge 1 percent and not do anything but hold three ETFs." We do tax-loss harvesting, budgeting help, retirement planning—essentially ensuring a client's entire financial house is in order. That said, I think there will be some fee compression in the advisory space just like everywhere else in financial services. Advisors will have to increase their value proposition. But ultimately, the end client determines the value. We work with all sorts of end clients. They know exactly what they are paying us. We are fully transparent.

—Nate Geraci

There is one notable factor that could complicate Vanguard's PAS success: it now has them competing with their own clients to a degree. It is possible that some advisors would be less willing to use Vanguard ETFs if they felt that they were a competitive threat to their business. That is why State Street, which also runs ETFs, has come out and made clear that it will not offer an advisory because it doesn't compete with its own clients. So far, it hasn't seemed to bother advisors much, but it is something to watch.

Another interesting aspect of Vanguard having an advisory service it is trying to grow is it will likely send Vanguard into many other areas it might not otherwise go, such as private equity, hedge funds, direct indexing, and perhaps even crypto. In order to compete with high-level advisors, Vanguard will need to have solutions for clients' demand for alternative investments. It could get interesting.

While Bogle praised PAS in one of his books, he went even further in our last interview and predicted that the advisor industry would ultimately have to scrap the asset-based percent model altogether. "This industry will get more and more professional," he said, "and less and less like a business. What will come along with that is more professional ways of paying fees. Pay fees on a visit basis by the hour. I don't know what it would be. But for an advisor, it seems to me that the flat percentage fee or even tapered percentage fee is not something that will sustain itself."

The Hourly Model

And this brings us to the hourly model, which is a small but growing mini-revolution inside the advisory world. In this mode, the client gets charged only for the advisor's time and nothing more.

Qualified advisors who bill for their time help to take us a giant step forward in shareholder capitalism, and it's how I think financial advice should always be rendered. At least 97 percent of the population would be better served by advisors billing for their time.
—Sheryl Garrett

Advisors have pushed back and said that they've given clients a choice and they *prefer* paying by percentage. Using Cullen Roche's example from above, ask yourself if would you rather pay an advisor 1 percent a year that automatically comes out of your account, or would you rather write a check once a year for $5,000? Some would probably pick the 1 percent even though the $5,000 is half the cost.

But you are an advisor. Isn't it your responsibility to enlighten your client? You are a fiduciary. You should be explaining why they shouldn't like the [seemingly smaller percent].
—Rick Ferri

The hourly model has yet to see the kind of impact that robos and Vanguard's PAS have seen—in fact, less than 1 percent of total advisor revenue comes from hourly fees, according to Cerulli Associates—it is making its voice heard. Time will tell if it is able to create a tipping point. Either way, though, there will be pressure in this neck of the woods for years to come.

I've been out there for a long time saying one percent on AUM is not only too high, it's also a dumb way to charge people. What you should be getting from your financial advisor is financial advice, and why the hell are you paying assets under management to get advice? You should be paying a fee for a service. If I want advice, charge me for the advice. I just think that model is doomed. It just makes no sense. The pushback I get is, "Well, I have 417 clients, and none of them have ever complained about it. It doesn't seem to bother anybody." Bogle's own story is a [counter]example. Indexing was nothing for years until all of a sudden it was everything. That is the way change happens a lot of times—gradually then suddenly. There are people chipping away at the 100 bps AUM fee, and they might just chip away at it until one day the whole just cracks from top to bottom, like some giant sculpture that falls apart right before your eyes.

—Jason Zweig

Brain Drain

What will be the end result of a financial industry with this level of wide-reaching cost migration across the board? Well, it is likely going to get smaller and force a significant reallocation of talent and brains in America. There simply won't be as much money spilling over to lure away some of society's smartest people. This scenario is Bogle's dream come true, as he wrote in *The Clash of the Cultures*:

In yet another distortion aided and abetted by our financial system, too many of the best and brightest young people in our land, instead of becoming scientists, physicians, educators, or public servants, are attracted by the staggering financial incentives offered in the investment industry. These massive rewards serve to divert vital human resources from other, often more productive and socially useful pursuits.

And again in *Enough*:

The enormous incomes received by hedge fund managers in the recent era and the staggering salaries and bonuses paid to investment bankers have inflamed the imaginations of many of the nation's graduates of our business schools and made Wall Street the preferred destination for their careers. The number of CFAs has reached a record of 82,000 [156,000 as of 2020]. Perhaps I should be cheered by such news. This is, after all, a calling to which I have devoted my entire career. I fear, though, that the motivation of too many of those rushing into finance is more aligned with what they can get from society than what they can give back to it; and it is a mathematical certainty that the costs of the services provided by their firms will exceed the value they create.

I think it is safe to say that many will applaud this assessment, given the steady diet of horrendous headlines they have been fed about the financial industry over the years, such as how the top twenty-five hedge fund managers make more than all of America's kindergarten teachers.

There's nowhere else you can make as much money as humanly possible without having that much talent for the most part. Look at what a good heart surgeon makes, and then look at what a top broker makes—it's ridiculous. Yes, they have ability, but where else can you have such lower ability and make that much more money? I feel like so many of the smart people trying to beat the market should be in medicine, or psychology, or other things where they can really use their intelligence. That would benefit so many more people.

—Anthony Isola

While Bogle was definitely proud of causing all this creative destruction, he wasn't totally unempathetic about the pain it would cause some. "I don't feel any happiness about that," he said. "No man is an island entirely to himself."

8

"Some Worry"

"I'm shocked by the need to defend the continued existence of what is often considered the most important financial innovation that has been created for individual investors."

When you get to the top—as well as mess with the establishment and its revenue—you are going to have a target on your back. As such, Vanguard, and the rise of index funds and ETFs that it ushered in, now gets blamed for all kinds of problems in the market—even things that haven't happened yet. Every few months someone will publish an article with a provocative headline about how "some worry" that passive or ETFs are causing a bubble, distorting the market, and even harming the planet.

The "some" in these pieces is typically an active manager, which is akin to the CEO of the Coca-Cola Company being worried that too many people are drinking water and that bad things could happen if they don't stop. Yet the headline will inevitably be "Some Worry Water Consumption Is Distorting Health."

Part of this is career risk. The people complaining about the fears of ETFs and index funds are either working as an active manager or supporting an active manager who has stayed within the mutual fund world, and it is easier to blame others than to solve the problem.
—Todd Rosenbluth

While there are occasionally nuggets of truth in some of these articles, as well as some good-faith concerns, about 70 percent of it is just histrionics and angst from threatened parties. Given that the growth of passive is largely a small investor uprising and makes almost no one inside Wall Street rich, it is somewhat odd that it gets purposely vilified by the media the way it does. It sometimes feels like a punching down, an effort to try to scare average retail investors for the sake of clicks.

While Bogle had a few worries himself, in general he largely saw the passive investing backlash as baseless attacks. After all, this was his baby, his mission. In *Stay the Course*, he complained,

> *Despite the success (or perhaps because of it), in recent years index funds have come under attack on multiple fronts. Yes, it seems ridiculous that an innovation that has enabled investors to earn their fair share of the returns generated in our stock and bond markets is now under fire, not only from jealous rivals who are associated with active fund managers, but from academia as well.*

It's very FUD (fear, uncertainty, doubt). These [worries] feel very much like fear generation on the part of people to justify their jobs rather than offer some alternative or better way. If the people who are putting forth those concerns had meaningful solutions to it that weren't "pay me more," I would be a lot more amenable to it.
—Dan Egan

Same as It Ever Was

Worries about indexing date back to day one. Right after Bogle launched the first index fund, the financial research firm Leuthold Group famously made a poster to give to its clients on Wall Street calling for index funds to be stamped out because they are "un-American!"

To be fair, employees of the firm later said it was a joke. I'm not sure I buy that, given the steady stream of similar attacks since. Regardless, Bogle actually relished these early attacks. They fueled him.

The idea of indexing at the lowest possible cost was blasphemous. And he took huge pride in this. He had huge posters around his office saying things like index investing was the infestation of communism. He loved that. He absolutely loved that.

—Jim Wiandt

But, of course, the idea of worrying about change and new things predates Bogle or index funds.

Anytime something new is introduced, people definitely get concerned because they don't know how it will impact everything they've known in their lives up to that point. Throughout all history, when humans were uncertain about the future, they tended to view whatever the new vehicle or innovation was through a negative lens. This has always been the case throughout history, but markets are still here and have continued to operate for some four hundred years. The markets have made it through two world wars, how many assassinations, pandemics—there's been no shortage of things that should destroy markets but do not. So I'd be hard-pressed to find something that would really affect markets to the point where they would stop functioning. So you should relax.

—Jamie Catherwood

Optimism Doesn't Get Clicks

And the truth is the vast majority of investors are relaxed, but the thing is, if you are in the media, *relaxed* doesn't get clicks. I know firsthand that if you write or tweet something that is negative, bearish, or expresses worries, it will get five times more reads and engagement than if you write something supportive or optimistic.

From a publication perspective, it sells when the headline is scary or tells you to be careful or wary of something. No one watches the news to find out that a kid walked to school safely each day.
—Todd Rosenbluth

When you combine some threatened livelihoods and a click-seeking media, you end up with some very fearmongering headlines. Some of my personal favorites from the last few years compared ETFs and passive with:

» *weapons of mass destruction*
» *the fault line for the next earthquake*
» *Marxism*
» *the misuse of antibiotics*
» *the Salem witch trials*
» *the next CDO (collateralized debt obligations)*
» *the song "Hotel California"*

While bias and histrionics are rampant in these attacks, it is still important not to slip into blind zealotry and just shut down or blow off any and all critiques. Though most worries never seem to play out, you don't want to miss something or be wrong.

Also, deconstructing these popular worries is a good way to learn about how index funds and ETFs fit into the broader picture of markets. So let's go through what I consider to be the eight biggest worries regarding passive:

1. Causing Stock Market Bubble
2. Distorting the Market
3. Never Been Tested
4. Creating a Liquidity Mismatch
5. Weak Hands
6. Too Many Indexes
7. Ownership Concentration
8. Bad Customer Service

One quick thing to keep in mind: Not all of these worries are aimed at passive as a whole. Some are aimed at ETFs, and some are aimed at Vanguard the company. But they are all largely a reaction to the rise of the Bogle Effect.

Causing Stock Market Bubble

The US stock market went up an astonishing 433 percent from the end of 2008 through 2020. The average price-to-earnings ratio of the index is about double its historical average. Naturally, people think it's a bubble and want to look for someone or something to blame (although I and my 401(k) are quite happy about it, to be honest).

While an accommodative Federal Reserve, earnings growth, buybacks, the increase in retail day trading, and good old-fashioned irrational exuberance are the likely catalysts fueling the rise in stock prices, some blame passive funds. They will point to the $3 trillion of flows into passive stock funds during this time. It sounds like a legitimate theory until you add in some context, such as how the stock market itself grew by *$43 trillion* during that same period to reach a total of $53 trillion.

Of that $53 trillion worth of US stocks, index funds and ETFs own 17 percent. The remaining 83 percent of stock shares are owned by households, active mutual funds, institutions, foreign investors, hedge funds, and businesses.

Assets in Passive Equity Funds vs. Total Size of US Equity Market

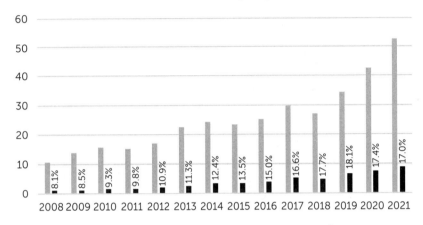

■ Size of US Stock Market ($T)   ■ Equity Index Fund + ETF Assets ($T)   % Ownership

Federal Reserve

These numbers surprise and trip people up a lot. It is easy to confuse passive's share of equity mutual fund assets (a substantial 50 percent) with its share of stock market ownership (a much tamer 17 percent). That said, while it is much tamer than people think, it is up from only 1 percent thirty years ago.

Ownership of the US Stock Market

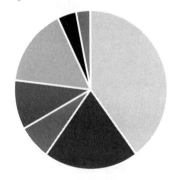

■ Households   ■ Mutual Funds
■ ETFs   ■ Pensions/Retirement Accts
■ Foreign Investors   ■ Business Holdings
■ Other

Federal Reserve

And what about that growth—surely the $3 trillion in flows had some effect on stock prices? It's true, all those flows went into funds that had to in turn buy stocks. However, there was almost an equal amount of outflows from active equity mutual funds that had to sell said stocks. This can be seen in one of the most famous charts of the past decade, which tracks the flows out of active and into passive.

Cumulative Flows for Domestic Active Mutual Funds, ETFs, and Index Mutual Funds ($B)

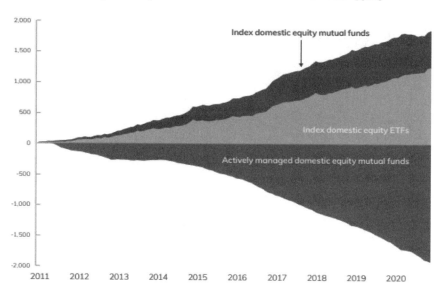

Note: Mutual fund data include net new cash flow and reinvested dividends; ETF data for net share issuance include reinvested dividends.

ICI

Thus, there's been largely a net zero effect on stock prices. Now, one could argue that index funds give a little extra boost to larger, mega-cap stocks since they are buying indiscriminately based on market cap versus an active manager who may use more discretion and buy based on fundamentals. But even those managers tend to buy large, popular names, so it is hard to give this too much weight (no pun intended).

A good way to think about it is that people are switching from an old format (active mutual funds) to a new format (index funds, ETFs), because at the end of the day, these active mutual funds hold the *same exact stocks*, more or less. For example, the top ten holdings of the actively managed Fidelity Magellan Fund are quite similar to the holdings of the Standard & Poor's 500 Index. Money is simply being transferred from closet indexing to actual indexing, from high cost to low cost.

Top 10 Holdings of the Fidelity Magellan Fund (as of September 2020)

	Security	Ticker	% Net
1	Apple Inc	AAPL US	6.88
2	Microsoft Corp	MSFT US	6.66
3	Amazon.com Inc	AMZN US	4.59
4	Meta Platforms Inc Class A	MVRS US	3.09
5	Alphabet Inc Class A	GOOGL US	2.62
6	Alphabet Inc Class C	GOOG US	2.55
7	NVIDIA Corp	NVDA US	2.35
8	Visa Inc Class A	V US	1.83
9	UnitedHealth Group Inc	UNH US	1.79
10	Home Depot Inc	HD US	1.78

Bloomberg

It's akin to the example in chapter five when people traded in CDs for MP3s and streaming. People are still consuming the same music, just in a different, arguably better, cheaper format. This is why blaming the stock market bubble on index funds or ETFs is like blaming MP3s for the rise of Nickelback.

Bogle made that point in a CNBC interview in 2018 to rebut the tired claim that Vanguard was going to crash the market because it was getting bigger and buying a lot of the big-cap tech names. "If you look at the hot stocks," he said, "US active managers own almost exactly the same [ones] as passive index managers. There's not much difference."

It's just a reshuffling of the chairs. Those stocks are going to be owned by somebody. They are out there in the marketplace. If they are owned by an index fund and they are packed away, how much impact is that going to have on price discovery? Basically zero. Also, you don't need a whole lot of trading for prices to be set. Only a little bit of the stocks trade every day.

—Rick Ferri

Now, to be fair, the passive ownership of stocks probably jumps up to 25 percent or 30 percent if we add in institutional investors such as pensions, endowments, insurance companies, sovereign wealth funds, and family offices. The reason we don't know the exact amount is that they tend not to use public funds and opt for separately managed accounts (SMAs) to get index exposure, and the data isn't public. These investors prefer to be private and off the grid, and some of the bigger ones can get their desired index exposures even more cheaply than an index mutual fund or ETF. That said, most of them have limited exposure to public equities in favor of more alternative investments.

And in case you are curious, passive ownership of the bond market is even smaller at 4.3 percent, although expected to grow over the coming years. And when it comes to gold, ETFs own a mere 1.5 percent of the global supply.

Distorting the Market

A companion worry to the bubble worry is that index funds and ETFs distort the market because when they see inflows, they mindlessly buy stocks purely based on how big the stock is with no regard for fundamentals. The idea is that stocks are not being priced correctly because of this and that the dog (index funds) is wagging the tail (stocks).

This worry can be traced back to December 1975—the same month Vanguard filed to launch its first index fund—in a letter to the editor in the *Wall Street Journal* from Mary Onie Holland, then the director of research at Chase Investors Management Corporation:

A proliferation of index funds, though accounting for ever-increasing amounts of investment monies, would lead to an inefficient market. A stock's price would become more a function of the monies flowing into index funds than a reflection of its investment merits. The efficient market hypothesis would be dead.

And it could have been written today (minus use of the word *monies*).

Even while passive is a popular target of causing-distortions criticism, it isn't alone. The Fed gets the distortion label a lot, as does the options market, as well as retail day traders. Well before any of us were born, the worriers were accusing other financial products of causing distortions.

As far back as 1935, there was concern over trusts owning significant amounts of stocks and the issues that could arise and how it affects pricing. They (the worriers) called for an immediate investigation from the stock exchange governing committees, and obviously we are still having the same concerns today.

—Jamie Catherwood

Thus, if we removed passive funds, the Fed, and retail brokers from existence, to some the market would still seem distorted. The truth is some expect the market to do certain things, and when it doesn't, it is distorted. Yet the truth is, distorted is arguably the natural state of the market. There have been booms, bubbles, and busts since day one and well before passive funds came along.

It's just the market. In the end, it's just supply and demand. Fundamentals matter in the ultralong term, but in the short run, sentiment drives everything.

—Wesley Gray

Most of the people who raise these worries are either the providers or users of active management, and if there are inefficiencies in the market and the price is distorted, that's how they make a profit—by being able to take advantage of such inefficiencies or errors. So I find it a little confusing that the very people who

should benefit from it are the ones saying, "Oh, look, here's the
danger with these things."
—Lee Kranefuss

Another problem with the tail-wagging-the-dog argument is that we see a steady stream of situations in which single stocks rise or fall quickly after a bad—or a good—earnings report or other relevant news, just as one would expect. And this happens to stocks that are widely held in index funds that are seeing inflows.

A good example is General Electric in 2018. Its price plummeted 50 percent during ten months for fundamental reasons—namely, weak profits combined with mounting debt—yet the ETFs and index funds that held it saw a torrent of inflows. So clearly the tail was unable to wag the dog, although it probably affected it a bit. Would GE have potentially plummeted a little bit more had it not been for the bids for the stock via index fund flows? Probably. Index funds do play a role, but they don't have authority over stocks or the market—they are largely just following active's lead.

GE's Price Plummeted Despite Inflows into ETFs That Held It

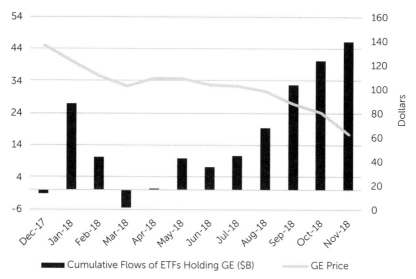

Cumulative Flows of ETFs Holding GE ($B) ———— GE Price

Bloomberg

Beyond GE, another indicator that active is the one setting prices is that we've seen a myriad of companies get kicked out of the S&P 500 Index—most recently Macy's and Capri Holdings. How could that happen given that the S&P 500 Index funds and ETFs are a mecca for passive flows? It's because active players didn't like what they were seeing in these companies and sold them, which decreased their market cap and caused them to get dropped from the S&P 500 Index in favor of a bigger company.

Stocks Recently Deleted from the S&P 500

	Deletion Date	Date Joined Index	Return While in Index	Index Ownership Est.
Helmerich & Payne Inc.	5/22/20	2/26/10	-33.30%	27%
Capri Holdings	5/12/20	11/1/13	-82.20%	24%
Macy's	4/6/20	11/30/95	-36.60%	24%
Cimarex Energy	3/3/20	6/20/14	-77.10%	14%

Bloomberg

Year after year, we are going to see stocks that are up 50 percent and stocks that are down and have lost money that are all part of the same S&P 500 Index, because the individual buyers of the stock are driving the price. Tesla is a perfect example. It was up like 1,000 percent in 2020 before it was added to the S&P 500.

—Todd Rosenbluth

The index isn't driving whether the stock goes up or down. What's driving it is the performance of the stock and its fundamentals. I don't think the indexes run the world.

—David Blitzer

A good way to think about it is that index funds and ETFs are in the back seat of the car that active players are driving. As we said earlier, they're freeloading a ride. Case in point: Apple and Microsoft are currently at the top of the S&P 500 Index, not because passive funds are popular but because their market cap is the biggest. And the reason their market cap increased is that their price increased. The reason their price increased is that active traders liked the stocks and bought them. And at some point down the road they will stop wowing active players who will sell them and then they will stop being the top two companies. The index is a dynamic, constantly changing organism thanks to active management.

There Will Be Tangers

In general, the distortion argument is weak, especially given the sheer size of the market and all the variables colliding into and offsetting one another. That said, there have been certain specific cases in the past decade in some smaller nooks of the market in which index fund and ETF ownership grew unusually large relative to their underlying holdings—like a medium-size fish in a small pond. When this happens, obviously the chances of them pushing the stock prices around increase. Although this is not just an ETF or index fund phenomenon—this happens with active funds and hedge funds on occasion, too.

One example of this small-pond situation is Tanger Outlets in 2019. This relatively unknown company that rents retail space in outlet malls became the first stock ever to be majority owned by passive funds. Nearly 60 percent of the firm's shares outstanding were owned by index funds and ETFs. This was a massive aberration from the roughly 17 percent of most stocks' shares owned by passive funds.

How did this happen? In short, the stock had something that many (smart-beta) passive funds wanted: yield. Tanger had a juicy dividend that had increased for twenty-five consecutive years, qualifying the stock for many popular dividend index funds and ETFs. And in a low-interest-rate era, dividend ETFs had become very popular. At the same time, active funds were selling the stock based on fundamentals and a negative outlook (renting outlet mall space amid the rise of online retail). Thus, there was an unusually high transfer of ownership from active to passive.

This very unusual situation naturally resolved itself when Tanger's market cap fell below the threshold needed to be included in the SPDR S&P Dividend ETF (SDY), its largest holder. Ultimately, the ETF had to dump 22 percent of Tanger's shares in one shot. There were some attempts to front-run this forced sale by hedge funds, but other variables moved the stock against them. The whole episode was a bit messy for a minute, but it wasn't a huge deal and life went on. The stock traded. Passive fund ownership is now below 40 percent.

Stocks with the Most Passive Ownership in September 2019

	Name	ETF Ownership %	Passive Ownership %	GICS Sector
SKT	Tanger Factory Outlet Centers Inc	43.65	58.79	Real Estate
WPG	Washington Prime Group Inc	27.18	43.15	Real Estate
UBA	Urstadt Biddle Properties Inc	23.81	39.99	Real Estate
MDP	Meredith Corp	28.71	39.73	Communications
STAR	iStar Inc	23.69	29.6	Real Estate
WRE	Washington Real Estate Investment	23.42	39.17	Real Estate
KRG	Kite Realty Group Trust	23.35	39.17	Real Estate
HT	Hersha Hospitality Trust	23.35	38.89	Real Estate
DRH	DiamondRock Hospitality Co	22.33	28.82	Real Estate
SCWX	SecureWorks Corp	31.06	37.47	Info Technology

Bloomberg

There will be more Tangers in the future, and they will be small-pond situations. Something like this won't happen to a stock like Apple or Microsoft for a long time, if at all. But it is worth monitoring.

How Big Can Passive Get?

One of the natural questions people ask now—and that analysts love to ponder and debate inside the financial bubble—is: How big can passive get before it's "too much"? What if *everyone* indexed? This is when you will typically see someone drop this quote from Bogle during a Yahoo! Finance interview:

If everybody indexed, the only words you could use are chaos, catastrophe—there would be no trading. There would be no way to convert a stream of income into a pile of capital or a pile of capital into a stream of income. The markets would fail.

However, they never include the rest of the quote in which he said the chances of that happening were zero and that he expects that indexing could grow to 75 percent before it would really do much to distort prices. Remember, we are at 17 percent via funds and potentially 25 percent via nonpublic funds. So there is a long way to go.

I wouldn't worry if 95 percent of the market was index funds. There will always be somebody to ensure that the market is efficient.

—Burt Malkiel

I don't have any worries about it. Will market efficiency be compromised? I don't think so. If it's at 80 percent and there are any active managers left standing and they find a cheap stock, they are going to buy it. And if they think it's expensive, they are going to sell it. So I don't think market efficiency is challenged by the growth of indexing.

—Gus Sauter

Passive Is Mostly a Myth

The other thing to keep in mind is that even if passive grew much bigger, almost none of it is truly passive or doing the same thing. Indexing is a big tent with many variations in how companies pick and rank the stocks. The formal definition of *passive* refers to a market-cap weighted basket of all the stocks in the market. Nothing really does that, with the exception of total market funds, and yet they only account for 10 percent of passive assets. The rest either track slices of the market or employ specific criteria and weighting schemes to achieve a goal.

The Tanger situation happened because of index funds and ETFs that selected and weighted the stocks based on their dividend, which is not passive at all, along with the fact that the funds are rules-based and not managed by a human. You can see how much gray area there is.

Indexing is not uniform, where everything is doing the same thing.
—David Blitzer

Even the S&P 500 Index, which is the first thing many people think of when someone says *index* or *passive*, technically isn't passive. Besides the large-cap bet being made, the S&P 500 Index is controlled by a human committee, which has ultimate discretion over what goes into and out of it. While it relies on a set of rules, it has—and has exercised—the power to delay a stock from entering the index, such as when it purposely denied Tesla's entry in 2020 despite the stock meeting all of its criteria.

The S&P 500, in my view, is not indexing. The S&P 500 is a passive way to implement active management. So, in other words, you are taking active bets on large-cap stocks, and you are betting against small-cap stocks. Indexing is investing in the total market—whether it is the total stock market, the total bond market, or the total global market.
—Gus Sauter

Never Been Tested

This fear tends to be aimed at ETFs and is probably the most absurd and easiest to refute of all the major worries, although I understand why it comes up. ETFs became really popular recently and can seem like a new creation to many newer market participants or the reporters covering them. But they've been around for about *thirty years*. Even Bogle, no fan of ETFs, did not think their durability and trading ability was a problem. His concern was that he thought they traded *too* much.

Total ETF Trades Since 1993 vs. Trades That Have Had Issues

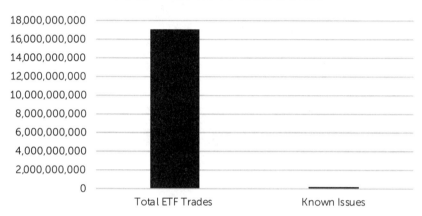

Bloomberg, NYSE

The fact is, ETFs have been tested—over and over and over again. All told, there's been $335 trillion worth of ETF shares traded since they were launched, in 1993. And with an estimated average trade size of $20,000, that breaks down to about seventeen billion individual trades with almost no issues to speak of. They have laid down some McDonald's-level numbers in terms of customers served.

ETFs have not only survived stress tests but they tend to thrive in them. ETFs saw increased volume in all the big market meltdowns, such as the bursting of the internet bubble, the week following September 11, the global financial crisis of 2008, flash crashes, the Federal Reserve–induced Taper tantrum of 2013, the UK's Brexit, the March 2020 sell-off caused by Covid-19 fears, and all sorts of other minor market spasms and exchange glitches. They tend to be the most liquid vehicles around in those severe market environments. Even the most sophisticated traders use them. I would start to worry if their volume went down in stressful situations. But it always goes up.

SPY's Daily Volume Spikes During Nasty Sell-Offs

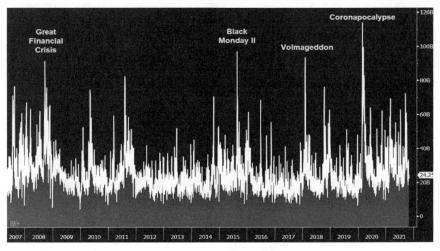

Bloomberg

Any remaining doubt about the viability of the ETF structure should be alleviated. That said, any narrative around ETFs causing bubbles or blowing up the market will make a salacious headline, so we as advisors will always have to provide education to counter it. I just think it is a tired narrative. I don't know what else needs to be seen for someone to have confidence in the structure.

—Nate Geraci

To be sure, there have been some hiccups, but they've typically been small and isolated and they usually get fixed so they don't happen again. The ETF track record speaks for itself at this point, so we'll just move on.

Creating a Liquidity Mismatch

Related to the "never-been-tested" worry is one aimed specifically at bond ETFs, which is that they will cause problems because of a liquidity mismatch. This is what the aforementioned "Hotel California" dig is all about:

you can check in anytime (when times are good and there's liquidity) but you can never leave (because liquidity goes away when the market is tanking). It's a logical concern based on a logical premise: bond ETFs tend to trade much more than the bonds they hold (which is totally true for most of them, especially junk bond ETFs, in which many of the bonds don't trade daily), and ultimately the underlying lack of liquidity will cause the ETFs to freeze up if there is a rush to get out.

Hedge funds in particular love making this critique. At Bloomberg, we actually keep a running list of high-profile hedge funds who worry about ETFs and passive investing. The list is always growing. Hedge funds have a unique relationship with ETFs. They trash them regularly but at the same time they are some of their biggest customers. They're basically frenemies.

While I do sometimes question the sincerity of the folks lobbing the accusations given that many compete with ETFs, this worry does make theoretical sense—how can something trade when the underlying holdings aren't? But that's the point. The ETFs are made to trade *even if* the underlying holdings aren't. And this is what we've seen time and again. Probably the ultimate example is when the VanEck Vectors Egypt ETF (EGPT) traded for about a month even though Egypt's stock market was closed during the Egyptian revolution of 2011.

The key is that ETFs are on an exchange, so they can act as a release valve in times of stress. We've seen this happen many times with bond ETFs. However, during periods of extreme volatility, it can appear as if the price of the bond ETF deviates from the net asset value (NAV), the calculated fair value of all the bonds that the ETF holds. This tends to happen the most with junk bond ETFs, such as the iShares iBoxx High Yield Corporate Bond ETF (HYG). This can look bad optically and cause some to wonder if the ETF is broken.

HYG's Premium/Discount Can Vary

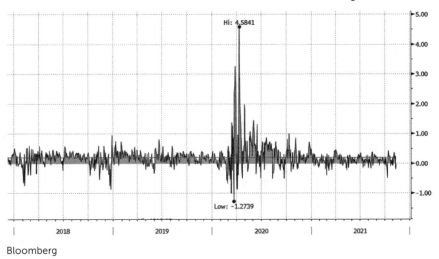

Bloomberg

The reason for the gap between price and NAV is that the ETF itself is trading in real time and thus reflecting all the latest market sentiment, whereas the NAV is calculated using some bonds that have not traded since the sell-off began and have pre-crisis prices. That said, the price of the ETF isn't totally pure either. It is the agreed-upon price by the market that includes what the market makers require to make money. I think that there's a ballpark of maybe 0.25 to 0.50 percent of market-maker cost embedded in the price on those wicked sell-off days as market makers tend to widen their spreads in times of distress and uncertainty. Even the father of the bond ETF, Lee Kranefuss, who defends their value-add to the market, admits they aren't perfect but that they help the situation. "You have to be careful to not have best be the enemy of the good," he says. "And there's a fundamental belief that isn't quite right that the ETF can't be more liquid than the underlying holdings. We'd always look at the fixed-income ETFs and think of them as having a big improvement in liquidity for investors."

Ironically, bond mutual funds are the real illiquidity-doom-loop risk that many think ETFs are. Mutual funds don't have that release valve of having their shares trading on a public exchange. Thus, if they start to see outflows, they will be forced to sell bonds into a frozen market at fire-sale prices, which will result in lower returns each day as their NAVs more accurately reflect reality, and that will result in more outflows until they will likely have to halt redemptions. We saw this begin to play out in March 2020, until the Fed stepped in and backstopped the market and provided liquidity.

Weak Hands

Another worry is that index fund and ETF investors are "weak hands" and will run for the hills the moment the market gets tough. And they will bring everything down with them. But every time we've had a sell-off, the exact opposite happens. Passive fund investors are more disciplined than just about anyone else. For example, passive funds took in about $200 billion in 2008 and about $450 billion in 2018—the last two down years in the market.

People who say this underrate the fact that passive fund investors tend to be self-directed. They chose to buy those funds. Thus, they are more loyal to the fund and more likely to understand the importance of staying invested in order to maximize their investments. On the flip side, many of the people in an active mutual fund were put into it simply because a broker was paid by them to do so. So there is less loyalty and perhaps not as much awareness of the importance of behavior.

Also, investors in active mutual funds tend to be much older. These are largely baby boomers, and they will likely sell more quickly given that they are closer to retirement, when they will need the money to spend. The next few sell-offs may show again that the weak hands are likely to be those in active mutual funds. Perhaps in thirty years that will change as the Gen X and millennial investors get ready for retirement and may start cashing out of their index funds and ETFs—but for the foreseeable future, look for passive investors to be the strong hands, not the weak ones.

Too Many Indexes

Some worry that there are too many indexes and ETFs. This is one fear that Bogle would agree with wholeheartedly. That said, I'll do my best to provide the other side of the argument.

From time to time, people will say something like, "Oh my God, there are more ETFs than stocks now!" First of all, that's not entirely accurate. There are about 2,500 US ETFs and about 3,600 US stocks. Further, about 1,000 of those ETFs do not hold US stocks but rather international stocks, bonds, or commodities. But what's baffling is that there are more than 7,000 mutual funds (18,000, if you include all the share classes), and no one seems to have a problem with that.

The other stat that gets people going is the number of indexes. The Index Industry Association published a 2018 report that said there are now *3.7 million* indexes—an increase of about a half a million from the previous year. It caused a collective explosion of heads and pearl clutching from the usual suspects with some crying out "peak passive," "this will not end well," and "smells like CDOs [collateralized debt obligations]."

On one hand, I get it—3.7 million is a shocking and absurd number and possibly scary to those whose livelihood is threatened by it. But there's a limitless number of indexes or ETFs that can be created based on a limited number of securities. The idea of limitless combinations being built from limited pieces exists everywhere. As Mebane Faber of Cambria Investment Management pointed out in response to all the worry, "There's also more words than letters." It's true—there are an estimated 171,146 words built from just 26 letters. The outrage! Further, there are an estimated 97 million unique songs that have been written using just 12 notes.

Yet of all those words and songs, only about 0.1 percent resonate with the public while the rest live in oblivion. The same is true of indexes. Only a microscopic number will ever be turned into investment products such as ETFs, and an even smaller group will attract substantial money. Thus, a lot of this is like worrying about something that exists in oblivion.

Many of these are reasonable strategies, like dividends or tech stocks. Whether they work or not we will all find out. That's the game. So I don't see any problem with the huge increase in different indexes.
—David Blitzer

Ownership Concentration

Now we are getting to some worries that are a little more complex—ones that even Bogle had mixed feelings about. The first is that there is a concentration of ownership among a few giant asset managers. Bogle worried that too few of them would own too much stock and would control too much of the voting shares of America's corporations. Bogle set off a huge debate in the industry with a column making this point in the *Wall Street Journal*, written a mere six weeks before he passed away. Here is how the column opens:

> *There no longer can be any doubt that the creation of the first index mutual fund was the most successful innovation—especially for investors—in modern financial history. The question we need to ask ourselves now is: What happens if it becomes too successful for its own good?*

Let's look at the numbers. On one hand, they are alarming. If you were to take almost any company in America and sort the owners of the company by their ownership percentage, Vanguard and BlackRock are going to be right up there. Vanguard is now the top owner of just over half of the companies in the S&P 500 Index and is in the top two of 78 percent. Vanguard and BlackRock are among the top three holdings of 90 percent of S&P 500 stocks. So yeah, it does seem like they are taking over.

Percent of S&P 500 Companies That Have Vanguard, BlackRock Among Top 3 Holders

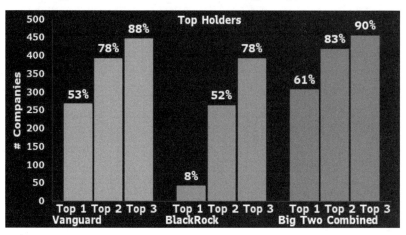

Bloomberg

That said, they each own only about 8 percent of a stock's outstanding shares. I say *only* because based on the numbers above and the rhetoric you hear you'd think they owned a lot more.

I don't care. I mean 8 percent is not a majority. There's still 92 percent they don't own, so why are we focusing on the 8? You need something like 40 percent of the market to have a real threat of influencing it.

—Rick Ferri

If you add Vanguard, BlackRock, and State Street together (the Big Three of passive), you get to that 17 percent number I discussed earlier. Yet if you combine the collective ownership of all active mutual funds, you get the same number. The only difference is that active mutual fund assets are distributed among several companies, whereas the passive fund assets are concentrated among the Big Three, which account for more than 80 percent of all index fund and ETF assets.

Top Owners of Apple Stock (June 30, 2020)

Holder Name	% Out	Mkt Val
Vanguard Group Inc/The	7.65	188 BLN
BlackRock Inc	6.13	150 BLN
Berkshire Hathaway Inc	5.49	134 BLN
State Street Corp	3.77	92 BLN
Fidelity Management & Research Co	2.12	52 BLN

Bloomberg

This says as much about the concentration of passive assets as it does about the rise of passive. Basically, Bogle wanted to see more competition in the passive world. Remember, back in the nineties he said he actually looked forward to the day when Vanguard's market share declined because it would mean that he had forced the rest of the industry to get cheap and become better stewards. He reiterated this point when he was on *ETF IQ* on Bloomberg Television, in 2017:

> *I wish there were more competition, to be honest with you. State Street is trying, but for some reason the numbers would suggest they're not succeeding very well. So what used to be an oligopoly, really of the three of us— Vanguard, BlackRock, and State Street dominating the index field—is pretty much becoming a duopoly. I say, "Come in, the water's fine." I wish people would compete, but it's a tough business to compete in. We need competition. Everybody needs competition. Competition sharpens you up. Competition drives away complacency. Competition makes you operate better. Competition gives you a nice fighting spirit. We need that. I was never bothered by competition. Even when Fidelity was three or four times [as big as] us, I used to think to myself, Let the best team win. And it did. We had to be patient.*

To be sure, there are flows going into Fidelity's and Schwab's passive funds. In addition, many big banks, like Goldman, J.P. Morgan, and BNY Mellon, have launched cheap beta knockoff ETFs that they can put their own clients into—instead of using Vanguard or BlackRock ETFs—which could help dilute the Big Three's stranglehold over time.

That said, as I write this, those flows are not quite strong enough yet to eat into Vanguard's and BlackRock's market share, which at the moment looks unstoppable. We have to assume they will keep growing. The question is, how much can they own of a stock legally?

The 10 Percent Rule

Well, there really is no rule for how much of one company an asset manager can own. The rule on the books is that a single mutual fund cannot own more than 10 percent of one company. Currently, the biggest mutual fund in the world is the Vanguard Total Stock Market Index Fund, and it only owns about 3 percent of Apple and most other stocks. So even that fund isn't even halfway to its 10 percent limit. But even if it were to hit it, Vanguard could theoretically just start up a Total Stock Market Part II Index Fund and keep growing.

Bogle thought this was one of the biggest flaws in the Investment Company Act of 1940, which regulates mutual funds. Back in 1940, there were only a handful of funds, and those companies only had a fund or two. Now there are massive fund complexes with hundreds of funds. Bogle thought there should be new regulation aimed at the complexes as well, but he stopped short of calling for the 10 percent limit to be applied to companies in the aggregate.

Until there is a public policy change, it is likely that Vanguard will double its ownership of stocks from 8 percent to 16 percent during the next decade. It could even hit 20 percent. But it's very doubtful that its ownership would grow beyond that, as that would mean it would own well over 50 percent market share of all fund assets. But it's possible.

We had SEC commissioner Hester Peirce on the *Trillions* podcast in 2020, and we asked if this concerned her. Peirce said:

> *There's a lot of concern about passive investing, and my theory is that if passive investing grows, then there is definitely going to be room for active managers to make a lot of money. If everyone is passive, the few people who aren't will be able to do quite well. So I don't think [the rise of passive] means the end of active or that markets can't function . . . Also, I think it's important to distinguish between Vanguard or BlackRock as asset managers and the particular funds they advise, because it is actually the fund that is the owner. The funds are managed separately, and each fund has its own objective, so they're not all managed in lockstep . . . so you have to look at it at a more granular level. That said, some funds do have quite a big percentage, and that is a growing phenomenon.*

Like many, she thinks the market will take care of this naturally, as active will have more opportunities to shine the bigger indexing gets, which will help maintain the balance. Also, if you are going to have a company that is "too big," you could do a lot worse than Vanguard.

Common Ownership

This brings us to a related worry about *common ownership*, which is a communist-sounding term that refers to a situation in which all the companies in a certain industry have common owners. And the rise of index funds is creating common ownership, given that an index fund—because it tracks the whole market—owns all the banks, all the tech companies, and all the airlines. So, if you are a bank, you share common owners (e.g., Vanguard and BlackRock) with your competitors.

The worry is that these common owners are incentivized to see the companies in the same industry raise prices in unison because it would maximize profits for the index fund shareholders. And if that happened, it would hurt consumers. Thus, indexing is potentially bad for consumers.

As logical as this concern may sound in the academic papers it appears in, it is hard to see the evidence, either in the data or as a consumer. And there have been no signs at all of collusion between Vanguard and BlackRock in wanting industries to raise prices. If you know index fund issuers, you know that kind of thinking is just not in their DNA. They aren't wired like that.

There are a number of holes in the argument that you have a small group of people making decisions and controlling what the airlines are doing and trying to do things that would help us, the index funds. First, I have a great deal of confidence that the three big players in the index field all fully understand and accept their fiduciary responsibilities. I absolutely believe that they embrace that. I can speak 100 percent for Vanguard, and I have no worries at all that Vanguard is going to act irresponsibly in respect to governance or anything else.

—Gus Sauter

Burt Malkiel, who sat on Vanguard's board for ages, said he's never seen a vote that would encourage anticompetitive behavior. He offers a good counterpoint that challenges the motive for this in the first place. "The same investment companies control a sizable portion of the common stock in every major company in the market," he says. "Perhaps banding together to encourage the airline companies to raise their prices would benefit the holdings of airline stocks. But this would mean higher costs for all the other companies in their portfolio that depend on the airlines to facilitate business travel."

In a way, owning all the stocks in the whole market acts as a self-policing mechanism, given that there would be a clear downside to colluding. But all this could happen indirectly—and without any collusion—according to one of the authors of one of the key papers exploring this issue, Eric Posner.

"The argument is not that the head of Vanguard is going to call up the head of United Airlines and say, 'I want you to raise prices. And don't worry, I've told American to raise prices as well,'" explains Posner. "The claim is that the CEO of United and your biggest shareholder (Vanguard) owns American as well as United. If you say to your boss, 'Guess what, I've cut our prices to get a huge market share away from American,' is the boss going to be pleased? And the answer is no because he owns both American and United."

While Bogle did express worry that there was a concentration of assets in a few passive giants, he wasn't sold on the common ownership concerns.

"They have these academics—one of whom I know very well—who are proposing that funds not be allowed to own more than one stock in any given industry," he told me. "I had breakfast with [two of the authors] about a year and a half ago, and I tried to talk them out of this crazy idea and I failed."

Bogle was concerned that this idea would have the potential to alarm lawmakers. "But you know, you get a ['some worry'] article like that in the *New York Times* and it has implications," he said. "People look at it. And the congressman looks at it and says, 'Does this give me something I can be elected on—by taking it on?'"

While worrying can come off as concerned and sober, it also can bring with it unintended consequences and hurt what is effectively a good thing going for small investors. In short, this is the worry about "some worry" articles.

Voting Power

The core of the concentration of ownership worry is really rooted in power. Owning that much of a company's stock gives you real voting power. Owners get to cast important votes on things like corporate goals, mergers, compensation packages, and many administrative issues. And in somewhat of a contradiction, Bogle thought passive funds were much better at this than active. He told Morningstar's Christine Benz in an interview:

I'd say traditional index funds are the last, best hope for corporate gov-
ernance . . . because they're the only true, long-term investors. Corporate
governance should be based on long-term factors affecting the corporation,
not a bunch of traders who want you to report higher earnings going to
try to get on your board for a minute, and in a moment . . . realign the
entire company and then all will be well. It just doesn't happen. In fact,
the reverse is more likely to happen . . . The old Wall Street rule was, if
you don't like the management, sell the stock. The new index fund rule is,
if you don't like the management, fix the management because you can't
sell the stock.

He even went so far as to propose that only shareholders who have owned the stock for more than three years should get to vote, as to not reward "renters" with any influence.

Not surprisingly, most active funds would disagree with Bogle's view. Some have even suggested that index funds are the real problem and they should not be allowed to vote. One of the loudest calls came from Janus Henderson Investors CEO Richard Weil in a *Wall Street Journal* Op-Ed titled "Passive Investors, Don't Vote," in which he called on the SEC to restrict index funds from getting to vote:

Passive-fund managers like BlackRock lack a strong incentive to cast
informed votes. Index funds retain shares of each company they hold at a
rate determined by the company's market value benchmarked to a certain
index. As a consequence, it matters little to them whether individual com-
panies perform well or badly; they are concerned with the performance of the
index overall. Passive investors don't engage the market with finely tuned
attention to each company. They don't help allocate capital specifically to
well-run companies with competitive advantages and long-term growth
prospects. Nor do they invest in discovering price disconnects between secu-
rities, undervalued assets, or future innovators. Rather than careful guides
for growing companies, passive investors are largely freeloaders.

Weil actually echoes many of the "worries" in this whole chapter. But if you talk to ESG analysts who study proxy votes for a living, they tend to be much more in tune with passive owners than active ones.

I would put a little more faith in passive [to vote in an ESG manner] because they have economies of scale. They come up with a thoughtful policy and then they can execute across thousands of companies they hold a stake in. They also have the expertise in engaging with these companies, as well as trying to meet them in the middle. Also, if you are a passive issuer and not going to sell yourself on stock selection but on how good a steward you are of capital, there's a much bigger focus now paid to how you are as a steward, which I think also pushes them to be more thoughtful in their voting.

—Rob Du Boff

This is our fiduciary duty. Someone has entrusted us with their assets in an active or index mandate. It's necessary that we exercise our fiduciary duty and vote along with what we think the long-term interests are because we are the ultimate long-term investors. And I think one of the benefits of index investing is typically we are twenty-five-year holders of the stock. As long-term holders of the stock, we are able to influence companies to think in five-, ten-, and twenty-year increments about how they create value because we want to manage it for the long term.

—Salim Ramji

While this ownership debate and the voting is a hot topic inside the industry, when you talk to actual investors outside the bubble, most don't even have an opinion or care that much.

I'm not going to really start worrying about whether BlackRock or Vanguard starts voting a certain way on things. I never had a client ask me how they are voting on this stuff.

—Ken Nuttall

"Who's complaining? The investors, they aren't complaining. It's a lot of noise over an issue that isn't really a problem."
—Rick Ferri

Their big size is and can be a major force in the industry to the extent that individual investors can't really move the needle on topics that are of direct interest such as corporate governance, say, on pay and board composition, business direction, or ESG topics. Not that their shareholders are in agreement, but there is the potential to transform something into effective action. To that end, it can be an incredible positive.
—Elisabeth Kashner

Having a Target on Your Back

All this attention on the topic has pushed Vanguard—and BlackRock—to get more vocal about how they approach voting. They are seeing increased pressure from all kinds of external forces and the media. When you are listed as the top owner of some of the most vilified companies and industries, you become a target.

For example, a 2021 *Financial Times* story titled "Vanguard Tops List of World's Largest Coal Investors" shamed Vanguard and BlackRock for being dirty and not addressing climate change. They even used an altered image of Vanguard's ship logo, adding smokestacks to twist the knife in deeper.

This is absurd for a number of reasons. First, Vanguard will top the list of owners of any industry given that it is the largest fund company and is largely an indexer. Second, it *has to hold* these companies. Third, some of its investors may actually like owning ExxonMobil, which reminds us again that Vanguard doesn't really *own* these companies at all—but rather is just the conduit for thirty million investors who have varying opinions. Finally, both Vanguard and Blackrock offer ESG ETFs that underweight fossil-fuel stocks, which give investors a choice.

It is a bit perplexing why these firms, which make very little money offering these funds because investors keep it, get so much heat while the demand side (e.g., wealthy climate activists who have private jets and multiple houses) gets so little attention or investigation.

People love to poke the big guy in the eye. But I think that's just a responsibility to take on and recognize that is how some people are—it's what sells books. But the reality is, you just recognize that, move on, and act responsibly. I have major confidence that the big index fund providers will act responsibly.

—Gus Sauter

If you want to be the industry leader, that's just part of life.

—Salim Ramji

On the flip side, this heat from the media also presents a huge marketing opportunity to look like the good guy. "There's definitely some marketing thought that goes into voting and how they want to position themselves," says Rob Du Boff, ESG analyst for Bloomberg Intelligence. "It's not all altruistic."

In the end, how these big passive firms vote is already tracked by institutions and could ultimately become part of the due diligence process down the road for some people in how they choose their index funds or ETFs.

I believe how a firm is going to vote as your proxy should be a fundamental reason for why you gave that company money. BlackRock is touching on this mostly through the megaphone of Larry Fink. And then everyone posts pictures of his private jet, so it's the wrong way to approach it. The right way to approach it is to have the front page of your company website list five key principles that drive how you vote, including a map of every single vote you cast in the last two years that lines up with those principles. That data is easily available.

—Dave Nadig

Let the People Decide?

One thing that has been suggested that Vanguard and BlackRock could do to help remedy this, which would kill two birds with one stone—ESG and common ownership—is turn the power back to those thirty million investors so that the votes are cast in a way that reflects the investors' will, as opposed to the company's will. BlackRock currently allows certain institutional investors to choose to vote the shares themselves if they want to. Why not do that for the small investors, too?

This would not only democratize the voting and allay a major worry about the growth of passive, it would also be a great defense against activist and media pressure on the likes of Vanguard and BlackRock to move in a certain political direction. After all, not all their investors live in New York City, where many of the advocates and the media live. If they sourced their voters, they could simply point to that and say that they represent their investors and are voting "the will of the people."

As these firms get bigger, I do think the corporate governance side and the voting will become a bigger concern. But I think it's something that can be solved through technology, so the end investors can start voting proxies or at least provide their general set of preferences for what they believe, so their shares can be voted on accordingly.

—Nate Geraci

Executive Pay

Until democratizing the voting becomes a reality, one of the ways passive giants can earn some good will is to tackle an issue everyone can agree on: CEOs are paid way too much relative to the average employee. This is a little off topic but needs a little attention since this book is about Bogle and this drove him crazy. Not just the gall of the CEOs taking that kind of pay but that Vanguard could do something about it.

On a real dollar basis, there's not much more hiring than there was in 1960 or 1970. And then you look at the other line. You know the line I'm talking about. How much that wonderful CEO thinks he's worth. I'm just not sure how a CEO can be worth, what are some of those big numbers, 18,000, 20,000 times the typical worker. I think this is the time for index funds of all funds because they're the only long-term holders, the only permanent holders, to stand up.

The "wonderful" dig is vintage Bogle, but it works because he's punching up. He had a front-row seat from which to watch CEOs, and he thought they wildly overstated their value relative to the workers who create the value for the company. He quoted Hellen Keller in his book *Clash of the Cultures* who said, "The world is moved along not only by the mighty shoves of its heroes but by the aggregate of the tiny pushes of each honest worker."

Bogle's relentless hammering of CEO pay seems to have resonated with Vanguard. The firm's 2020 Stewardship Report states that "sound compensation policies and practices linked to performance that extend well beyond the next quarter or year are fundamental drivers of sustainable, long-term value. Companies should provide clear disclosure about their compensation practices and how they link to performance and to the company's espoused strategy."

That would mean nothing if there was nothing backing it up. But the company appears to be walking the walk having voted down certain pay packages. One specific example is Alphabet, where Vanguard has voted "no" repeatedly against the "magnitude and structure of the equity plan awarded to the CEO." They found the pay was misaligned with performance and withheld support for the proposal as well as for the chair of the compensation committee.

You could write a whole other book just analyzing institutional ownership and voting. But suffice it to say that Bogle cared deeply about keeping greed in check at corporations, and Vanguard and BlackRock now have an opportunity to do just that. Whether they fulfill on the promise of being the "last hope" for good stewardship—which includes applying it to themselves—remains to be seen though.

Bad Customer Service

Another one of the more legitimate concerns regarding the rise of passive is whether these companies will be able to provide the kind of customer service needed to serve their millions of investors. If the fees are so low, where will the money come from to provide the support needed for the investors?

I've been asked, "What could possibly bring down Vanguard?" And really the only thing I can think of—and really one of the only complaints I've heard about them from people—is their customer service. Can their customer service scale up enough to help their clients when they need it?

—Ben Carlson

Thirty million investors is *a lot* of people. That's over 10 percent of all adults in America. And Vanguard only brings in about $5 billion a year in revenue. That may sound like a lot, but it's bare bones versus most of their active peers. For example, Fidelity's annual fee revenue is in the neighborhood of $20 billion, and it has only half the assets of Vanguard. Of course, the lack of revenue is exactly why people love Vanguard. But it does bring up the legitimate question of how it can handle the service aspect of the business as well as keep up with technology.

Vanguard has a ton of legacy computer systems. I talked to some IT guys who had recently retired, and it is keeping some of these legacy systems together with baling wire. It doesn't have the money that Fidelity, Schwab, or Robinhood have to upgrade. Or it may have it, but it isn't going to spend it. And it has a lot of technical problems. On big trading days, its website goes down regularly. I've had a lot of leader complaints of account values being wrong. That is really serious.

—Erin Arvedlund

I've been writing about this for years. Vanguard's service is just abysmal. Fidelity is way better with service. Look, if you are going to have low fees, it has got to come from somewhere. And it is not coming from reusing paper clips. It has off-loaded a lot of its service to people who are low paid. It gives nobody responsibility. You can't shove all these things into a tiny funnel. There's going to be a roadblock somewhere.

—Dan Wiener

Some of the people I interviewed for this book reported having bad experiences personally, and they are largely fans of the company. A quick scan of Yelp shows that Vanguard gets a mere 1.5 out of five possible stars, which is the same rating as the Walmart on Christopher Columbus Boulevard in Philadelphia, which one review compared to the Seventh Circle of Hell. Here's a review of Vanguard's customer service from one investor:

I've been with Flagship service for more than twenty-three years and with Vanguard for more than thirty-seven years. On November 25, the day before Thanksgiving, I was on hold for more than thirty minutes. I called again and was placed on hold for thirty-plus minutes. I did the transaction online, which takes two business days. My wire transfer can only be done with a representative. Can we get more representatives before and after the holidays?

Here's another one:

Fees are low but the price you pay is lousy customer service. An example is, I called today to ask questions about transferring $30,000 more of my money to them but was placed on hold twenty minutes so I hung up. Their competitor, where I have money stored, picked up right away. Diversification is the key.

Even some on the Bogleheads website have complained. That's not a good sign, given how devoted they are. Here's an example comment I found on the forum:

Vanguard's "customer service" if you want to call it that, is subpar for other providers. Customer service is only available during business hours M–F (doesn't work when my husband is a surgeon and is generally unavailable business hours). Lots of their documentation has to be requested by phone, sent by email, then printed, and mailed back. They never processed our request for me to have limited authority on my husband's account. Had to resend by mail. Oh, and the three-to-seven-day hold on funds with backdoor Roths IS UNNECESSARY AND ABSOLUTELY INFU-RIATING. BOO VANGUARD.

This is perhaps in contrast with how Bogle describes the service in his books and speeches, where he reiterates that the crew remembers that the investors in the funds are "honest-to-God human beings." He told the crew this in 1991:

Caring about our clients, I should add, calls for personal service. We must go out of our way to empathize with their needs and concerns. Too often in this late-twentieth-century environment, rules and procedures have replaced judgment, recorded voices have crowded out human responses, and interminable elevator music has taken the place of a prompt response. To be sure, we need some of this modern-day efficiency, but if we let our humanity go, all too soon our clients will follow. And that would be that for Vanguard.

Fast-forward to today, and while Vanguard has said it is increasing expenditures in this department, it is an ongoing issue that it—as well as other passive giants—will have to work on, as its customer base grows much faster than its revenue thanks to the Great Cost Migration.

Customer service and technology are Vanguard's Achilles' heels.

—Erin Arvedlund

9

Bogle vs. Vanguard

"That got me into a lot of trouble around here."

My very first in-person meeting with Bogle was on the day after he had written an Op-Ed in the *Financial Times* in December 2016 that was somewhat critical of ETFs and how much they traded. Before I could even get to any of my prepared questions, he started talking about the fallout internally from a companion article to the Op-Ed about how Bogle "warns" about ETFs. It was clearly on his mind, and he wanted to vent:

Did you read the article that came out with [the opinion piece]? That got me into a lot of trouble around here . . . Usually [the Vanguard execs] shut the hell up. They don't talk to me, by the way. They talk to the press . . . It says I'm taking on ETFs or some damn thing. I said to people here who were criticizing it, "Would you just do me a favor and read my Op-Ed and underline any sentence you don't agree with?" There's not a single sentence anybody would disagree with. All of the sudden it's "an attack"! Even [Vanguard's then-CEO William] McNabb writes me and says it's the most concerted attack on ETFs he's ever seen. And I'm amazed. What I'm saying is just facts and data. I said ETFs are fine just as long as you don't trade them. Well, broad-market ETFs are all fine, so long as you don't trade them. All that other junk I don't have an intelligent comment about.

Notwithstanding the media's efforts to fan the flames with the companion piece to the Op-Ed, Bogle did in fact choose to write a very public column critiquing ETFs, which is one of the fastest-growing areas at Vanguard. So here you have the founder—and face—of the company slamming a successful part of the company from his office that is literally on campus. Who does that? Bogle does. And he did it consistently since the day he stepped down as CEO, in 1996, and resigned from the board three years later, in 1999, to set up the Bogle Financial Markets Research Center.

Bogle's war of words with Vanguard and the gaps that developed between them are worth exploring in an effort to better understand the man, as well as where Vanguard may be headed in this post-Bogle era.

Most of Bogle's problems with the company stemmed from what he saw as the firm's ambition for more and more growth, such as its push into ETFs. His "enough" mentality was against that, plus he had seen the problems that can arise from becoming too concerned with asset growth. "Looking back on my career," he said, "I've made some really stupid judgments, and I think 100 percent of them were when I had a marketing hat on."

I don't think he necessarily agreed with all the changes that have gone on at Vanguard. I think he's said he worried about it getting too big.

—John C. Bogle Jr.

A Rift at the Top

Bogle's ongoing friction with Vanguard was likely also due to hurt feelings and a bruised ego over the way he was pushed out from the board. At the same time, he was having a falling-out with his successor, Jack Brennan, who aggressively expanded the company into many new areas while overseeing a massive growth in assets from 1996 to 2009. By all accounts, Bogle was not happy with and perhaps also jealous of Brennan's success and resentful of his decision to go into ETFs.

Vanguard had a policy that the age limit for a board member was seventy, which Bogle was in 1999. He thought an exception would be made for him since he was the founder, but they wanted him out. There were stories that he was becoming increasingly difficult at board meetings, coming in with all kinds of studies and data and dominating the meetings and driving people crazy.

Bogle gave his side of the story in *The Clash of the Cultures*:

> *As 1999 began, the board seemed determined that I leave the board at year-end, following my seventieth birthday, a standing policy that I never imagined would apply to the firm's creator. I let the directors know of my surprise and dissatisfaction, and I awaited their decision. Then in August a journalist telephoned me to let me know that he had learned the board would allow no exceptions to the policy.*

The journalist was from the *Wall Street Journal*, which ran a story about "a possible rift at the top" at Vanguard. The news spread like wildfire and many shareholders (aka Vanguard investors), who tend to revere Bogle, expressed disappointment and even outrage. The board eventually relented and said he could keep his seat, but he decided he should just go away due to all the trouble it was causing. That was when he decided to resign.

They pushed him out. Brennan then took a lot of the credit for the asset growth. So his two original orphans were embraced as the darlings of the retail investment community and he was no longer head of the company. He liked to take shots at them when he could. He was also uncomfortable with the asset growth at the end. His Frankenstein [monster] had gotten away from him. He worried this would create bureaucracy, and clients wouldn't be human beings.
—Erin Arvedlund

In the end, it may be impossible to untangle what parts of Bogle's public differences with Vanguard were because of his resentment toward the way things unfolded versus Bogle just being his typical uncompromising, outspoken self over what he saw as right and wrong.

The greatest bulk of Vanguard's success, at least from the vantage point of gathering assets, came after Bogle was gone. And, to be honest, I think it always bothered him that Brennan turned out to be a good steward of what Bogle had built. His resentment was really bitter. He was just fuming mad, and he just ranted and raved, and he sounded like Captain Queeg. He wouldn't refer to Brennan by name. I mean, the company was his entire life, and you can understand why he was so upset about it. I think a lot of the tension never really left from the time he was forced out till the time he died. I think a lot of it stemmed from his anger about how Vanguard treated that transition.

—Jason Zweig

Vanguard's Assets ($B) During Each CEO's Tenure

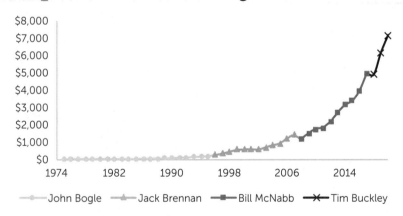

Stay the Course by John C. Bogle

The Old Guy Won't Shut Up

And so, just as the "bifurcation period" at Wellington had Bogle at odds with his own handpicked partners, Bogle would soon become the biggest critic of Vanguard and his handpicked successor for the next twenty-five years. It was something of a dysfunctional family for a while, with the founder—who was physically there on the campus still—firing off shots in the press at current management and slamming some of the products and strategies that the company offered, most of which he created, including smart-beta, international funds, and ETFs, which all involve many of the employees' daily roles and were hugely successful asset-wise. I used to say that Vanguard is so in the zone that its inflows were "Bogle-Proof" in that even its founder's stream of critiques couldn't stop the money from coming in. But he wasn't going to be denied expressing his opinion.

Jack Bogle had very strong ideas on just about everything. I can't think of much that he didn't have a strong idea about.

—Gus Sauter

Bogle acknowledged his opiniated style and the dysfunction but saw Vanguard, not himself, as the problem. As he explained to a crowd at a Morningstar conference in 2013, "[Vanguard] has a problem. Here's this old guy who keeps saying what he thinks. People say to me, 'I understand you disagree with Vanguard.' Absolutely not. I'd never do that. Vanguard disagrees with me."

The best part about covering him in the later years was that he had enough distance from the company that he was able to be its biggest booster but also its biggest critic. He was unhappy with the growth of "product" in the mutual fund industry. So when I knew there was a story about Vanguard that it might not like, he would be my first call. And he loved to swap gossip.

—Erin Arvedlund

I know people love Jack Bogle, and you don't want to besmirch a legacy. But Jack changed his tune about Vanguard when he got tossed. That's not to say the tune was false originally and now he was being honest, but he was devastated by being tossed out of that place. They even left Burt Malkiel on the board, even though he was beyond the age when they said Bogle had to leave. He got pissed. They screwed with him, and he turned on them.

—Dan Wiener

On one occasion when Bogle was writing his last book, *Stay the Course*, he requested to review the corporate minutes of the Vanguard mutual funds during the time he served as chairman, and the company denied him access. Perhaps it thought he was just going to make more of a headache for Vanguard if it gave him the minutes. It seemed to be a sign of the distance between them. Here's how Bogle described it when he was asked about his relationship with Vanguard in one of his final interviews in 2018 on the *Bogleheads* podcast with Rick Ferri:

> *To be candid, I don't have much of a relationship with Vanguard because I'm out. I don't participate in the management at all, and I think that's appropriate. I get no information. I have no access to its records. But that's fine, because I don't run the place anymore. I moved over to let other people run it, and they are running it. If they ever want my advice, they know they can get it anytime. But they think they know more because they are in the business more currently on a daily basis. But, look, when you leave the position of CEO—even if you are the founder—the new guys want to take over, should take over. And the old guys should move out of the way. I didn't (totally) want to move out of the way because . . . I am still—for better or worse—the face of Vanguard to many people, the shareholders, and the media.*

Bogle had several concerns about Vanguard, and going through a few of these specific issues will help us better understand the post-Bogle Vanguard and how it has evolved since his passing.

Vanguard's Size

Bogle was clearly uncomfortable with Vanguard's ballooning size, which I highlighted in depth in chapter one. But he was complaining that it was getting too big back when I met with him in 2016, when it had less than *half* the assets it has today. "My objective around here is not to get to $3 trillion," he said. "In some ways that is an appalling number, particularly for someone who has written a book called *Enough*. Do we really need more? More. More. More. Oliver Twist."

While Bogle expressed concern about Vanguard's growth, he remained critical of the asset-management industry for not being fiduciary enough or cheap enough. In a way, Vanguard's growth shows that others agreed with that criticism and became Vanguard investors. Thus, there was definitely some degree of contradiction in his critiques. One of his specific worries over getting too big was that it could lead to an inhuman bureaucracy, something that he had seen happen to many companies over the years. As he told the crew in a 1989 speech:

> *In my few dark moments, my greatest fear for Vanguard is that it becomes a giant, impersonal, boring bureaucracy, where nobody cares about anything or anybody. It is incumbent on our entire management team to fight to our dying day to hold back the great tide of process—of paper, policies, regulations, and procedures—that could overwhelm all that we have tried to achieve.*

He also mentioned in a 1993 speech that he had read an article in *Chief Executive* magazine that talked about how the larger and more mature a company grows, the less entrepreneurial it is likely to become. It begins to focus upward to satisfy each level of management and inward on the company itself rather than focusing downward to give employees more responsibility and outward to service the client.

In his last book, *Stay the Course*, Bogle spoke about Brennan's talent and their close relationship and squash matches. When it came to describing his stint as CEO, however, Bogle was polite but the strain and disapproval of the aggressive expansion was obvious:

Some of his accomplishments in that role include bringing marketing into a far more prominent place in the Vanguard spectrum, as well as instituting firm-wide data-driven performance management. Brennan also made the final decision to create Vanguard's ETFs and was ultimately responsible for building an organization to support them. While my decision to bring Vanguard into the international business had been timid, he initiated a broader approach to our foray into the world markets.

ETFs Rising

ETFs were arguably the biggest ongoing bone of contention between Bogle and Vanguard. Bogle was not a fan, as I explained in chapter six. He purposely said no to ETFs even when he was asked to launch the very first one. And then Vanguard launched them just a few years after he left the board. Bogle did not take it well.

He had been put on the outside at Vanguard, and then ETFs were launched and he disagreed with them from the very start. When [Vanguard ETFs] were first launched, there were competing press releases from the Vanguard camp and from the Bogle camp. It was ludicrous, comical.

—Jim Wiandt

Today, ETFs are the main growth engine for Vanguard, taking in a much greater percent of Vanguard's flows than they make up in assets. Had it not launched them, Vanguard would not have been able to reach as many people and help spread low costs in other places, a fact even Bogle conceded. That said, ETFs definitely took away from the index mutual fund. In fact, after Bogle passed away, Vanguard allowed investors to move from the mutual fund share class into the ETF share class, which had become cheaper. It is hard to imagine this not agitating Bogle.

It is important to note, though, that the best-selling ETFs at Vanguard, the ones the company uses the most in its client portfolios, are the most plain-vanilla, Bogle-friendly strategies.

"Look at what Vanguard is doing with its portfolio-level products and in its life strategy funds," says Elisabeth Kashner, vice president and director of ETF research and analytics at FactSet. "Look at where the largest flows are going in the ETF space, and you'll see Jack Bogle's legacy everywhere.

"The robo is going to use four funds," she continues, referring to Vanguard's premade portfolios for its digital advisory clients. "What's not in those portfolios is Vanguard's style funds, sector funds, none of its strategy funds, none of its active factor funds, and none of its active mutual funds. That's not what it is building its next-level business on. It is building it on Jack Bogle's legacy front and center. So, in the big picture, it is Bogle all the way down. Although in the fund-level product development, Vanguard is definitely doing some things that Bogle would consider a distraction."

Voting Record Disclosure

Another situation that found Bogle at odds with Vanguard was in 2002 when he wrote an Op-Ed in the *New York Times* in favor of a new regulation that would require mutual funds to disclose their voting records, given that Vanguard was a pretty big owner of many companies. This was right after the Enron scandal, so Bogle applauded the new rule because "investors had a right to know" how their shares are being voted. Most fund companies didn't want to disclose their records. He called their reticence the Silence of the Funds.

Just two months after Bogle's Op-Ed, Vanguard then-CEO Jack Brennan and Fidelity then-CEO Edward "Ned" Johnson III coauthored their own Op-Ed in the *Wall Street Journal* that argued *against* the new regulation. Brennan and Johnson didn't like the fact that the new rule singled out only mutual funds and not other institutional investors like pension funds and insurance companies. And this, they said, would make mutual funds the "prime pressure point" for activist groups with an axe to grind.

So here you have Bogle's handpicked successor teaming up with the CEO of one of its biggest, fiercest competitors, Fidelity. You don't see that every day. Both sides had valid points. It is better that voting records are transparent, but on the flip side, it should be a rule for all institutional owners. The regulation *did* result in mutual funds being singled out by activist groups, who by and large do not understand the concept of index investing.

Bogle would criticize Vanguard's voting record for years to come after this, citing studies that showed how Vanguard, along with some other big fund families, was passive in its voting and didn't show enough disagreement with management. He called out Vanguard directly in his book *The Clash of the Cultures*:

> *But what surprised me—and, I confess, disappointed me—was that the two index fund providers—Vanguard and BlackRock—were both notably passive in their voting policies . . . The singling out of Vanguard as the least-shareholder-friendly manager—[that] the firm ranked number 26 out of the list of 26 hardly gladdens my heart.*

That was complete hypocrisy because when he was running Vanguard it was at least as silent. He started beating Vanguard up for doing what he had always done when he was running it. It was ridiculous. It always made him look bad. He got away with a lot because of who he was.

—Jason Zweig

Of course, this was about twenty years ago. Fast-forward to today, and it is clear that Vanguard has evolved into a much less passive shareholder. It should be credited for being very transparent and detailed about its voting and engagements.

Quantitative Investing

One of the areas that Bogle pioneered for retail investors but then largely soured on in his later years was quantitative investing (aka smart-beta). These funds largely try to systematically capture factors in the market, which are characteristics of stocks that have been shown to explain outperformance historically, such as momentum, value, size (small companies), and quality.

Bogle was way ahead of this trend when he launched the Vanguard Quantitative Portfolios fund, in 1986, the first retail quant fund. Since then, Vanguard has expanded its factor offerings to include a large suite of funds.

It has a whole department for this called the Quantitative Equity Group (QEG), which has a healthy—albeit modest for Vanguard—$50 billion in assets. The thirty-four-person team oversees forty-one mandates, including factors and liquid alternatives (hedge fund–style strategies). At the end of the day, there are clients who like to invest this way.

Yet Bogle would routinely pooh-pooh the strategies. I tried asking him in one of our interviews whether—even if he didn't believe in the factor strategies' efficacy—he could take some pride in Vanguard bringing low costs to the category? "Well, as a matter of principle," he replied, "if you say no matter what junk there is out there, Vanguard should start it because it would be the cheapest junk, is not what I find to be an appealing marketing proposition."

International Investing

International funds is another area that Bogle would routinely blow off as unnecessary despite the fact that Vanguard is a leader in that sector (with $1.1 trillion in assets) and that Bogle himself spearheaded that expansion back in the early eighties. He didn't think you needed to invest in foreign stocks. He would frequently say he didn't own them in his own portfolio. Here is his rationale in *The Little Book of Common Sense Investing*:

> *My view that a US-only equity portfolio will serve all the needs of most investors was (and still is) challenged by, well, everyone. As the argument goes, "Isn't omitting non-US stocks from a diversified portfolio just as arbitrary as, say, omitting the technology sector from the S&P 500?" I argue the contra side. We Americans earn our money in dollars, spend it in dollars, save it in dollars, and invest it in dollars, so why take the currency risk? Haven't US institutions been generally stronger than those of other nations? Don't half the revenues and profits of US corporations already come from outside the United States? Isn't US GDP likely to grow at least as fast as the GDP of the rest of the developed world, perhaps at an even higher rate?*

Now, on one hand, he has largely been proven right. An investor who went heavily into US funds and lightly or not at all into international funds would have gotten better returns. On the other hand, hindsight is twenty-twenty, and most—including Vanguard, which has written papers advocating for international stocks—feel that you need some international exposure. This was also one of those issues that even his most ardent supporters disagreed with him on.

My biggest disagreement with Jack over the decades was on international.

—Ted Aronson

There are good people and good companies in other countries. If there is a great company coming out of Brazil, I want exposure to it. If there is a great company coming out of Ireland, I want exposure . . . And I don't believe in international because I think it is going to beat the US or anything; it is just a very comfortable "I don't know." I mean Rome fell, so how do you know that the US is going to forever be the best?

—Dan Egan

Post-Bogle Vanguard

Since Bogle passed away, Vanguard has made a few changes that are worth mentioning as well. For example, right after Bogle's death, the company changed the language on Vanguard's mutual ownership structure in its legal documents by stripping out the term *at-cost* as well as dropping *mutual mutual* (one of Bogle's favorite terms) to describe itself. It also dropped the claim that it offers a "no profit" contrast to the "for profit" ways of its peers.

Immediately after Bogle's death, it changed the language in its offering documents that it was no longer a nonprofit.

—Erin Arvedlund

The company says it was just trying to simplify disclosure, although it admitted it was not asked to do so by the SEC or the IRS. An ex-Vanguard attorney who was quoted in a story on the topic by Joseph N. DiStefano in the *Philadelphia Inquirer* said "at-cost" pricing would risk violating Federal tax law, while Barry Ritholtz suggested it would help the firm avoid "nuisance" litigation.

Is this just a company getting bigger and making sure it is tighter with its language, or is it a way to transition away from Bogle? While the timing certainly seems suspect, it's really hard to see this as some nefarious move to make more money. In fact, since all of this happened, Vanguard has continued to lower fees as it normally does on its funds while launching an ad campaign that touts how you can "become an owner." While Bogle was not a fan of advertising, the message shows the "mutual mutual" is very much alive and well regardless of what people want to call it. Further, it has already gotten the entire industry to offer near-free passive funds. That ship has sailed.

The Ship Logo

Speaking of ships, another example of the company shedding some of its Bogleness is its recent decision to retire the ship from the firm's logo—a superficial but arguably symbolic move that probably would have stung a bit for Bogle. The HMS *Vanguard* was a British naval ship captained by Lord Nelson that helped defeat Napoleon. Bogle got the idea from a book he had received about British naval battles. As he wrote in *Stay the Course*:

> *When I turned to the saga of the historic Battle of the Nile, I was impressed. There, Lord Nelson's fleet sunk almost every French fighting ship, while losing but a single English frigate, still the most complete naval victory in history. Napoleon's dreams of world conquest were over . . . With neither a second's hesitation nor a single consultant, I decided that "Vanguard" would be the name of the firm I would soon create.*

The ship was huge for Bogle. It was like the visual manifestation of his eighteenth-century soul. He went as far as to say that Vanguard had a "heritage that comes from a naval battle fought by Great Britain nearly 200 years ago." The ship had become ingrained in the DNA of the firm and all the language metaphorically. In virtually every company speech he ever gave, there is a direct or indirect reference to the ship. He talked of "headwinds" and "tailwinds" and referred to the staff as the "crew." Further, most of the buildings on Vanguard's campus are named after ships in Nelson's fleet, such as Goliath, Majestic, Swiftsure, and Victory—where Bogle's office was located. He even had paintings of ships in his office.

So why did the company decide to drop the logo from its website and printed documents a year after he passed away? Apparently, it had hired a branding firm to help it modernize the firm's brand imagery. And as part of that, it decided to do away with the HMS *Vanguard* ship image, which hadn't been changed since 1981.

Modernizing? That sounds to me like they are washing away his imprimatur.

—Erin Arvedlund

The boat stuff is just Jack. He had a fascination with it, and that's what drove the culture. The galley, the crew. That's just a thing, but Vanguard getting rid of the ship and downplaying this stuff is further shifting away from the Bogle legacy.

—Dan Wiener

While it is hard not to see it as a distinct move away from Bogle, it is also a cosmetic change and basically inconsequential. And, let's face it, warships aren't exactly part of the broader culture anymore.

I'm inclined not to make anything of it. I will cast all my judgment on what Vanguard's products and policies are, not on what its logo is. I don't think there is some symbolic "screw Jack Bogle" in the move. I think someone was just like, "This is antiquated, and we need to get younger investors." I don't make much of it.

—Jim Wiandt

My guess is, Bogle would not be in support of removing the ship. Although to come full circle, Bogle's mentor, Walter Morgan, didn't care for the name *Vanguard*. He said it sounded like a troupe of acrobats. What is new becomes old eventually. The times change. Bogle even acknowledged the need to progress away from tradition. Here's how he put it in a speech to the crew in 1994:

> *Tradition has a negative side as well. It can substitute inertia for action: it can encrust and stultify. In short, however vital in the past, tradition can cast a pall over the future. T.S. Eliot put it well when he said, "Tradition is not enough; it must be perpetually criticized and brought up-to-date."*

Private Equity

Vanguard and private equity don't have a lot in common. One is about serving up publicly traded securities for a superlow cost to largely retail investors and the other is about serving up largely illiquid private investments to institutional investors in expensive funds. That is why people were surprised—and intrigued—when Vanguard announced a partnership with the private equity firm HarbourVest about a year after Bogle passed away.

I could almost see Bogle turning in his grave over the prospect of a Vanguard private equity fund.
—Robin Powell

In Vanguard's defense, its reasoning for the partnership is pretty logical. First, the number of publicly traded companies has been cut in half from about eight thousand in the mid-nineties to under four thousand today. This is because many firms are choosing not to go public or wait much longer before they do, as evidenced by the growing size of IPOs. This has increased interest in private equity—even among retail investors who are looking to capture the value created by American businesses—something Bogle preached in regard to public equities.

Number of Domestic Equities Listed in the US

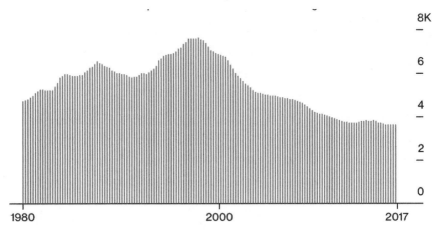

Jay R. Ritter, Warrington College of Business, University of Florida; University of Chicago Center for Research in Security

Second, Vanguard is looking to build up its advisory service and out-sourced CIO model for institutions, so it needs a private equity offering to be competitive. Third, perhaps private equity is an area that could use a little Vanguarding. While it is unlikely that we will see a literal Vanguard PE fund, there are indirect ways that Vanguard can offer it and perhaps apply some cost pressure. The fees in this space are really high, making active mutual funds of the eighties seem like child's play.

I joke with my buddies that when I die I want to come back as a private equity guy. I don't want to be a quant manager with no fees and pressure from Vanguard.

—Ted Aronson

The Big Things

Despite Bogle's constant ongoing friction with the new leadership and his criticism of certain product lines within Vanguard, the company and its employees still seemed to love him. At the end of the day, they knew he was on their team. Plus, when it came to the big things and the core principles, the company was largely still carrying on Bogle's low-cost and indexing legacy just fine.

He never lost the respect inside Vanguard. He was just doing his thing. Some of it was based in reality, and yeah, we want people to trade less and do buy and hold, but some of it was that he was just wedded to what he had built.

—Jim Wiandt

Internally at Vanguard, I really do think there was a sense of commonality over the big things, although there were smaller issues where they would have dustups. I would say the question of how to proceed in the advisor space was probably a big bone of contention.

—Christine Benz

Bogle the Manager

One of the reasons Bogle retained respect inside the company despite his frictions with it in public was that by all accounts he was a good manager and CEO to his employees during his tenure. This is an underrated part of his life because without the ability to hire the right people, organize them, retain them, and rally them, his experiment and mission would have likely stalled quickly. That leadership skill set combined with his analytical mind, vision, and communication skills is a rare combination. But when it all comes together in one person, it can change the world.

And in Bogle's case, he also had the unique challenge of trying to balance the inherent tension of employee compensation with the mission to lower costs and Vanguard's structure. Early in the company's rise, he could sense unease among the crew that the low-cost mantra would be bad for their paychecks. Bogle addressed it in a speech to the crew in 1991:

At Vanguard, there is a concern among some of our crew members— actually about one in every four of you—that compensation is less than it might be relative to other financial services organizations . . . In reading your comments in Crew's Views, I was stung by the fact that some of you believe your compensation is less because of our determination to maintain our low-cost-provider status. It is not so. The fact is completely reverse; our low-cost advantage is the root cause of the payments you are about to receive. It is this advantage that serves as the basis for our unique partnership arrangement and that is among the principal forces in our enormous asset growth.

This partnership arrangement is called the Vanguard Partnership Plan and was introduced to address this compensation worry. Bogle promised that it would be at "par plus plus plus" and he has seemingly done that. The returns of the plan have actually doubled the market, according to Jeffrey DeMaso of Advisor Investments, who talked about it as one of our guests on *ETF IQ* in 2019:

A lot of people don't know that Vanguard has this profit-sharing plan that started back in 1984 as a way for Jack Bogle to reward all the employees, and it is largely based on the difference in cost between their funds and the industry average. We were asking how it compares to be a partner at Vanguard versus an investor at Vanguard, and that distribution in the partnership plan has really increased about seventy-two-fold since 1984. Compare that with an investment in the S&P 500 Index, which is up about thirty-three-fold.

Vanguard doesn't disclose what people make there. But it has to attract talent as well, and running the biggest index fund in the world is a huge responsibility, and those people have to be highly compensated.

—Jared Dillian

Many people who entered Bogle's orbit—namely his assistants—became lifers and top executives (including CEOs) at Vanguard, helping to build and grow the company into what it is today. Most, if not all of them, really bought into his vision.

People who came to Vanguard often came with a sense of idealism. I thought I was going to go back to law school and be a public defender. I had no intention of spending my career at Vanguard. But you got there, and you would hear the sermons. Jack delivered a regular dose of sermons. I ended up staying for thirty-three years, but then you are damaged goods. You have a way of thinking about the world. You have a way of critically thinking about data and about the alignment with the client. The longer you are there, the harder it is to see the world differently.

—Jim Norris

In order to walk the walk with both clients and employees, Bogle also purposely limited the perks normally given to bigwigs at asset management firms, such as largely eliminating first-class flying, reserved parking, and an executive dining room.

Bogle reminded me a lot of a military leader. He embraced many of the same principles, like lead by example, officers eat last. I think that's why he was successful. Because a lot of people who are in finance are the opposite of military leadership. Nowadays it has become more standard, but back then it was unique. Back then it was all master of the universe, stomp on people's heads in the greed-is-good era.

—Wesley Gray

Same Direction

I personally witnessed this grassroots respect for Bogle inside the company with everyday employees on Vanguard's campus. After that first interview, he invited me to join him for lunch at the campus dining hall. As we walked over from his office to the cafeteria and passed employees, you could sense the respect and warmth from them: "Hello, Mr. Bogle," "Good afternoon, Mr. Bogle," "How are you, Mr. Bogle?" And they didn't appear nervous—as can happen with young employees in the same vicinity as the founder—but seemed very at ease and genuinely happy to see him. And then in the dining hall, he picked a table right in the middle of the cafeteria like he was any other employee (which was quite a sight, since he probably raised the average age of the room to thirty-one years old).

Even Brennan, who arguably bore much of Bogle's angst over the years, seemed to really love and appreciate the company and culture that Bogle had set up. He said as much in a speech to University of Notre Dame students in 2016:

> *I am spoiled because I was fortunate to spend a career at a place where the only thing that matters is character, integrity, and ethics. That's how you get hired. That's how you progress. That's how you ended up as a leader in our organization. I got to do that. And not many people at my age at the end of a forty-year career can say that. And say it with such confidence.*

Conversely, there has been nothing but positive reviews of all the CEOs who have run Vanguard since Bogle left. It isn't easy to grow a company while keeping its DNA intact, but Vanguard's management has largely done just that.

Obviously, different people are going to develop a company differently. And I think Jack Bogle and Jack Brennan were both absolutely necessary for Vanguard to be what it is today. Jack Bogle had the vision to create the company, and Jack Brennan did it. He made it happen. Vanguard wouldn't be where it is today without Jack Brennan, that's for sure. McNabb [CEO number three] did a fine job following up as well, and Buckley [CEO number four] is doing a good job so far from what I can see. So yeah, they are going to take things down a slightly different path, but they are going in the same direction.
—Gus Sauter

In the end, I think Bogle's view toward the company, both when he was running it and after he left, can be best summarized by this line in *Enough*: "My hope, then, is not merely that Vanguard will endure, but that it will deserve to endure."

10

The Art of Doing Nothing

"Higher trading activity is the investor's enemy. It's been proven a thousand times over."

I remember reading an article about U2 back in the early nineties in which the lead singer, Bono, said that writing a song was as easy as walking down the street but that writing a *good* song, a hit song, was much more difficult. The same could be said of passive investing. Buying an index fund or an ETF is as easy as clicking a button, but holding it for ten years—let alone a lifetime—is a whole other story. That is why Bogle made behavior an ancillary piece of his low-cost and indexing sermons. Because investors can have the ultimate dirt-cheap portfolio, but if they can't control themselves from trading said cheap funds at the wrong time, all those cost savings will go right out the window.

The proper term for this concept is *behavioral finance*, although I prefer the "Art of Doing Nothing" (which was yet *another* title I almost gave this book). Along those lines, I also like the phrase *chasing patience*, which I first heard from Michael Batnick of Ritholtz Wealth Management and is a riff off the habit many investors have of chasing performance. Both ideas point to the fact that doing nothing is a deliberate act and ironically much harder than doing something. Whatever you want to call it, it is the next phase of this investor enlightenment era that Bogle had a big hand in ushering in.

Navy SEALS

As we learned earlier in the book, Vanguard investors in particular are already good at the art of doing nothing. In fact, relative to the average investor, they display some Navy SEALs–level discipline as evidenced by the fact that the funds see inflows come rain, sleet, or snow.

Vanguard has some of the best-behaved clients out there. Bogle was intent on bringing in the right people and the right clients, and he didn't want these Johnny-come-lately types. That's what we have tried to do with our business. Because if you bring in the wrong client and they're a headache, you are wasting everyone's time.
—Ben Carlson

While Vanguard and passive funds generally attract the type of investor who may be more aware of behavior than most, Bogle's pounding the drum on this point surely helped the cause as well. Bogle distilled it down to its bare essence in one of our interviews. This is basically his $E = mc^2$:

The whole thing about indexing is—as a wise man has said a thousand times—it gives you the magic of compounding returns without the tyranny of compounding costs. That's when it happens in the long run. That's why lifetime is the most important holding period for everybody.

He changed behavior. He was so effective at his "no trading" and "Why should you trade?" and his tyranny of humble arithmetic. No one could talk about that better.
—Ted Aronson

And just to be clear, when I say "doing nothing," it doesn't necessarily mean never doing anything, although that really is about 99 percent of it. It really means sticking to a plan and trading on your terms rather than on emotions like fear and, especially, FOMO—the fear of missing out.

Something Worth Holding

Beyond his message, however, Bogle's even bigger impact on behavioral finance was in giving investors something *worth* holding on to: an index fund. Just providing the low-cost index fund to the marketplace helped change behavior for the better. For many, when the market is falling, there's not the thought *I'm in the wrong fund, I should switch* because many realize it's hard to do better than owning the total market for three basis points. So they do nothing. You can see this in the flow data, as the most disciplined investors are the passive investors. They rarely, if ever, flinch.

I think Bogle did have a role in behavior. His influence, apart from his role of pushing down fund fees, was that he created this sort of frictionless investment product. The beautiful thing about index funds is, I could recommend that a young investor buy index funds and never do anything else and never see them again for the rest of our lives but still have a sense that I had given them a good piece of advice. And that's what I think is one of the underrated and under-discussed aspects of Bogle's legacy, that if you buy an index fund portfolio and do a little bit of rebalancing along the way, you literally have no reason to make changes to it.

—Christine Benz

Improving investor behavior was no easy feat, however, given the opposing forces at work, which is why Bogle would say doing nothing is "simple but not easy." It is essentially a battle against human nature. People are wired to do something. We are wired to want to buy things when they are popular and sell when they're not. It just feels right instinctually. And it doesn't make matters any easier when brokerage platforms are designed to encourage trading and an entire media apparatus is motivated to get clicks and eyeballs by amplifying sell-offs, stoking fear, and framing market coverage in the ultrashort term. I know this firsthand. I'm guilty of it, too.

Selling the Drama

A prime example of this is when CNBC rolls out its "Markets in Turmoil" special every time stocks have a bad couple of days. The font and colors it uses for the segment title make it look like the opening credits of a horror movie. It creates a visceral reaction to panic and sell. But doing that has proven to be the absolute dumbest move during the past decade, as the market has always rebounded quickly. To this point, some have even used it as a tongue-in-cheek indicator to buy more.

Reasons to Sell

S&P 500 Index

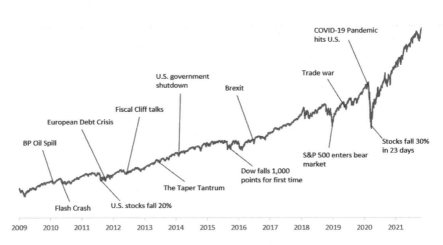

Michael Batnick

The media will also use pictures of pissed-off grizzly bears along with superlatives like "worst week since 2007." They'll also quote the Dow Jones in points rather than percentage because it sounds scarier. "Dow Falls 500 Points" is going to get your attention much more than "Dow Falls 1.4 Percent." They will also show short-term charts that are crashing down and all red, but if they just zoomed out to the medium- or long-term view, it would add much-needed context and likely show how microscopic the current decline is.

No surprise, Bogle wasn't a fan. Here's how he put it in *The Clash of the Cultures*:

Less understandable, however, is the fixation of financial journalism on the momentary movements of the stock market, in which every sudden rise or fall is treated as a newsworthy event, even though the trading activity merely reflects the transfer of stock ownership from one investor to another.

On the flip side, the media will also try to make you envious about missing out on specific investments that are doing well, publishing articles about how if you'd bought $10,000 of this one-in-a-hundred stock twenty years ago, it would be worth some crazy-high amount today. What are you supposed to do about that? Build a time a machine? Or start buying every IPO that comes on the market? Such articles make you feel that you need to do something. In either case, you are left with a lot of fear and FOMO, both of which can inspire bad decisions.

The media also tends to cover only that which shines brightly or crashed badly and ignores the boring stuff. I call it the 95/5 Phenomenon, which is that 95 percent of the media coverage is based on holdings that typically make up 5 percent of most people's portfolios and vice versa. You will be hard-pressed to find much coverage of the Vanguard Total Stock Market Index Fund, despite the fact that it is the most popular core holding in America. Meanwhile, things like meme stocks, themes, and crypto will dominate the coverage for days.

The 95/5 Phenomenon

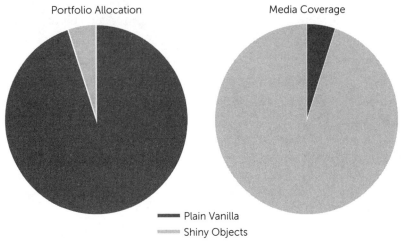

Portfolio Allocation   Media Coverage

Plain Vanilla
Shiny Objects

Eric Balchunas

A Show About Nothing?

Of course, we can criticize the media, but what else are they supposed to do? If they built the coverage around long-term investing and wealth creation, it would get boring quickly and they'd lose clicks and viewers and thus advertising dollars. Plus, to be fair, some people just like trading. It may not be proven to work well long term, but that's their right. So while a show about nothing worked for *Seinfeld*, it probably wouldn't work for CNBC—although it is fun to think about.

Give me Jim Cramer's CNBC show and here's what I would do: I'd come out each night and say, "Own a broadly diversified portfolio of low-cost index funds around the world. Rebalance once a year. See you tomorrow." Then I have fifty-nine minutes and forty-eight seconds left to kill.

—Barry Ritholtz

This topic was explored in the book *Clash of the Financial Pundits* by Joshua Brown and Jeff Macke, which includes about a dozen interviews with people in the financial media, both print and broadcast. They explore some of the trials and tribulations of covering the markets, as well as the inner workings of their roles. But when it comes to discussing their own investments, many admit to just buying and holding an index fund. One example is Henry Blodget, who rose to fame as a stock analyst for Merrill Lynch during the nineties internet boom. His job, before getting banned for fraud, was to help mutual fund managers pick stocks so they could beat the index. He said it doesn't work, but you can't say that out loud on TV:

> *It is crazy for individuals to try to pick stocks, and it is crazy for individuals to try to pick mutual fund managers or hedge fund managers who can beat the market. For 99 percent of individuals, it's just devastating to their financial performance. Really what they should be doing is keeping their money in low-cost index funds and only rebalance once every couple of years, and that's it. And yet the problem is, as a brokerage firm, as an advisor, as a media pundit, you can't just go on and say everyone should buy index funds. Stop trying to figure out what's next for Yahoo or Google or Apple. Just buy index funds and forget it. Financial TV would just have to fold up the tent.*

Bogle would argue that folding up the tent would be a good thing. He went even further in *The Little Book of Common Sense Investing*, channeling John Lennon in his vision of a behavioral utopia: "Imagine a day when nobody sold anything, and the stock market lay fallow, silent all day long."

Free Trading!

Bogle's vision of stock market dormancy is at odds with the media as well as retail brokerages, who are largely incentivized to get people to trade. And they do it through gamified interfaces and commission-free trading.

In chapter six, we mentioned how Bogle said ETFs were "like handing an arsonist a match." Well, if that's true, then making all trades commission-free is like handing an arsonist a flamethrower. But this is the current state of the major retail trading platforms, such as Fidelity, Schwab, Interactive Brokers, E*TRADE, and, of course, Robinhood, now offering largely "free" trading on just about everything.

This trend is mainly a result of how democratized trading has gotten—it's *so* easy and *so* cheap. There's a clear correlation between the cost of trading coming down and the rise of retail trading volume. Just like Vanguard's average expense ratio during the past forty-five years, the cost of a trade on Schwab—to use it as an example—has dropped steadily in parallel from $70 to $0 today.

The Cost to Trade Stocks Through Schwab

Era	Cost per Trade via Schwab
1970s	$70
1990s	$30
2000s	$13
2020s	$0

Bloomberg News

Breakdown of Trading Volume in the US by Investor Type

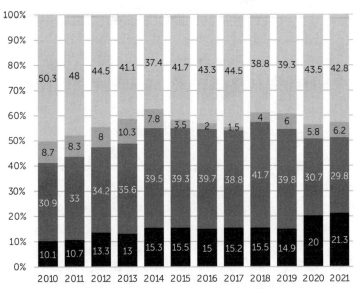

Retail ■ Institutional Buy-Side ■ Bank ■ Non-Bank Market Makers/HFT

Bloomberg (Larry Tabb)

Retail makes up about 20 percent of all equity trading today. This is up from 10 percent ten years ago. Retail is now a bigger trading force than hedge funds and mutual funds are. While the trend was in place for a while, it got a significant boost in 2020, as many people found themselves bored at home during the Covid-19 pandemic with no sports on TV and "stimmy" checks burning a hole in their pockets. Throw in the fact that the Federal Reserve was injecting the markets with liquidity, and it was a perfect storm for an explosion of trading.

This all happened a year after Bogle passed away, and it was probably for the best that he wasn't around to read about it—although his comments would have been epic.

The free-trading stuff, he would have—his head would have exploded.
—Ted Aronson

He would have thought it was an abomination. He would have sounded like Jonathan Edwards or one of those seventeenth-century preachers reading fire and brimstone at the pulpit. It would have been anathema to him.
—Jason Zweig

"An Orgy of Speculation"

We know Bogle's take would have been colorful because his past comments on trading have been. He saved some of his most biting, savage language for trading, referring to it as a "loser's game," a "socially useless activity," and "an orgy of speculation." If he were to have made a Ten Commandments of Investing, I'm pretty sure Thou Shalt Not Trade would be in the top three—perhaps even number one.

In a 1999 *New York Times* Op-Ed (at the height of the internet bubble), Bogle calculated that active mutual funds capture only about 75 percent of the annual stock market return but that individual DIY traders fared worse, capturing only about 65 percent of the market's return after costs. He contrasted that with the 99 percent captured by buy-and-hold index fund investors. In other words, as bad as he thought active mutual funds were, he thought trying to be your own active manager was even worse.

In addition to the near impossibility of timing the market consistently well, there are also costs involved. A small toll called the *bid-ask spread* is paid for each trade (even if there is no commission). It is essentially the difference between what a market maker will sell a stock or ETF for versus what he or she will buy it for. Spreads vary but they are usually pretty small, like a penny or two, but they can be bigger for less liquid or exotic securities or derivatives.

"Each buyer is accompanied by a seller and is a zero-sum game until you take out the croupier's cost," Bogle said. "There's no way around that. So trading makes money for Wall Street. It does not make money for the two parties. It's called rent-seeking in economic terms."

Bogle was appalled at how much trading had increased since he entered the industry. After he left college in the 1950s, the annual turnover of the entire stock market (the volume of stocks traded in dollar terms divided by the total sum of the market cap of all stocks) was about 15 percent. It rose to 100 percent by the late 1990s, only to hit 250 percent in 2011. In 2020, it was 317 percent. To break that down, this means that there was $120 trillion worth of stock (and ETFs) trading, yet the total market cap of the stock market was "only" $38 trillion.

Bogle often pointed out that all that trading activity was a massive mutation away from Wall Street's original function of connecting capital to businesses. He brings in the data in *The Clash of the Cultures*:

Total equity IPOs have averaged $45 billion annually over the past five years, and secondary offerings providing additional equity capital have averaged about $205 billion, bringing back total stock issuance to some $250 billion. The annual volume of stock trading averaged $33 trillion during that period, some 130 times the volume of equity capital provided to businesses. Put another way, that trading activity represents 99.2 percent of what our financial system does; capital formation represents 0.8 percent.

A quick counterpoint: While data shows trading does hurt one's overall returns, it isn't illegal and can sometimes be fun, just as going to a casino is legal and fun. People typically know they will probably lose in a casino but go anyway for the experience. And the market makers, or croupiers, are generally nice people who do a good job of facilitating trades for a fair price. They are also absolutely crucial in a sell-off to step in and provide liquidity when there isn't much. They are the oil that greases the whole machine.

Vanguard's Role

Despite Bogle's crusade against trading, Vanguard ironically played a role in ushering in this free-trading era when it shocked the world by announcing in July 2018 (more than a year before most of the other brokerages went commission-free) that it would allow 1,800 ETFs to trade commission-free. That went much further than any other major platform at the time and it felt like a game-changing moment. CNBC went as far as to say it "might be the boldest experiment in the history of retail investing."

Almost everyone who saw this news just spotted *Vanguard* and *free trading* in the same sentence and was scratching their heads a bit given Bogle's outspokenness about the dangers of trading. This seemed very much against the DNA of the company. On the flip side, lowering costs *was* in Vanguard's DNA, and it was a move that seemed in tune with the way it used the mutual ownership structure to lower fees on funds and advice. Some thought it was a way for Vanguard to force the rest of the platforms to go commission-free on all ETFs, too, which would put Vanguard's ETFs on more of a level playing field and thus increase their distribution.

While it didn't happen overnight, eventually other platforms—namely Interactive Brokers, Schwab, E*Trade, and Fidelity—did follow suit and then some. Many upped the ante by adding in commission-free stocks and options, and so on. There was a torrent of press releases and announcements from brokerage platforms with each one seemingly offering more free-trading than the next. It is how we reached the commission-free utopia, or perhaps dystopia, that we are at today.

Free Is a Helluva Drug

The move from cheap to free trading may seem small in cost, but it is massive psychologically, as people tend to lose their minds a bit and act irrationally when it comes to free stuff.

Psychologically, people overconsume free things. Literally going from something costing one cent or two cents to free drives a dramatic change in how you regard it, and in really dumb ways. You will wait in line far longer than you should for free things. You will drive further—spending gas money for something that is free. Bogle was all about driving the cost down and down, but there is an event horizon, like a black hole, that you hit at free. The laws of physics don't work the same way anymore. This leads to apathetic collateral damage for the consumer. As with Twitter, Facebook, or anything that is free, they aren't trying to hurt you, but they don't care if they do. Robinhood doesn't care if you are successful at trading, it just wants you to trade. So I think low cost is better than free. And I think Bogle would have ascribed to this.

—Dan Egan

In a market as complicated as the stock market, and given the way that it is operated, if you are not paying a fee, then you're the product. It's the most common saying out there, but it's true. It's a zero-sum game. People are in this to make money. So you are paying for it in some way. I don't think you have to be a genius to know that nothing is free on Wall Street.

—Brad Katsuyama

They have to make money some way. And there are a few ways they do that. One is by selling the order flow (your buy or sell orders) to market makers who are willing to pay for retail order flow because retail tends to trade with wider bid-ask spreads so they can make more money. This is Robinhood's model. Another way is by sweeping the cash lying around in your account into a fund yielding less than what the company can get in a money market fund and pocketing the difference. That difference is called *net interest income*, which is how Schwab, which deserves the most credit for ushering in this low-cost trading era, makes about half its revenue.

> It's framed as superlow-cost, pro–end investor, and there's all this crap going on with payment for order flow, and God knows what else is happening under the hood. There are massive amounts of trading activity, which, of course, is stupid by and large. It is destroying value for end investors. Bogle would have hated it all, no question, in so many ways.
>
> **—Jim Wiandt**

Beyond those moneymaking methods, some companies also use free trading as a loss leader to get you in the door, then try to upsell you on pricier services or active mutual funds. To be fair, though, this concept happens throughout our retail economy—like at grocery stores—and customers tend to understand it and shop accordingly.

The Robinhood Army

Beyond trades being pitched as free, there's also the gamification of trading, which can make "doing nothing" much more difficult. Many of today's young retail traders grew up playing video games, watching YouTube, and making memes, and they are now applying all they've learned to the stock market. The media refers to these risk-seeking young traders as the Robinhood Army, although they can be found on many of the other trading platforms as well. But just as *Kleenex* is widely used for any generic brand of tissues, *Robinhood* has become synonymous with young, risk-seeking, YOLO (you only live once) traders.

These traders love the rush of quick gains and tend to prefer single stocks, options, and leveraged ETPs (exchange-traded products) to the more boring, plain-vanilla ETFs or mutual funds. While their bravado mixed with naivety has caused a lot of pearl clutching among the old heads, they have time on their side and are getting a high ROE (return on entertainment) as well as an education about markets.

The question remains whether people are slowly developing a full-blown addiction. The fact is, the folks designing the platforms and interfaces for these young traders are incentivized to increase the proverbial nicotine, such as dropping green confetti when users make a trade, emoji notifications, constant updates of stock-related articles, and free stocks in the shape of lottery tickets.

Think about how hard it is to put Twitter or any social media platform down. These apps are built by the same people. They are geared toward providing dopamine hits.

—Nate Geraci

Free trading, trading apps, the gamification of trading—all that points to more people getting active in the market. Those apps have been geared toward an emerging class of trader, the millennial. So I'd say it is a factor, a new type of trader—giving them access and then making them want to trade as much as possible.

—Brad Katsuyama

It has reached the point at which there have been some calls to reverse the commission-free trading trend, given how tempting it makes trading.

Fees are not the enemy of investors. Trading commissions are a good thing. High commissions are a good thing. One of the reasons I went to a full-service broker is because I wanted to pay a five-cents-a-share commission and pay hundreds of dollars of commission on each trade, because it would discourage me from trading. It would incentivize me to buy and hold things.

—Jared Dillian

If your time horizon is forty years, if you take a young person's view of the market, it is crazy to try to time it.

—Michael Lewis

History Rhyming

And while free trading and gamification may be new, the idea of losing one's mind from trading too much in a bull market is not new, and each generation will likely learn that the hard way. Case in point, here's an excerpt from a *Forbes* article from January 1999, which could have been written today:

> *Each day a five-million-strong mob of online investors is proving that when it comes to stock picking, might makes right. In their world, everything you have learned about rational pricing—earnings or book values or even revenues—is meaningless. Don't worry about the long haul. Trade for the moment. Make a killing. Hey, everyone else in the chat group seems to be doing so.*

It goes back even further than that, too. "Robinhood echoes the bucket shops of the twenties," argues Jamie Catherwood, a client portfolio associate at O'Shaughnessy Asset Management, "because those were almost pure gambling, where you bet on the direction of stock prices' movement but you weren't actually invested in those stocks. It was like paper trading taken to the extreme. And it was almost all younger people and those who didn't have the ability to buy at the higher lot levels required by the brokers at the time."

The young day traders of today will likely ultimately convert into conservative buy-and-hold investors, as did the generations before them. This is what happened to me and many of my Gen X friends in the nineties. Not only are you sobered up by a correction, but you also tend to get very busy with life as you get older. With a career, a house, and a family, the desire for long-term wealth creation can easily outweigh the short-lived dopamine rush from a good trade. Just like the supercomputer in the movie *WarGames*, many younger investors will learn that "the only winning move is not to play."

The rise of platforms like Robinhood has been beneficial in the sense that they are bringing new investors into the fold. Because it can be tough to get younger individuals to get excited about investing. These younger investors are going to expect the ride and returns

that they saw in 2020 to continue into the future. And will a broad-based index fund provide enough juice for them? How do we pivot them there? That's the challenge.
                                                                            —Nate Geraci

---

There is definitely some truth that we go through these boom-and-bust cycles of retail interest. We are right in the middle of one of these bubbles. Some percentage of these folks are going to get their you-know-whats handed to them, but they are interested enough in the market to find out what the game really is, and they'll find Bogle's hack.
                                                                            —Dave Nadig

---

The Big Long

On the opposite side of the spectrum from these young YOLO retail traders is a whole new generation of behavioral-minded advisors who consciously study and practice the art of doing nothing. They tend to be index fund investors and avid followers of Bogle as well as the research from the academic world. I refer to their mindset as the Big Long because they are like the hedge fund guys from the film *The Big Short*, folks inside the system who see something others don't. But in their case, that something isn't impending doom or a bubble but rather a pot of gold at the end of the rainbow decades away—even if it isn't as cool as being a skeptic.

Just as the 1987 film *Wall Street* made everyone want to be a master-of-the-universe get-rich-at-all-costs type, *The Big Short* made it fashionable and sophisticated to call out bubbles, tops, and potential problems in the market. People can get their name into the press by saying things are going to hell, because putting the words *bubble* or *blowup* into a headline will guarantee clicks.

Calling out how screwed up everything is can also be a risk-free move reputation-wise. People lose nothing by making this call. If anything, they are seen as smart. For whatever reason, being negative when it comes to the market sounds smarter—and even more caring—than being an optimist. And no one ever goes back and calls them out for being wrong. No one calculates the opportunity cost in lost returns that investors would have incurred if they listened to the naysayers. It's free PR with little effort and no downside. And it can tempt investors to sell or trade when they shouldn't.

But while buying and holding index funds or ETFs may not come across as intellectually sophisticated as calling out bubbles, shorting stocks, or speaking in Greek symbols about the options market, it has proven to be a great strategy for building wealth. These Big Long advisors have learned to identify, ignore, and even mock the onslaught of negativity and worry. They are the hedgehogs. They know one great thing. They think more like gardeners than gamblers.

We had the dot-com crash and then 2008, so within ten years we had these two 50 percent bear markets. So top calling became its own industry. I do think the Big Long thing has taken hold in the wealth management industry, though. Even the wirehouses are moving more toward a long-term asset allocation strategy, as opposed to just trying to sell you these securities or active mutual funds.
—Ben Carlson

This isn't to say that every once in a while the skeptics don't have a point or aren't proven right. Even Bogle praised the Big Short folks who called the 2008 meltdown and thought they deserved to be compensated. His problem was with all the so-called gatekeepers. In *The Clash of the Cultures*, he spends dozens of pages skewering the entire system, namely Congress, the SEC, the Fed, rating agencies, accountants, the media, security analysts, and mutual fund directors, all of whom he thought had failed miserably in their roles.

The Behavior Gap

The problem with constant skepticism and negativity is that you could become poor (and crazy) thinking about and betting that things will blow up. It is just no way to manage your—or someone else's—nest egg. Part of the art of doing nothing is to acknowledge that there will be sell-offs—just as part of life is acknowledging you will get flat tires and catch colds. The secret to surviving these sell-offs is preparing for them both mentally and portfolio-wise. Seeing through the speculative-return smoke screen that distracts most people is the key to capturing the full share of investment returns that lies beneath.

The single biggest value an advisor can provide is on the behavioral side. Advisors are human like everyone else, so their biggest role is to be that steady hand. That's 90 percent of investing. You can minimize costs and taxes and have good allocation, but none of it matters if an investor can't stick to a plan. The future of the advisory profession is all behavioral based.

—Nate Geraci

Advisors sometimes talk about this value-add of behavioral coaching in terms of a *behavior gap*, which is essentially the difference between what the fund reported returns are versus what returns the investors actually got based on the flows. The behavior gap is what Bogle used all the time to try to take down ETFs, since many of them do show these differences. Anyone who has ever invested probably understands the behavior gap all too well.

Some studies have gone even further by looking at brokerage data as well as fund assets to break down where the gap comes from. One of the most-cited studies is a 2011 paper by Terrance Odean of the University of California, Davis, and Brad Barber of the University of California, Berkeley, that broke new ground about how counterproductive trading can be to your wealth.

"Barber and Odean were the ones who put a stake in the heart of a lot of stuff," says Dan Egan, vice president of behavioral finance and investing at Betterment. "Because they didn't just focus on fund flows, they actually got individual investor and broker data for tens of thousands of households and were able to say this part of it is due to concentrated speculation and this part is due to commissions and trading. That paper has spawned numerous subsequent ones."

When you are in this profession, you are working against both the market and client expectations.

—Ken Nuttall

It's a 24-7 fire hose of information, and social media has magnified it. So it does make the job of behavioral coaching more difficult as well, because clients and investors do see it. The challenge is, the advisors have to be able to drink from that fire hose—because they need to know what's going on in markets—but not themselves react to what they are drinking, and add context for the clients.

—Nate Geraci

One of the companies at the forefront of helping investors with this art of doing nothing is the robo-advisor Betterment, which conducts study after study on investor behavior to figure out how to help investors not make mistakes. They're effectively the anti-Robinhood in that they are trying to keep you from doing too much. They've found that using colors and pop-ups showing the tax impact of various trading moves has been an effective way to stop investors from selling every time the market has a bad day.

Color can motivate you to do bad things and good things. We use color to say, "Are you on- or offtrack for the goal you are trying to achieve?" If it is orange, you can change how much you are saving, the target date—things you can control. Green is about the future, not the past. Color is only used to encode things you can control. You can't control the market.

—Dan Egan

Dumb Money No More

And all these efforts are working. We can see it in the flow data for Vanguard, as well as in the low-cost ETFs from BlackRock and Schwab that advisors like Betterment use in their portfolios. If you separate the Big Long

ETFs from the more liquid ETFs that are frequently used by the easily spooked trading crowd, the data speaks volumes. The retail buy-and-hold crowd, which many refer to as the "dumb money," looks much smarter in retrospect. Trader ETF flows are correlated with market moves, but Big Long ETFs are not correlated with anything. They just keep investing, rain or shine.

Flows into ETFs Used by Traders vs. Ones Used by Buy-and-Hold Investors

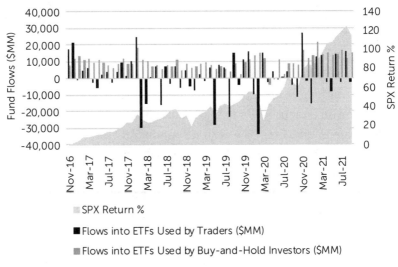

SPX Return %

Flows into ETFs Used by Traders ($MM)

Flows into ETFs Used by Buy-and-Hold Investors ($MM)

Bloomberg

All one has to do is overlay these flows with a chart of the S&P 500 Index to see how smart it was in retrospect to keep calm and carry on during the downturns.

All of this is a real sea change compared with the old days when your broker would be incentivized to trade your account—or even churn it— since he or she was paid that way. In one of our interviews, Bogle talked about how lethal old-school brokers could be to your long-term returns. "If somebody brings you to a mutual fund—a salesman, and so on," he said, "he's going to want to move you when things go down . . . so having that intermediary . . . is a disruptive force against long-term holdings."

And while there's some debate about how much to charge for helping investors hang in there, it is clear the Big Long advisors have taken Bogle's message to heart, and their clients are better off for it.

He helped to solve the problem of investing by identifying three things that matter more than anything else: your cost structure, what you own, and how you behave. If you deal with those three things, you will be a successful investor. There are a variety of ways to achieve that goal, but the only one that is close to a sure thing is the one that Jack Bogle came up with.

—Barry Ritholtz

CONCLUSION: BOGLE'S LEGACY

*"History will judge Vanguard, not by how many tens of bil-
lions of assets we manage but by how we played the game.
And we have played the game the right way—our way."*

Istory is going to be very kind to Bogle. Despite his flaws and having made a virtue of necessity, he is largely seen as a genuine champion of the small investor, as well as a huge disrupter of a massive
industry. While there are a handful of legendary investors whose legacies
will carry on, Bogle is likely to rise to the top of the list over time, given that
his success wasn't in playing the game well but rather in changing the game
for the better.

There are many factors that will help grow Bogle's legacy. First and
foremost is Vanguard, which is in its prime and will likely be around well
after our lifetime. The overall growth of index funds, ETFs, and passive—
and all the investors who use them—will also add to his legacy, given that
most people associate Bogle with them. The Bogleheads group, which is
bigger and more wide-reaching than most people think, will also help further his legacy.

Beyond those obvious legacy builders, which I highlighted in previous chapters, there are a few other, perhaps less obvious, ones that are worth looking at, including Bogle's books, quotes, and scholarship fund, along with some of the people in the industry who are carrying on the Bogle torch in their own way.

Bogle's Books

Bogle was a prolific writer, as well as a good one. He wrote about what he knew, and he put his unique voice into his books. Having both spent time with him in person and read his books, I can tell you they are very similar experiences.

He was a tremendous writer. I think the key thing that makes his books so good is that they are infused with this sense of conviction. They all have a thesis. They are data dependent. Also, I don't think you can overstate his well-roundedness as a human being. He was conversant in many of the great books, and he was a great communicator. All that contributed to his books being really important in the annals of financial literature.

—Christine Benz

He was always writing his own speeches, too. I remember him as being a big reader. He loved crossword puzzles. He was always a word guy. When his kids asked him what would be a good major in college, he didn't say economics, he'd always say English. And when we asked him why, he'd say the ability to communicate clearly, cogently, and concisely is probably the most important skill you can have for the rest of your life and everything else falls from that. He certainly did that himself.

—John C. Bogle Jr.

While Bogle always wrote, he did not necessarily plan on becoming an author. Yet he ultimately spent more time writing books than he did running Vanguard. He ran the company from 1974 to 1996, a twenty-two-year period. He wrote his first book in 1993, and his last one was published in 2018—a twenty-five-year span in which he penned a plethora of books.

And it is quite possible that none of it would have happened without a young woman named Amy Hollands.

The First Book

In the early nineties, Hollands was a twenty-five-year-old acquisitions editor at a small publisher. Her job was to find thought leaders in the financial industry with an iconoclastic message and a big platform. She had just helped publish a book on Charles Schwab and was looking for someone else to approach. Bogle was a no-brainer, but he would not be easy to land.

After multiple letters and phone calls, Bogle finally agreed to meet with Hollands.

"He's larger than life physically and personality-wise," Hollands recalls. "I was shaking in my shoes. He asked me why anyone would want to read this. He was very humble in his own way. I explained to him that this is exactly what people need to know. They need to know that Vanguard funds will help them over the long term. This book was a way for him to walk investors through the impact of fees on their overall returns. I had to go back a couple of different times."

The problem was that Bogle was still running Vanguard and simply didn't have a lot of time for such a big venture. As he describes it at the beginning of *Bogle on Mutual Funds*:

> "Thanks Amy, but maybe later," I told her. For at the time, I was quite overwhelmed with the task of building Vanguard . . . We had just begun to emerge as an industry leader. "I'd love to do it. And I know I can do it," I told her, "but right now I can't possibly find the time to write a book." So, Amy came back a year later with the same plea. And then again a year after that.

Amy finally broke through in the spring of 1992. Bogle's schedule had eased a bit. And his heart problems had returned, which made him wonder how much time he had left. Hollands was going to get him help.

"I was prepared to find him a ghostwriter," she says. "Most people in his position don't care quite so much about the content or the execution as much as having something to represent their thinking. But that would not suffice for him. Jack Bogle was a very precise, exacting person, and words really mattered to him."

Editing Bogle

Still, Bogle leaned heavily on his assistant Jim Norris, who has said that he became so used to writing in Bogle's voice that he forgot his own. (Norris would ultimately go on to run all of Vanguard's international business.)

To start, Hollands and Norris had to filter out some of Bogle's eighteenth-century Princeton man tone to make the book more approachable. Hollands remembers him saying things like "to the manor born," the meaning of which she had to look up. (It is from *Hamlet* and means being born into a life of wealth and privilege.) Bogle also wanted to have gold-edged pages in the book (is that vintage Bogle or what?), as well as a red cover, which is a no-no in the publishing world, according to Hollands. In the end, the book did have a red cover, although the gold-edged pages were nixed.

When *Bogle on Mutual Funds* came out, in 1993, it was largely a critical and commercial success. Both Bogle and Hollands were pleased, and the memory of this was tattooed in each of their brains forever. For Bogle, this would kick off a torrent of writing, with many of the books addressing the same themes.

Bogle even joked about this at a miniconference he had with Burt Malkiel at Princeton to discuss common ownership concerns. Malkiel said that he had written the same book twelve different times (in reference to his twelve editions of *A Random Walk Down Wall Street*). Bogle responded with, "I'm not sure I don't do that either."

Most of Bogle's books contain the Wellington story, some active mutual fund bashing, and a general attack on corporate America and the lack of stewardship from the agency owners (e.g., mutual funds, pensions). Each also has its own unique sections and style that differ from the others. He wrote till the very end, too—publishing his last book only three months before his death, at the age of eighty-nine. And that book, *Stay the Course*, is easily one of his best. While all of his books are well-researched and chock-full of data, they progressively got more human. Bogle wrote in his own inimitable voice more and more with each book.

Ranking the Books

Prior to writing *The Bogle Effect*, I had only read a couple of Bogle's works. But I was able to read the rest in preparation. It felt like I was studying for my Bogle Level III exam, although his books are *much* more enjoyable than a textbook because he is a good writer and uses a myriad of references and includes a lot of data and truth bombs. You rarely read a section without nodding along, thinking, *That makes a lot of sense*. What he says rings true today, and it will likely ring true in fifty years.

While I tried to work in excerpts from each book throughout *The Bogle Effect*, I would recommend hearing them straight from the horse's mouth. To help, I've ranked eight of his books based on their quality and my enjoyment of them.

1. *The Little Book of Common Sense Investing: The Only Way to Guarantee Your Fair Share of Stock Market Returns* **(2007)**—This is his best-selling book, and there is a good reason why. It's the tightest and most practical of them all. Everything comes together in this book. This is his *Sgt. Pepper's Lonely Hearts Clubs Band*, the defining work, a classic. It stays in the how-to-invest lane, but in a way that is vintage Bogle.

2. *Stay the Course: The Story of Vanguard and the Index Revolution* **(2018)**—This is the last book Bogle wrote, and it reads that way. It is largely a memoir and a chronological journey through the story of Vanguard—from Wellington, the first index fund, and the launch of bond funds to the ETF "invasion" and multifactor ETFs—with him narrating the voyage. If *The Little Book of Common Sense Investing* contains Bogle's philosophy in a nutshell, this is the Vanguard story in a nutshell. They work well as a one-two punch.

3. *Enough: True Measures of Money, Business, and Life* **(2008)**—This book is probably Bogle's deepest as well as his most personal. In the intro, he shares a lot of insight into where he came from and what made him. This was the book I used the most to help inform

chapter four, "Explaining Bogle." The word *enough* is where you end up when you go on a mission seeking out why Bogle did what he did and why he chose to walk a less beaten path in contrast to his peers. He was happy with what he had, at least materially. The grass was already greener on his side of the fence. This concept is powerful and at odds with much of Wall Street as well as the broader corporate world.

4. *Bogle on Mutual Funds: New Perspectives for the Intelligent Investor* (1993)—This is Bogle's first book. It is arguably the most practical but the least personable, as he was still busy with Vanguard duties at the time and had to rely on his assistants for help in writing it. If a professor were teaching a college course on investing and mutual funds, this would serve as a great textbook for the class. It educates the reader on a wide range of topics from how to think about bond yields to inflation and dividends. It also addresses how to approach picking a mutual fund. It was cutting-edge at the time. Of course, it favors index funds but in a textbook kind of way. The Twelve Pillars of Wisdom section is the highlight for me. There is some real hard-won knowledge in those.

5. *The Clash of the Cultures: Investment vs. Speculation* (2012)—This is easily one of the most impressive books Bogle wrote. Many of his books stick to familiar areas, but this one expands well beyond mutual funds into the global financial crisis of 2008, and he utterly skewers all the "gatekeepers" in the system for failing miserably. He also looks at the retirement crisis and executive compensation. Many of the problems he points out come from a culture of speculation and greed, hence the name of the book. I especially liked that he doesn't just slam everything but also offers solutions and prescriptions to make things better.

6. *Character Counts: The Creation and Building of the Vanguard Group* (2002)—This is mostly a compilation of Bogle's speeches and letters to the crew, as well as some important letters and his thoughts on running Vanguard. The speeches span from 1980 all the way to 2001. On one hand, the speeches tend to echo one another and can become a little repetitive, but on the other hand, it is really

interesting to hear what his exact words were during various periods. He is amazingly consistent, with a singular focus and vision despite a fast-changing financial world evolving around him in the eighties and nineties.

7. *The Battle for the Soul of Capitalism: How the Financial System Undermined Social Ideals, Damaged Trust in the Markets, Robbed Investors of Trillions—and What to Do About It* (2005)—This book has Bogle in one of his most cynical moods. He spends pages and pages hammering corporate America. It is a thoughtful yet cantankerous reaction to the dot-com bubble burst and Enron-type corporate fraud. This book is almost like the prequel to *The Clash of the Cultures*, which was largely a reaction to the 2008 financial crisis. In both books, he lets everyone—corporations, the media, mutual funds—have it about the parade of "disgusting scandals" in business.

8. *Don't Count on It! Reflections on Investment Illusions, Capitalism, "Mutual" Funds, Indexing, Entrepreneurship, Idealism, and Heroes* (2010)—This book is largely a collection of essays and speeches that Bogle gave at various places. The overarching theme is that the business and investment worlds have lost their way due to a worship of numbers; for example: the business world's obsession with quarterly earnings numbers or active management's obsession with building strategies based on past performance, or even how we have changed the way we calculate inflation and unemployment numbers to make them seem better than they are. This was the last Bogle book that I read in my research, so for me it seemed to largely repeat the themes in his other books (not to mention, it is a whopping 580 pages!).

Top Ten Quotes

Beyond Bogle's books, there are a handful of his Ben Franklin–esque investing aphorisms that will likely outlive us all. I specifically didn't include many of these in the book until now because I had exclusive quotes, and I wanted to keep things fresh. But here are ten of his most famous lines:

1. "Don't look for the needle in the haystack. Just buy the haystack!"
2. "The stock market is a giant distraction to the business of investing."
3. "Where returns are concerned, time is your friend. But where costs are concerned, time is your enemy."
4. "The miracle of compounding returns is overwhelmed by the tyranny of compounding costs."
5. "Before costs, beating the market is a zero-sum game. After costs, it is a loser's game."
6. "Fund performance comes and goes. Costs go on forever."
7. "The winning formula for success in investing is owning the entire stock market through an index fund—and then doing nothing. Just stay the course."
8. "Don't do something—just stand there."
9. "The grim irony of investing is that we investors as a group not only don't get what we pay for, we get precisely what we don't pay for."
10. "When there are multiple solutions to a problem, choose the simplest one."

The Bogle Scholars

Bogle's legacy will also live on in the scholarship funds he set up at Blair Academy and Princeton. The Bogle Brothers Scholarship was established by Jack at Blair Academy in 1968 in honor of his brothers, David (a twin who died in 1994) and William. All three Bogle brothers attended Blair through scholarships. The scholarship is given to "boys and girls of special promise to obtain necessary funding for their Blair education." Students must demonstrate financial need, academic ability, character, and determination. There have been 161 Bogle scholars since its formation.

In 2016, with the help of a generous contribution from his son John C. Bogle Jr. and John Jr.'s wife, Lynn, he also set up the John C. Bogle '51 Fellows in Civic Service program at Princeton. One of his greatest pleasures in life was seeing these young scholars blossom.

"He loved going back to Princeton and talking to the students," says Bogle Jr. "He would thrive in that environment, going back to the school, meeting these kids, finding out what they are doing, or talking about his life or career. He was really energized by this. He would go on for hours as long as these kids would want to hang around."

I spoke with two of the Bogle scholars, and not surprisingly they were very appreciative of the gift of education. They also seemed to genuinely like the guy.

"Mr. Bogle was incredibly generous, and being a scholarship student himself, his focus was on making sure other students had the same opportunities afforded to him," says Victoria Bailey, a Bogle scholar who is now a financial advisor. She was inspired to get into finance because of Bogle, but more importantly, it was going to Princeton that changed everything for her. "My mom was a single mom working three jobs. Mr. Bogle was my benefactor and helped to actually pay [for me] to go to Princeton. There's no way I would have had the confidence to apply to or been able to afford Princeton if it weren't for him. He changed the entire trajectory of my life. I'm forever indebted to him."

Another Bogle scholar, Anthony D'Amato, pursued a career in music and is a successful indie rocker. He has put out four albums and has worked with musicians such as Conor Oberst, aka Bright Eyes. (Side note: Oberst's song "First Day of My Life" was my wedding song. Small world.)

"I'm a professional musician," says D'Amato, "which was different from most of the Bogle scholars who went into finance, tech, or entrepreneurship. He always made sure to ask [me] questions about it. And he took an interest in it, even though it was clearly outside of his wheelhouse. But he would engage with lyrical themes and ask specific questions about the writing—that to me really showed he was an endlessly curious guy."

Bogle followed many of these scholars as they made their way in the world. And he made an effort to keep up with them through letters and get-togethers. Everyone I spoke with equated him to a genuinely curious and proud grandfather who wanted to hear about everything they were up to. Case in point: When Bogle heard D'Amato had put out an album called *The Shipwreck from the Shore*, he asked for a copy. A few weeks later, D'Amato got this email back from Bogle, which he allowed me to print in full:

Hi, Anthony,

Thanks for sending your CD (DVD?). Hard as it may be to imagine, this antique relic of Blair and Princeton, without a hint of musical talent (but a love of music, from symphonies to country rock), loved every song—now played many times over.

The rhythms were exciting and easy on the ear and the lyrics surely poetic. I do confess to wondering about the themes of lost love, sadness, and death from someone of your (relatively) young age. At my age (eighty-five), singularly moving (though I've had just one true love, and we've now been married for fifty-eight-plus years).

I realize full well that applause from someone my age may not be a good sign for popularity with your (as they say) target audience. But there it is! Keep up the good work, and I wish you the continued success that you so richly deserve.

Best, always,

Jack B (also known to some of your Princeton contemporaries as the "Chief," my grandkids' name for me) B '47, P '51

P.S. Last Sunday, we went to a concert featuring Mahler's Second Symphony (Requiem), conducted by Yannick Nézet-Séguin. Unforgettable, majestic, enthralling, dramatic. (That's our maestro.)

Bailey says that she and Bogle also wrote to each other frequently. "He was always so quick to respond," she recalls. "The fact that he replied was always amazing. Despite who he was, he was always very personable and met you at whatever level you were at and just would have these great conversations as if you were the only person in the entire world. He was incredible, and the fact that he dedicated himself to doing these scholarships for people had this amazing ripple effect. My goal now is to do the same thing for other students. As soon as I have the ability to, I want to be able to offer a full ride back to students and give them the opportunity that I had. It's life changing."

Bogle also looked at the scholarships as a way to preserve his legacy. As he wrote in *Enough*, "Small as they may seem, these human touches in a now giant enterprise will, I'm certain, help to preserve the legacy I've tried to create."

The Bogle scholars show that Bogle was not just a philanthropist in the sense of saving investors' money through Vanguard—you could argue that he was the greatest of all time, given the trillions in savings—but an altruist in the traditional sense as well, with both his money and time.

Carrying the Torch

One question I pondered while writing this book is: Who will be the next Bogle? Or was he a total anomaly? Almost everyone I interviewed said he was an anomaly—even people who acknowledged the good work many others are doing. It was just too hard to see anyone else as even close to him.

He was a true anomaly. There's nobody like him anywhere. They broke the mold. They're never going to get another one.
—Jared Dillian

That said, there are some people out there who deserve to be highlighted, who are doing Bogleian things—being a champion for investors, driving disintermediation, and disrupting the status quo. Many of them were inspired by him as well.

Here's a look at ten people—outside Vanguard—who I think are worthy of highlighting.

Anthony and Dina Isola

Anthony and Dina Isola are a husband-and-wife team at Ritholtz Wealth Management trying to save schoolteachers from losing hundreds of millions a year in fee-ridden—and arguably predatory—annuity products. They are looking to replace what amounts to underwhelming returns being eaten up by inflation in products that charge 2 to 5 percent a year with simple, low-cost ETFs that cost a combined 0.08 percent. They also offer full financial planning for another 0.40 percent. Their pitch is for teachers to pay one-fifth the fee while getting more service and likely doubling or tripling the dollar amount when they retire.

"Vanguard has the best funds to offer the teachers," says Anthony Isola, "because I can explain to them that outside shareholders aren't going to get rewarded. *You* are going to get rewarded with lower fees because you are the shareholder. Having that 'we're all in this together' theme is very important. This is the exact antithesis of what they are getting now. Going from a crappy annuity from some insurance company to a Vanguard index fund, you are making a quantum leap. You aren't improving your life a little—it's like you went from the outhouse to the penthouse."

Tyrone V. Ross Jr.

While Bogle's impact on investors is undeniable, only half of Americans are investors. The Bogle Effect has yet to reach the other half of the country, and it needs to. Missing out on those market returns has really exacerbated the wealth gap in this country.

Who Owns Stocks? (as of 2021)

Households by Net Worth	% Ownership of Stock Market
Top 1%	54
Top 90–99%	35
50%–99%	10
Bottom 50%	1

Federal Reserve

Bogle was well aware of the wealth gap and had been worried about it for a long time. In *The Clash of the Cultures*, he wrote:

Ultimately, such a system is all too likely to bring social discord to our society and engender a harsh public reaction to today's record disparity between the tiny top echelon of income recipients and the great mass of families at the base.

Enter Tyrone V. Ross Jr., the cofounder and CEO of OnRamp Invest, which helps advisors invest in crypto (another disintermediating force). But Ross's overarching passion is his endeavors through his nonprofit, Evolve, which aims to help with financial literacy and get the rest of the country invested.

"I wake up every day with the goal of wanting to leave a legacy of financial education," says Ross. "I think as an industry and as a country we've ignored it long enough. We know half of the country doesn't invest in stocks. We know half of the country is financially illiterate. It's always been geared toward those who speak the language of money. If you speak the language of money in a capitalist society, you will thrive. If you don't speak the language of money, you will suffer.

"So my goal is to make financial education accessible. No matter your color, no matter your zip code, you should have access to it and the ability to get it on your terms . . . Children start picking up financial concepts at three years old. By age seven, research shows, the whole scope of what you think, feel, and know about money is set. And yet we are still doing that stupid stock-picking class for seniors in high school. It makes no sense."

Bogle would be completely in tune with Ross's education efforts. In *The Battle for the Soul of Capitalism*, he wrote, "When we should be teaching young students about long-term investing and the magic of compound interest, the stock-picking contests offered by our schools are in fact teaching them about short-term speculation."

Ross's solution is twofold: First, you have to educate kids when they are younger. He has created *Learn to Money*, a ten-part video series that teaches financial basics such as money, credit, debt, and checking accounts. He is looking at getting it into schools. Second, he proposes and is lobbying for a government fund attached to any child born in the US, which would hold a diversified portfolio (likely of dirt-cheap index funds) that will grow. Individuals will not be able to touch the fund until they are out of high school and have also passed a national financial literacy curriculum. This would help bring the other half of Americans into the market, as well as provide an incentive for them to get educated.

Again, Bogle was very close to having the same idea. He wrote in *The Clash of the Cultures*: "Create a public sector DC [defined contribution] plan for wage earners who are unable to enter the private system or whose initial assets are too modest to be acceptable in that system."

Ross wasn't directly inspired by Bogle, but he was well aware of his impact and is happy to be carrying on his legacy, albeit not to investors but to people not yet invested.

"I love what Bogle did," says Ross. "If you talk about our industry and what people have done for finance and people in general, it's him and then everybody else. It's amazing what he did. It is hard to overstate. I do love how he made it easy to participate and how the company eats its own cooking. It's all in—there's no outside influence."

Brad Katsuyama

Brad Katsuyama is the CEO and cofounder of IEX Group, the Investors Exchange, which he set up to give investors a new way to trade that protects them from front-running and scalping by high-frequency traders. The big stock exchanges are set up to sell high-speed technology and advantages that benefit a minority who pay for them. Katsuyama equates them to the referees playing a role to determine the outcome of the game. IEX is trying to level this unlevel playing field.

"Right now, every exchange pays a rebate to a broker to send them an order," says Katsuyama. "Last year, an estimated $3.7 billion was paid out. IEX is the only exchange that doesn't pay that rebate. Rebates are paid to subsidize brokers for poor execution quality. And the execution quality is so bad because of the speed advantages that the exchanges sell. So it's all linked. We wanted to give people the best execution possible and protect them from latency arbitrage and these predatory activities."

His story is famously told in the book *Flash Boys* by Michael Lewis, and it echoes Bogle's story in many ways. First, Katsuyama would likely have remained an executive at a big established company if circumstance hadn't intervened and inspired him to take a different road. Second, he has a natural instinct to help the client over himself. And third, he has chosen to operate outside of a system of kickbacks, which means his journey won't be a short one but rather one that requires patience, relentless dedication, constant educational efforts, and hopefully a few breaks along the way.

"What gets me out of bed every day is that we understand how this market works," says Katsuyama. "We understand how investors are losing, and we know how to fix that. There's an entire apparatus set up around calling that crazy, saying that everything is fine, it works great for everyone, and the customer has never had it better. I just don't think that's true. There are moments in life when you look at yourself and ask: Was I put on the planet to take this next step? And I think, for me, I felt that way."

Sheryl Garrett

Sheryl Garrett is the cofounder of Garrett Investment Services and the founder of the Garrett Planning Network, a nationwide network of advisors that offers financial advice but charges for it on an hourly, as-needed basis, like a lawyer or accountant. While that may seem more expensive, it is typically much cheaper than an advisor who gets paid a percentage of assets, and it opens up the door to less wealthy clients, whom fee-based advisors can be naturally disincentivized from serving. Also, this service ensures that the advisor is paid only for their time and work. This sounds logical, but it is somewhat revolutionary for the advisory business as I discussed in chapter seven.

Given the lower fees and populist sentiment, Bogle would have been totally behind Garrett's efforts. In fact, I asked him about the advisory business in our last interview, about six months before he passed away, and he basically echoed what Garrett is doing. This would be music to Garrett's ears, as she was very inspired by Bogle, whom she called her North Star.

"You know how kids grow up with their favorite sports figure?" says Garrett. "When I was a young adult, Jack Bogle was my hero, my superhero of industry. I cried when he passed away . . . In all of my work, Jack Bogle continues to be a central thread. He's been like my North Star. If I do something that Jack would approve of, I'm going to be happy with it. If I do something that Jack wouldn't approve of, my moral compass wouldn't be happy with it. And I can't quite say that about any other human being."

Rick Ferri

Rick Ferri, who was quoted a lot in this book, is quite literally carrying the Bogle torch as the host of the *Bogleheads on Investing Podcast* and president of the John C. Bogle Center for Financial Literacy. On top of that, he also founded and runs his own firm, Ferri Investment Solutions. Ferri has said he wants to be "the Jack Bogle of the advisory business" by challenging the 1 percent fees just as Bogle challenged them in mutual funds. He has started an hourly advice service for DIY investors, where he charges for portfolio construction by the hour.

"The amount of service and time that advisors spend on clients' accounts doesn't line up with the fees they charge clients," says Ferri. "There is a misalignment. Not all, but a lot of advisors are overcharging clients."

Ferri is very much like Garrett in this mission to have advisors paid for their time and effort and nothing more or less. Garrett even said they "are the head of each other's fan club."

Ferri is also known for taking this fee fight right to advisors on social media. Just as Bogle would drop uncomfortable punk-rockery in front of an audience of active managers, Ferri does the same on Twitter. He is known for riling up and debating the advisory world on a consistent basis by tweeting out bombs like, "Advisor fees are the last bastion of gluttony in the retail investment industry."

Jerry Schlichter

Jerry Schlichter took on Fortune 500 companies and won. Very few people can say that. He was able to prove that many of America's biggest companies were letting their employees get charged much more than they should have in the company's 401(k) plans. His lawsuits have resulted in companies completely reworking their plans with lower-cost fund options for the participants. Despite the fact that his lawsuits would have helped employees, the companies involved were not going to take this lying down.

"I knew what is involved," says Schlichter. "I had taken on chemical companies. They decide to try to bury you with work and costs. I knew they would come after us. What that meant is, as a small law firm in St. Louis, we would need a monster line of credit to finance this and to persevere through what I knew would be a long battle, a nuclear war. My two partners and I at the time put up our houses, everything we had, to get the line of credit. Then in 2006 we brought cases against some of the biggest companies in America—Boeing, Caterpillar, Lockheed Martin International—all over the country. It shook the industry."

Schlichter ended up getting $1.5 billion worth of settlement money while getting many plans to change to cleaner share classes and lower-cost index fund options. He also did something Bogle was unable to do—he won over the US Supreme Court, which, in a rare nine–zero decision, agreed with Schlichter that under the Employee Retirement Income Security Act (ERISA), a company (or university, etc.) that uses 403(b) does have a fiduciary duty to monitor investments and remove imprudent ones.

"When beginning this journey, I called Jack Bogle and talked to him because I saw such a connection between his goals and what I decided to do," says Schlichter. "Bogle told us we were on track and doing the right thing. We use Vanguard in our litigation as the gold standard. To win these cases, we had to prove that there are options available that are prudent and that are substantially less expensive. Without Jack Bogle doing what he did, we would have had a harder time trying to show what's out there in the market that could be available for a retiree."

Robin Powell

Robin Powell is an independent and vocal advocate for low-cost passive investing in Europe. His blog, *The Evidence-Based Investor*, is dedicated to being an independent educator of both retail and institutional investors to teach them many of the same principles Bogle advocated for. He was compelled to do this because, as we discussed in chapter one, most financial professionals and other intermediaries outside the US are incentivized to keep this information buried.

To help, Powell writes, speaks, and even makes documentaries. One of his documentaries, *Index Funds: The 12-Step Recovery Program for Active Investors*, is about the benefits of low-cost indexing and the problems with high-cost active mutual funds. This would have been right up Bogle's alley.

Powell, like Bogle, has also experienced the backlash that occurs when one threatens the status quo revenue stream of an entire industry. He was actually kicked out of a conference that he was asked to speak at because his presentation was too pro-indexing.

"You can really put noses out of joint if you aren't careful," says Powell. "About five or six years ago, I went to do a presentation in Leeds [UK] at a marketing company for the fund management industry. And I don't think they really did their research on me. But I gave the opening speech of the conference, and it went down like an absolute bomb. Sometimes you can just tell when you are bombing. It all went quiet. There was polite applause at the end. Then the organizer pulled me to one side and said, 'Robin, I'm ever so sorry but we're going to have to ask you to leave. We really weren't expecting you to come out and say that.'"

Dan Price

Dan Price is the CEO of Gravity Payments, a low-cost credit card processing company. Bogle would have loved this guy. He is in every way the opposite of the CEOs Bogle railed against in many of his books, who took insanely high salaries and made out like bandits. Price, on the other hand, imposed a $70,000 minimum salary at his company and purposely cut his $1.1 million salary to $70,000. Here's Price on Twitter:

> At my company the highest-paid person makes 3× the median worker, down from 36x in 2015. Since raising wages and slashing my CEO pay, our business tripled.

Price's company is in stark contrast to the average CEO-to-worker compensation, which was 351-to-1 in 2020, according to the Economic Policy Institute, which is even higher than it was when Bogle wrote about it in many of his books. Price, who looks a bit like Jesus, was also able to keep everyone at the company employed during the Covid-19 pandemic, despite a big hit to revenue. All this has made a real impact on employee lives and set off a chain reaction of goodwill.

Dan Egan

Dan Egan is the vice president of behavioral finance and investing at Betterment, a robo-advisor with about $29 billion in assets. Not only does it serve up advice and planning for a Vanguardian fee of 0.25 to 0.40 percent, it has also been spearheading ways to develop interfaces to keep investors from trading on impulse or fear—or overtrading in general. Like Bogle, Egan worries that investors will trade at the wrong time and ruin the compounding effect. Egan's whole job is to fight this temptation and keep investors from being their own worst enemies. He is on the complete opposite side of the spectrum from a platform like Robinhood, which is designed to encourage trading. Egan is the yin to Robinhood's yang.

"We also tactically make [investors] aware of pieces of information they should know about before they make a decision," says Egan. "A lot of clients will come in if the market is going down, and they'll try to market time—either increase or decrease risk based on what the market might do. So we will calculate the tax impact of the move they are about to do. All of a sudden, this decision has a very specific cost associated with it . . . When we show people the tax-impact preview, 80 percent to 90 percent of the time they do not go ahead with the allocation change."

Egan and Betterment have likely saved investors countless dollars through these interfaces, although Egan doesn't get a ton of compliments. He's like a shadow ninja looking to protect investors from harm without being seen. What he lacks in public appreciation he makes up for by feeling good about his work, which is not always that easy.

"It is a feeling of good alignment between you and the people you are trying to help," says Egan. "I've worked—and I know friends who have worked—at other places where the incentives aren't necessarily aligned. It's more like sell the product, make the sale, get the commission, etc. And that takes a toll on you. You can have friends and family asking if they should be using your investment, and you are like, 'Hmm, not really.' Being able to be proud to put your money into it and recommend it goes a long way . . . We are freeing people up, like Bogle did with index funds, but with planning."

Nerina Visser

Nerina Visser, an independent ETF strategist based in South Africa, spent the first part of her career working for an investment bank and servicing institutional clients. It was a fine job, and it put her on a secure career path. But then her life changed when she heard Deborah Fuhr, a veteran, world-traveling ETF expert (whom I interviewed for the book), speak at a CFA conference in 2007.

"We already had ETFs in South Africa for seven years by then, so I knew what they were and how they worked, but I didn't quite get it," says Visser. "And I often refer to that presentation by Debbie as my road-to-Damascus moment in the ETF industry because it was the first time I really got it and could see what the instrument could do."

Visser decided then that she would dedicate her life to helping smaller retail investors assemble low-cost ETF portfolios. While this type of thing is common now in the US, it is not in many other countries, especially South Africa, where the vast majority of investors use brokers who get paid a commission by a mutual fund company. The average expense ratio for a fund is typically between 1.5 and 2 percent, which blows away US expense ratios—even in the eighties and nineties.

"I think, as you get older, you realize you need a little more in life than just the money," says Visser. "There's got to be some purpose to what you do. For me, the major passion is providing the access to investment markets and investment opportunities. For the longest time, the average investor was completely priced out of the market. So, for me, it is about bringing down costs and providing access, especially in a country like South Africa, where there is a massive gap between the haves and the have-nots."

Like Rick Ferri in the nineties in the US, it is the epiphany-receiving Nerina Vissers who will help ensure that the Bogle Effect spreads throughout the rest of the world.

Judging Bogle

If you are reading this, it means you made it to the end of the book. Congratulations! Take a deep breath and know that I wholeheartedly thank you. Hopefully, I was able to show you just how mind-blowing Bogle's story and effect is. It's hard to think of someone else—in any industry—leaving their neck of the woods in so much better shape than they found it. And it's only just beginning. We don't even know the full extent of his influence yet.

There's no question that the Bogle Effect is so dominant today, and the good news is that it will just continue. It is a pendulum in motion, and inertia will keep that thing moving. And so his legacy will live on for generations.

—Gus Sauter

How did Bogle think of his own legacy? He addresses it in *The Clash of the Cultures*:

Of course, the jury is still out on my legacy. But I confess that I can't worry about how others may appraise it. Yes, I've erred. Yes, I've come up short more times than I care to count. But if, at the end, I'm deemed to have failed, at least I will have failed despite the rush of great enthusiasm; despite the high achievement of having my most important ideas—the mutual fund structure, the single-eye focus on rock-bottom costs, the index mutual fund, the abandonment of sales loads, and the creation of a new structure for bond funds—proven beyond doubt; and despite championing the worthy cause of serving our nation's citizen investors "economically, efficiently and honestly"—the very words that I cited in my Princeton University thesis more than six decades ago. All too soon, it will be time for history to be the judge.

Consider this book one of the first attempts to be that judge.

ACKNOWLEDGMENTS

Writing a book is not a solo effort, and I would like to acknowledge those who helped make this possible: first and foremost, my wife, Trang, for urging and pushing me to do this, knowing it would put more on her shoulders at home and with the kids. She is also the best sounding board for just about anything, including the book process. There's no way this could have happened without her.

I also want to thank Gina Martin Adams, the chief equity strategist—and my manager—at Bloomberg Intelligence, who, along with global research directors David Dwyer and Drew Jones, encouraged me to go for it as well. Having support and interest both at home and at work was crucial, given how time-consuming an undertaking this was.

I also want to thank Joel Weber, the editor of *Bloomberg Businessweek* and my cohost of the *Trillions* podcast, whom I bounced the book concept off a few times while it was just a thought in my brain. He got it right off the bat, and that early encouragement was important. I also want to thank my literary agent, Farley Chase, who gave me invaluable advice on the proposal—as well as help navigating among publishers.

In terms of the actual book itself, the biggest thanks goes to Athanasios Psarofagis, James Seyffart, Graham Sinclair, and my mom. Those are the poor souls who read the first version of the book, which was double(!) the length it is now. That is right up there with someone asking you to help them move. But their feedback was very useful in the early stages. From there, Vy Tran at BenBella Books was instrumental to and amazing in the development, arrangement, and editing of the text. She effectively made my manuscript look and read like a real book.

I'd also like to thank Freddy Martino of Vanguard, who, along with Mike Nolan, helped with some hard-to-get data, as well as some fact-checking. I know I probably annoyed Freddy with all my requests but he never let it show. And finally, a special shout-out to Lauren Davis, without whom this book would not have happened. She asked me to speak at a Bogle tribute in October 2019. Not only did the PowerPoint presentation that I made for that event give me the outline and idea for the book but speaking in front of and talking to many of Bogle's longtime colleagues and peers also made me believe that perhaps I could be the guy to write a book about him. And that's what I spent the next two years doing.

INDEX

ABOUT THE AUTHOR

Eric Balchunas is a senior ETF analyst for Bloomberg Intelligence where he writes for and leads the fund research team. He has more than fifteen years' experience working with ETF data, designing new functions, and writing research and articles. He also helped to create the first TV show solely focusing on the opportunities, risks, and current events in the ETF industry, *Bloomberg ETF IQ*, as well as a podcast, *Trillions*. He is a *Bloomberg Opinion* contributor and the author of *The Institutional ETF Toolbox*, published by Wiley in March 2016. Balchunas holds a bachelor's degree in journalism and environmental economics from Rutgers University. He currently lives in Philadelphia with his wife and two sons.